Craig Anderton
Christian Deinhardt

Cubase SX/SL—Mixing & Mastering

Craig Anderton
Christian Deinhardt

Cubase SX/SL—Mixing & Mastering

Order No. WZ 00739
International Standard Book Number: 0.8256.2720.6

EXCLUSIVE DISTRIBUTORS:

Music Sales Corporation
257 Park Avenue South, New York, NY 10010 USA

Music Sales Limited
8/9 Frith Street, London W1D 3JB England

Music Sales Pty. Limited
120 Rothschild Street, Rosebery, Sydney, NSW 2018, Australia

Printed in the United States of America by Vicks Lithograph and Printing Corporation

Publisher: Peter Gorges
Cover art: MoTYPE, Cologne, Germany
Editor: Reinhard Schmitz
Interior design and layout: Uwe Senkler

Welcome ...

Steinberg unveiled the first version of Cubase VST in early 1996. The idea was simple yet brilliant: With Cubase VST, Steinberg put a tool into the hands of recordists that enables us to produce professional-sounding tracks using just a computer and audio card— no costly recording hardware required.

Cubase VST was endowed with virtual instruments; the range of its functions grew steadily until its user interface was bursting at the virtual seams with features. Time for a new Cubase.

The torch was handed over at the 2002 Frankfurt Musikmesse. Cubase VST was mothballed; Cubase SX/SL was born. If you're an old hand at VST looking to ease on over to SX/SL, think again. Cubase SX/SL is a completely new program rather than a major update. As such, it calls for some woodshedding. If you're a newbie, you don't need recalibrate your sequencing sensibilities; all you have to do is get hip to what Cubase SX/SL is here for—to make music.

That's exactly what this book will do for you. It gets to the point without a lot of blather, and that point is to create great sounding songs in Cubase SX/SL. This requires more than merely program handling skills. You need to know how to make the most of effects, mixer automation options, and VST Instruments. And Cubase SX/SL is more than a sequencer. It puts a virtual audio studio at your fingertips, so it's important to learn the techniques of music production. This book will help you to become proficient at recording, arranging, mixing, mastering, and burning tracks on CD.

Here's wishing you lots of fun and success with your Cubase SX/SL-powered music productions. We sincerely hope that alongside providing valuable insight, this book inspires you to use that knowledge creatively.

Craig Anderton
Christian Deinhardt

Table of Contents

Part 1 Cubase Essentials

Part 2 Basics of Mixing and Mastering

Part 3 Equalization, Dynamics, and Reverberation

Part 4 Using Effects in Cubase

Part 5 Specific Techniques

Part 6 Mastering with Cubase SX/SL

Part 1

Cubase Essentials

Chapter 1

How to Set Up Your System

PC components can be combined in countless configurations. This makes it all but impossible to recommend specific peripheral devices or even models of computers. Nevertheless, I will share a few useful tips for choosing a computer and its constituent components. In this chapter, I'll also walk you through the process of installing Cubase SX/SL and configuring it for the tasks ahead.

1.1   The Computer

As a minimum requirement, Cubase SX/SL mandates a 500-MHz Pentium III or equivalent AMD processor and 256MB RAM. Though this minimal configuration will get Cubase SX/SL running, don't expect fire-breathing performance. If you want to finish tracking before your pension plan kicks in, opt for a Pentium IV or an equivalent AMD processor and 512MB RAM.

The great processor debate—AMD or Intel—has become irrelevant. Today it simply doesn't matter. Intel was the better choice up to a few years ago, but AMD has since caught up; its processors are now on par with Intel's offerings. What's more, computers sporting AMD processors are generally the better bargain.

At the time of printing, new computers shipped with hard disks boasting around 80GB. You're on the safe side with this breed of hard disk because a minute of stereo audio material requires about 10MB of storage space on your hard disk. Subtract some real estate for the operating system and installed programs, and the 80GB disk leaves plenty of space for audio data. However, your best bet is to dedicate a separate hard disk to audio data. Time to start thinking about installing a second hard drive ...

Your computer should also be equipped with a CD burner, which more often than not is a standard feature of the latest generation of computer.

If you prefer to use external hard disks or CD-ROM drives, budget for the purchase of a separate SCSI or FireWire interface. At the time of publication, FireWire is the preferable choice. It's faster and the range of connectable media is greater.

Let me share a few tips gleaned from long experience with Windows computers:

Opt for a separate AGP graphic card rather than the frequently touted option of on-board graphics. This affords you the freedom to choose a graphic card. You could even go for a dual-monitor card, which connects two monitors to your rig. The ability to spread the Cubase interface out over two monitors is a righteous luxury well worth the added price. This reduces clutter and enhances the views.

Virtually every main board of recent make sports an integrated sound generator. Though this breed of on-board audio card will get the job done, the audio quality ranges from mediocre to atrocious. To make matters worse, the appalling latency of such cards makes it all but impossible to play virtual instruments in real time. Budget for a quality audio card when drawing up your music computer wish list. More tips on choosing the right audio card await you in the following chapter. I also recommend that you go to a qualified music store for first-hand advice. A reputable dealer will also be happy to help install the gear.

1.2   The Operating System

Cubase SX/SL runs smoothly on Windows 2000 or Windows XP. If you're considering Windows XP, both Home Edition and XP Professional will do. The Professional Edition has no advantages when working with Cubase SX/SL. Home Edition is cheaper, so feel free to cut corners and opt for the latter.

Though Cubase SX/SL 1.03 and later versions run on Windows 98, the experience is unlikely to be memorable. Try running SX/SL on Windows 98 if you must, but waste no time updating your operating system.

1.3   Audio Hardware (Audio Card)

An audio card may be chock full of hip features, but it won't do anything for you if it can't talk to Cubase. The only way to interface the two and ensure they speak the same lingo is to use a card with an ASIO driver.

ASIO (Audio Stream Input Output) is Steinberg's solution to the driver problem. It's designed to blast through the performance barriers that Windows operating systems are so adept at putting up. This translates into truckloads of audio channels, comparatively light CPU loads, and reliable synchronization.

In addition, audio cards with ASIO drivers are hands-down winners in the latency stakes. Every digital audio system issues audio data with a certain amount of delay born of CPU processing time. This lag is called latency. Some on-board audio cards' latency ranges from 500 to 700ms, which is utterly unacceptable for audio applications.

For these reasons, buy an audio card with ASIO drivers. To shine some illuminating light into the dark and tangled audio card jungle, Steinberg regularly benchtests cards and publishes findings on the support pages of the Steinberg website.

1.4   The MIDI Interface

Many audio cards ship with an integrated MIDI interface. This type of card usually offers one MIDI input and one MIDI output each. A special cord connects to the integrated interface. It's furnished with a connector for the audio card's game port on one end, and two connectors for the MIDI input and MIDI output on the other. A MIDI interface on the audio card is the cheapest way to connect a computer to the external MIDI world.

However, experience teaches that the performance of integrated MIDI interfaces won't inspire admiration in even the most forgiving musician. The fact is, they frequently cause considerable headaches, so I can't recommend their use in good conscience.

The only solution worthy of endorsement is a separate MIDI interface such as the Steinberg Midex 3 (one in, three outs) or Midex 8 (eight ins and outs). Steinberg interfaces offer something called LTB (Linear Time Base), a technology that delivers better MIDI timing than interfaces that are integrated using conventional Windows drivers.

Most contemporary external MIDI interfaces connect to a USB port on the computer. Counting the Cubase dongle, you're already dealing with two USB devices. To connect further USB devices, you may have to buy a USB hub, depending on the number of USB ports available on your computer. Head for your local computer store; the hub will cost you just a few units of whatever your local currency may be. Note that you can connect the Cubase dongle and a USB MIDI interface to a single hub without running into trouble.

1.5   Installation

Cubase SX/SL installs automatically using the installation CD. Once the installation routine starts, all you have to do is type in your name and the serial number of your Cubase version.

Acrobat Reader version 5.05 is required to view the online manuals. Install it alongside Cubase if it's not already installed on your computer.

> The installation routine asks if you want to install older VST plug-ins, among them the virtual synthesizers JX-16 and CS-40. Definitely accept this offer and don't let the installation program's somewhat misleading dialog confuse you: This message doesn't pertain to the JX-16 and CS-40; these are installed even if Cubase VST has never run on your computer. It would be a shame if you missed out on these virtual sound generators because both are great-sounding synthesizers.

A USB dongle protects against software piracy. Note that you must install Cubase first. Plug the dongle into a USB port on your computer only after installing the program and rebooting the computer. If you plug the dongle in before installing Cubase, Windows identifies the new USB device, but can't install it for lack of a driver.

1.6   Keeping Up to Date

Take the time to update Cubase before you begin working with it. Steinberg strives to steadily improve Cubase SX/SL and doesn't charge for every advance along the way. Free updates are posted regularly on the Steinberg homepage for your downloading pleasure. Often these updates are bug fixes that clean up the mess left by programming errors that are discovered after the official release date. However, it's not uncommon for such updates to contain improvements and extensions.

First, find out which version you're running. To do this, go to the HELP menu and select the option ABOUT CUBASE. A window opens; the version number of your SX/SL appears at the top right of it.

The easiest way to find the current version of Cubase SX/SL is to connect to the Internet and go to HELP > STEINBERG ON THE WEB > PRODUCT UPDATES. A click on this option is all it takes to get to Steinberg's update server.

Cubase		
Cubase SX	**Info**	**Download**
Version 1.051	Version History (10 KB) about fixes.	ftp Server Steinberg
Platform: PC	Please click on the download link and	
Update	follow the instructions.	
File size: 16 MB	Updates only earlier Cubase SX versions,	
	but NO Cubase VST versions.	
	To update from your Cubase VST version	
	please contact your local dealer.	
	Mackie Control Support.pdf (1.531 KB)	

The Steinberg website's update page.

Check also if the hardware drivers for the audio card and MIDI interface are up to date. Outdated drivers are frequently an avoidable nuisance. It pays to occasionally drop by the vendors' web pages to check for updates.

1.7   Preparing for MIDI

Cubase automatically identifies and integrates the MIDI interface and device drivers once they have been properly installed to your system. Double-check to make sure by going to DEVICES > DEVICE SETUP. There you'll find the ALL MIDI INPUTS and DIRECT MUSIC panels. They show the MIDI input and outputs configured on your system.

Set up a standard MIDI port. To do this, select DEFAULT MIDI PORTS and define a port for the MIDI input and the MIDI output. Cubase uses this setting for all newly generated MIDI tracks as well as for importing standard MIDI files.

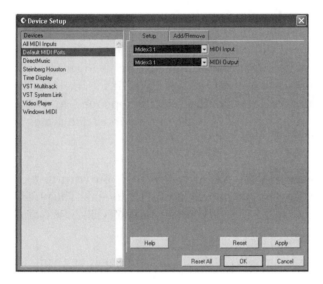

The place to define a standard MIDI port is here.

Under FILE > PREFERENCES > MIDI you'll find the option MIDI THRU ACTIVE. Make sure that this option is activated; otherwise, incoming MIDI data won't be sent to connected sound generators.

If your recording keyboard also serves as the sound source, set its mode to "Local Control Off." Otherwise, every note will sound twice, first when you strike a key and again when Cubase triggers a sound after receiving the first note. "Local Off" severs the connection between the keyboard and the internal sound generator. When activated, the keyboard receives commands sent via MIDI only, in our case, from Cubase.

1.8 Gearing Up for Audio

If you own an audio card with a stereo input and a stereo output, connect the output to your monitoring system. Route it directly to an amp or an active speaker system or via an intermediary mixer. If you intend to track with other audio sources such as synthesizers, microphones, guitars, and so forth, you can hardly get around using a mixer. More on this later.

Connect a signal source to the audio card's input.

You may prefer to connect the sound source that you want to record directly to the audio card's input. I advise against it, though. The problem is that you're unlikely to get a decent input signal, especially if you aim to record using a microphone.

Your better bet is to patch a mixer to the inputs, preferably one with "subgroups." A mixing console like this offers a master output designed to connect to your monitoring system as well as additional selectable outputs for each mixer channel. In the interests of convenience, connect a (stereo) subgroup to your audio card's input.

Here's an example illustrating why this is a good idea: Say you're ready to record in Cubase and the sound source is connected to mixer channel 1. Then all you have to do is route channel 1 to this subgroup. Most mixer channels offer special buttons that let you do this. This means that your setup is ready to record at the touch of a button. A mixer's subgroups may also be routed to the master output. This means you can record and monitor the signal at the same time.

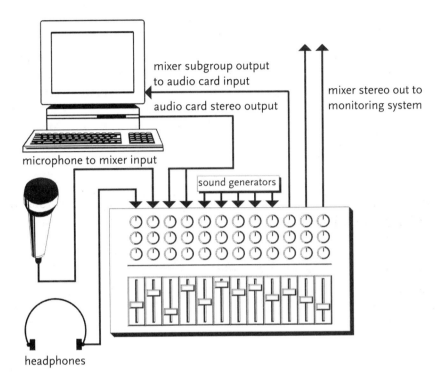

mixer subgroup output
to audio card input

mixer stereo out to
monitoring system

audio card stereo output

microphone to mixer input

sound generators

headphones

This is how a mixer is connected to subgroups.

If your audio card offers several separate inputs/outputs, you'll surely address these via a mixer. When choosing a mixer, ensure that it offers a sufficient number of input channels and subgroups.

Now we'll enter some basic settings for Cubase SX/SL. First let's check the audio card settings.

1   Go to DEVICES > DEVICE SETUP and select VST MULTITRACK.

2 Go to the ASIO DRIVER pop-up menu and select your audio hardware (audio card). If a dedicated ASIO driver is available for your hardware, be sure to use it. This driver is easy to identify—the name of the hardware is preceded by the designation ASIO. If your audio hardware doesn't come with a dedicated ASIO driver, use the ASIO DirectX driver.

3 If you aim to run several audio applications on your computer, activate the option RELEASE ASIO DRIVER IN BACKGROUND. Cubase will then enable the audio driver as soon as another program accesses it.

4 If your audio hardware supports direct monitoring, you can switch the DIRECT MONITORING option on.

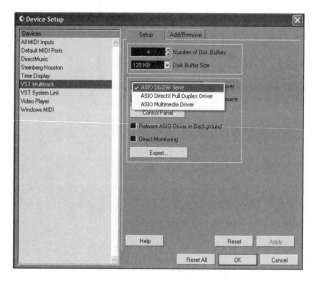

The place to configure your audio card in Cubase SX/SL is here.

1.9 How to Personalize Cubase

Cubase offers diverse options for adapting the program look & feel to suit your requirements. For example, you can have the computer load your personal working environment automatically when the application is launched. This is the first step to working successfully with Cubase. For one, an interface that you know and like provides a familiar environment. For the other, it's far more convenient to have the program load your preferred presets automatically rather than setting up the user interface for every session.

Let's first check out Cubase SX/SL's new file format and learn how Cubase stores data—particularly audio data—on the computer's hard disk. A good working knowledge of data management prevents potentially disastrous data loss.

1.10 Customized Data Management

In contrast to Cubase VST, Cubase SX/SL doesn't expect you to fuss with songs and arrangements or fret over the destination directory for your audio tracks. Instead, Cubase SX/SL works with "Projects." It automatically saves all data related to a given project in the same directory on hard disk. All you have to do is indicate the desired directory.

If you haven't created a folder for your SX/SL files yet, now is a good time to do this.

1   Generate a folder on your hard disk and name it *Cubase Projects*. You'll create subfolders later, one for each project.

2   Open Cubase SX/SL. If a project or template is loaded automatically, close it so that you're looking at an empty Project window.

3   Select FILE > NEW PROJECT. A directory offering various templates appears. Choose Empty.

4 A dialog box appears prompting you to select a destination folder for all data related to your project. Open the *Cubase Projects* folder and generate a subfolder within it using the Create button. Name it as you see fit, for example *Test*. Make a habit of naming these directories for the song they contain. We don't have a song yet, so *Test* will have to do.

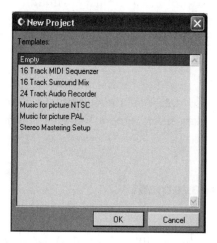

This is how you can create a blank project.

From now on, all data pertaining to this project will be filed in this directory. Cubase takes this a step further, automatically generating further subdirectories as the need arises. For example, it creates a subdirectory called *Audio* without further prompting. As soon as you begin carrying out functions and generating data within this project, Cubase adds further subdirectories such as *Edits*, *Fades* and *Images*.

As you can gather, Cubase provides for clearly organized folders from the start, conscientiously rounding up and corralling all of the project's data. All you have to do is play by the rules and generate a dedicated directory for every project.

1.11 The Perfect Desktop

The SX/SL application interface offers scores of functions and an abundance of information. Though features and functions are arranged clearly and structured logically, it's still a good idea to tailor the interface to suit your tastes.

1 Zoom the Cubase window all the way up so you can use the full screen. If you're working with two monitors, zoom up the window on both screens.

2 If you have yet to create a project, generate a new blank project now, and zoom the project-window all the way up.

3 Show the Inspector, Event Infoline and Overview by activating the first three buttons on the top left of the Project window.

4 Right-click the Track List. The Quick menu appears. Select ADD AUDIO TRACK. Cubase generates a new audio track.

5 Grab the line between the Track List and the Event Display and drag it to the right. Note how the control feature array changes in the Track List. Select a two-line view ending with the R/W buttons in the upper line.

6 Use the horizontal zoom slider at the bottom right of the Project window to view a section of the bar line. Move this fader and watch the Ruler. First select an eight bar section. Click the downward pointing triangle located to the left of the horizontal zoom slider. The Zoom Preset menu appears; it lets you to store the setting that you have just entered using the Add command. Name this section of the bar line, in this case, "8 Bars." From now on, you can call up this setting directly via the Zoom Preset menu. Create as many different zoom presets as you please and store them in the same way.

7 Add tracks to the Track List using the Quick menu (right mouse button) until the Track List comprises 16 MIDI tracks and 8 audio tracks.

8 A hidden menu lets you adjust the vertical track view. To do this, click the downward pointing triangle located above the vertical zoom slider. It zooms the vertical view to the desired number of tracks or track height. Try the different settings. You can also change the vertical view manually using the zoom slider or directly in the Track List. Grab the dividing line between two tracks with the mouse and drag it up or down. The height of every track changes when you press and hold [ctrl]. Experiment with the various options for a while, and then please select "Zoom Tracks 2 Rows" from the menu offering vertical view options.

9 Open the mixer via DEVICES > MIXER. It always shows the tracks that have been generated in the Project window. Every track that you create also appears in the form of a mixer channel. Position the mixer anywhere on the screen. If you work with two monitors, you may want to place the mixer on the right screen and the Project window on the left screen. If you work with one monitor, the mixer appears on top of the Project window. For reasons of space, you should close the mixer once you have positioned it on your screen. Cubase recalls where the mixer was placed.

10 Select DEVICES > SHOW PANEL and situate this window anywhere on your screen. The Devices window affords you fast access to key areas. Experience teaches that it's a good idea to leave this window open.

The Devices window.

You have just personalized your first desktop. Let's store your setup as a window layout so your settings don't vanish into the digital ether. To do this, select WINDOWS > WINDOW LAYOUTS > NEW. Name your configuration, for example "Standard," and click OK.

From here on out, you can call up this window layout via the WINDOW LAYOUTS menu. An even faster option is to press the key combination [alt]x [Num] on your computer keyboard. "Num" stands for the number block of the keyboard and "x" for the number of the layout. [alt][1] [Num] calls up your first window layout.

Now save a second configuration. To do this, open the mixer and save the window layout under "Mixer." [alt][2] [Num] calls this layout up.

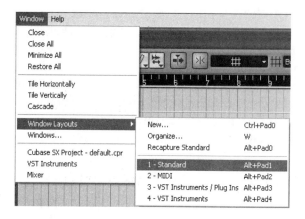

Window layouts are easily created and called to the screen.

1.12 A Standard Project of Your Very Own

The steps described above provide the perfect blueprint for creating a standard project. A standard project is loaded automatically when the program launches. This lets you get to work immediately in a familiar environment.

While window layouts save visual elements only, standard projects save both visuals and contents. These contents include tracks that you have generated, virtual sound generators that are available in the VST INSTRUMENTS rack, and effects assigned to VST SEND EFFECTS.

If you want to store a specific configuration as a standard project, proceed as follows:

1   Select FILE > SAVE AS.

2   Indicate a memory location, in this case the Cubase program directory, which is generally "C:\Programs\Steinberg\Cubase SX" (or SL). Enter the file name *Default;* the program automatically generates the file extension *cpr* for "Cubase project."

We're not quite finished yet. To prompt Cubase to open the standard project when the program is launched, we must enter the following setting:

1   Select FILE > PREFERENCES.

2   Select User Interface, and then the option "Open Default Project" from the "On Startup" pop-up menu.

1.13   Templates—the Right Workplace for Every Purpose

Cubase SX/SL lets you create, store, and recall templates. Whenever you generate a new project via FILE > NEW PROJECT (key command $\boxed{ctrl}\boxed{N}$) in Cubase SX/SL, a directory offering templates opens.

Templates are largely the same as the aforementioned standard project in that they contain settings required for different working situations. For example, you'll generate different versions of your standard project in the form of templates when you change the number of tracks, say 16 audio tracks for an audio template or 16 MIDI tracks for a MIDI template. Save this template under a meaningful name via FILE > SAVE AS TEMPLATE. Your templates are added to the template directory.

You may at some point want to delete or rename templates. At the time of printing, this could not be done in Cubase, so you must do it manually in Windows Explorer. You'll find the templates on your hard disk in the Cubase program directory's *Templates* subdirectory.

The program presets that we defined earlier prompt Cubase to load the standard project automatically when the program is launched. Cubase SX/SL can also execute other functions during program launch. For example, in order to view the template directory at the start of the program, select the option "Show Template Dialog" in the "User Interface" section of the Preferences.

Chapter 2

First Steps in Cubase SX/SL

Before we get to the main course—making music with Cubase—let me whet your appetite and take you on a whirlwind tour of the sonic kitchen, familiarizing you with its layout. Though most steps described in the following section apply to both Cubase SX and SL, I will point out functions that are available in Cubase SX only.

2.1   The Project Window

The Project window is Cubase SX/SL's most important window. Providing a sweeping view of the entire project, it lets you navigate throughout the project and determine its basic settings.

On the vertical plane, the Project window is divided into tracks; on the horizontal plane, a Ruler runs from left to right. Every project has a dedicated Project window. If you have opened several projects, you can access the various projects via the Activate button. You'll find this button at the top left of the given Project window.

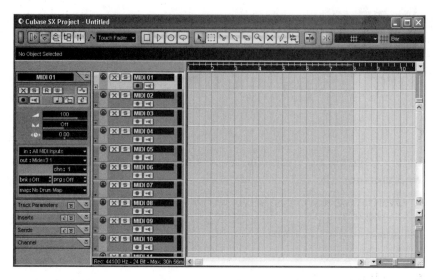

The Project window.

The Project window is partitioned into several areas:

- The Toolbar: The Toolbar contains tools that perform various functions as well as icons used to open further windows.

  The first five icons on the left are buttons that open the Inspector, the Infoline, the Overview, the Pool, and the mixer. The next four icons control key transport functions such as start and stop.

  These are followed by nine tools that do things like cut, paste, and select objects in the Project window.

  Next comes the icon for automatic scrolling. When it's activated, the content of the Event Display follows the current song position. The buttons for the Snap function, Snap mode, quantize value, and color pop-up menus are located at the end of the Toolbar.

  I won't trouble you with explanations of the various icons and tools now. We'll use the Toolbar extensively, and hands-on practice is more fun than dull theory.

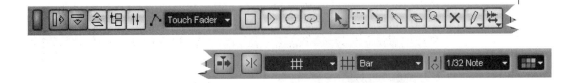

- The Overview: It shows MIDI parts and Audio Events—that is, Cubase's musical components—in small boxes. Drag the blue rectangle in the Overview to quickly move to a specific  position within your project. Reduce or enlarge this rectangle to change the view of the Event Display. Open and close the Overview using the third button from the left in the Toolbar.

- The Infoline: The Infoline presents information regarding the object selected in the Project window. The values for this object can be edited directly in the Infoline. Open and close the Infoline using the second button from the left in the Toolbar.

- The Inspector shows control features and parameters for the selected track. Its content depends on the selected track type (MIDI, audio, etc.). For some track types, the Inspector is divided into different panels that are opened and closed via the arrows at the top right of the respective "card." Press and hold [ctrl] down while clicking to view several panels at the same time. Press and hold [alt] to show or hide the Inspector's panels. The first button on the left in the Toolbar opens the Inspector.

- Located in the left section of the Project window is the Track List containing name boxes and different setting options for the tracks. The Track List offers different control features for different track types. You may have to change the size of the track in the Track List to view all control features. To enlarge the view, drag the dividing line between the Event Display and the Track List to the right.

■ The Event Display and the Ruler are located in the right section of the Project window. The Event Display presents a graphical view of track contents as they appear along the Ruler. These contents can be edited in various ways.

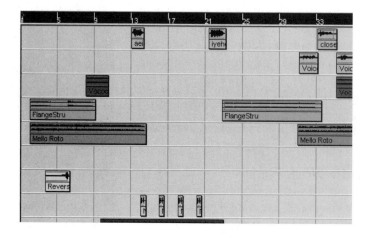

2.2   The Transport Panel

The Transport Panel controls recording and playback processes in Cubase. Its functions are much like those of traditional tape machines. Next to the actual transport functions, you'll find further elements such as the Locators for setting the starting and ending points of Regions in the Transport Panel, buttons for punching in and out, as well as Cycle mode and MIDI activity displays.

In the following chapters, we'll work extensively with the Transport Panel. Though we'll take a closer look at its functions as we come to them, I'll preview some key functions now.

You can show and hide the Transport Panel via the Transport menu or F2. The transport functions start, stop, recording and cycle can also be executed via the Toolbar. This is generally the preferred option when you have hidden the Transport Panel for reasons of space.

You can configure the Transport Panel view to suit your taste. To this end, click the Transport Panel using the right mouse button. A menu opens that lets you show and hide specific areas. Experiment with different settings and observe how the view changes. When working with this book, I recommend that you show all areas in the Transport Panel. This is easily done by selecting the menu option SHOW ALL.

2.3   How to Work Fast

The ability to work quickly is the key to successful recording. If you're constantly having to search for specific functions or don't know the shortcuts that let you work swiftly, the fun factor for you and your fellow musicians will be negligible. Of course, it will take practice to learn how to find the required functions quickly and surely. Though practice may lead to perfection, I have found that even users who are very well versed in Cubase do things in roundabout ways or have acquired inefficient working habits. This applies mainly to routine chores such as editing values or executing frequently used functions such as starting and stopping.

Often a key command is the fastest option; other chores are best done using the mouse. It's in your best interests to find a good compromise between mouse and keyboard handling. Though personal preferences dictate which approach suits you best, allow me to share a few tips that in my experience speed up working pace.

2.3.1 Using Key Commands

Cubase offers a shortcut for almost every command. Key commands are managed in the Key Command window. It opens via FILE > KEY COMMANDS. At the left of the window, you'll see listed various categories such as Edit, File, Editors, and so forth. Individual commands are listed on the right in the COMMANDS section of the window, next to the respective category. In the KEYS section on the right of the window, you can see which key combination has been defined for a specific command. If you want view all standard key commands, click the Show List button. A window listing all available key commands opens.

You'll find it very easy to define key commands of your own. To do this, select a Cubase function in the CATEGORIES and COMMANDS columns. Click the in "Type new Key Command" box and press the desired key or key combination on the computer keyboard. The defined key command appears and can be assigned using the Assign button. Cubase will let you know if the key command that you have entered has already been assigned elsewhere. You have the option of substituting your key command for the previous shortcut or defining another key command.

If you add or change a key command, it's stored globally rather than locally as a part of a project. This means that the new assignments apply to all projects. You can restore all preset assignments at any time using the Reset All button. In addition, you can export key commands as a file with the file extension ".key." These files can be imported into every project. This lets you restore your personalized key assignments swiftly and easily via the Export and Import buttons, for example, if you want to dump projects from one computer to another.

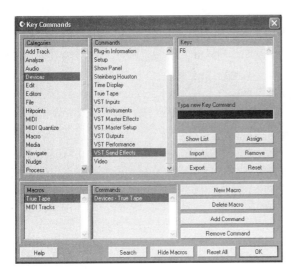

This is where key commands and macros are defined.

With practice, you'll soon discover which combination of mouse and keyboard handling works best for you. I strongly recommend that you heed this bit of advice, though: Always control frequently used transport functions with the keyboard because this speeds up your pace of work tremendously. A list of the commands for essential transport functions follows.

Command	Key(s)
Show/hide Transport Panel	[F2]
Start	[enter]
Stop	[0] (Num)
Start/Stop	[⬯] (Space bar)
Record	[*] (Num)
Rewind	[−] (Num)
Fast forward	[+] (Num)
Return to zero position	[.] (Num)
Cycle on/off	[/] (Num)
Auto punch-in on/off	[i]
Auto punch-out on/off	[O]

2.3.2   Using Macros

The macros in Cubase SX/SL are superhero key commands—they can carry out several functions at once.

Call up macros via EDIT > MACROS. Initially, this menu offers no options because macros have yet to be defined.

To create a macro, select FILE > KEY COMMANDS and click the Show Macros button at the bottom of the window. This loads functions for defining and managing macros into the window.

Generate a new macro via the New Macro button. It will appear with the initial name "New Command." Double-click to rename it. The Add Command and Remove Command buttons let you combine different key commands in the macro. Note that you are free to define macros as you please. It's immaterial if a key combination is assigned to the given Cubase command; so don't let the names of the buttons confuse you.

Note also that a macro is executed sequentially from top to bottom. A hopefully enlightening example follows:

1 Create a new macro and name it "Add tracks."

2 Select "Add Track" in the Categories column. Then select "Audio" in the Commands column. Click the Add Command button.

3 Repeat this step, selecting "Add Track > MIDI" the second time around, and "Add Track > Audio" the third time.

4 Close the Key Commands window by clicking OK and call up the macro via EDIT > MACROS > ADD TRACKS. Cubase adds three tracks to the Project window in the sequence defined in the macro.

As this little experiment demonstrates, you can define frequently used workflows very easily as macros. Make a habit of using them and your working pace will pick up considerably.

2.3.3 Using the Mouse

If you don't own a mouse equipped with a wheel, rush right out and buy one now. There are countless functions in Cubase SX/SL begging to be manipulated via mouse wheel, which also significantly speeds up proceedings.

Try the mouse wheel out now. In the Transport Panel, click on the value for the Left or Right Locator and dial the mouse wheel. The value changes. Move the mouse pointer to the horizontal or vertical scroll bar and turn the mouse wheel. This controls the scrolling function.

Try using the mouse wheel all over the Project window by clicking values and control features and turning the mouse wheel. This editing option won't work everywhere, and it's not the best solution for every editing chore. See for yourself where the mouse wheel works best for you.

In Cubase SX/SL, you can also enter all values via keyboard. To this end, all you have to do is click the value with the mouse and type in the new value. This is a departure from VST, which required double-clicking to select values.

In some areas of Cubase, you'll find control features that serve to enter values. Some of these remain hidden until you activate them via mouse. This is the case in the Inspector. Go to the Inspector, click the small blue bar below a MIDI track's volume control, and hold the mouse button down. A fader appears that lets you adjust volume level.

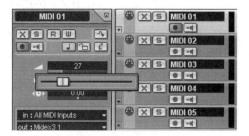

Entering values using a fader.

Note that the right mouse button plays an important role. It opens something called a Quick menu at many places throughout the program. This menu is a shortcut serving to carry out functions and select tools. Try it out: Click anywhere in the Project window using the right mouse button. Don't worry about the contents of the Quick menus for now; just try to remember where they appear.

The Quick menu of the Event Display.

Chapter 3

Recording

We'll look how to get music into Cubase SX/SL in the following sections.

The focus is of course on recording, specifically the different methods of recording MIDI and audio material. This chapter deals with the particulars of recording in Cubase rather than generalities such as which microphone is best for recording a saxophone or how to record a drum set. If you need answers to questions like these, there are many excellent books and tutorials readily available.

Another option for getting music into Cubase is to load prerecorded material offered on CD in the form of audio data, for example, drum loops. This is another important skill alongside actual recording, so we'll also examine how this is done.

3.1   Recording MIDI

Once you have set up your MIDI environment properly, nothing stands in the way of your first MIDI recording.

First, quit Cubase and re-launch it. The program loads your standard project with 16 MIDI tracks and 8 audio tracks, if you followed my advice and stored this configuration as a standard project. No worries if you didn't: Simply load a blank template and generate a MIDI track by selecting PROJECT > ADD TRACK > MIDI.

Cubase uses the MIDI inputs and outputs that you defined under DEVICES > DEVICE SETUP > DEFAULT MIDI PORTS for the newly created MIDI track. You can verify this by checking out the two Inspector options "in" and "out."

These two options also let you use other inputs and outputs. In order to assign a MIDI input to a track, open the input pop-up menu by clicking "in" in the Inspector. Cubase lists all available MIDI inputs in this menu. Generally, these entries require no modification. For purpose of the examples below, I assume that you're working with just one recording keyboard and have defined the input to which this keyboard is connected as the MIDI input.

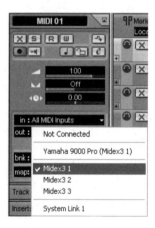

Selecting a MIDI output.

Arm the MIDI track so that it's ready to record. To do this, click the Record Enable button. It's the button sporting the dot. Once armed, this button lights up red.

Standing by and ready to record.

This is a good time to call your attention to two more program presets:

■ If the option "Show Tips" is enabled under FILE > PREFERENCES > USER INTERFACE, Cubase shows the function of a control feature in plain text when the mouse points to it. Try this out: Drag the mouse pointer to the Record Enable button. A tiny window pops up offering a description of this button. This feature is particularly helpful in finding specific functions when you begin using the program on your own.

■ A track can be armed automatically as soon as you select it. Another program preset is responsible for this function. Under EDIT > PREFERENCES > EDITING you'll find the option "Enable Record on Selected Track." The selected track is armed automatically when this option is enabled.

Back to the business of recording: First check your settings by playing a few notes on your keyboard. The level meter in the Track List should show a green bar signaling the arrival of incoming MIDI signals. Also the MIDI activity displays at the far right of the Transport Panel should light up—the upper red bar for the MIDI input and the lower green bar for the output.

> The red bar should light up even if Cubase is not armed for recording. It indicates that Cubase is receiving MIDI data. If this is not the case, check your MIDI interface's settings.

As the final step of recording preparations, you must define a MIDI output to which you want to send recorded and MIDI thru data. This determines which MIDI sound generator plays your music. Use the "out" menu in the Inspector to select a MIDI output. The standard setting is the preset MIDI port. A mouse click opens a list of all activated MIDI outputs.

If you have interfaced your external sound generator with Cubase via the MIDI Device Manager, it will also appear in this list. The MIDI input and output are automatically configured accordingly if you select your sound generator.

You can define the MIDI channel in the MIDI output menu. You may opt to work with a multi-timbral sound generator. This breed of device includes all GM/GS and XG-compatible instruments and can receive data via 16 MIDI channels. For example, you could route a bass sound via channel 1, a piano via channel 2, an organ via channel 3, and so forth. The drum sets of GM/GS/XG-compatible sound generators are addressed via MIDI channel 10. If you're working with a GM/GS/XG-enabled instrument, step through all MIDI channels in Cubase while playing your recording keyboard. You'll discover that initially a piano sound is audible on all channels. MIDI channel 10 is the exception; here you'll hear that various percussion instruments are distributed across the keyboard.

Select a sound that you want to use for your first recording. If you prefer something other than a drum set, select MIDI channel 1 for the MIDI track, and choose a sound. To do this, click "prg" in the Inspector.

If you have interfaced your sound generator with Cubase, a list of sounds will open. You can select the sound conveniently by its name. Check this by striking a chord on your keyboard. The selected sound will be audible.

If you have not interfaced a sound generator, you must select programs by entering numbers and possibly using the menu for the sound bank labeled "bnk." If you're working with a predefined instrument, the menu for the bank is hidden because the bank select settings have already been loaded to the Midi Device Manager.

You're almost ready to record your first track. You probably want to activate the metronome so that your track is in time and tight. Switch the metronome on via the Click button in the Transport Panel. Under TRANSPORT > METRONOME SETUP you can adjust the click as desired; at the left of the window, you can select a MIDI click or an audio click.

The MIDI click has proven beneficial in practice. Your best bet is to assign a drum sound such as hi-hat cymbals, rim shot, or side stick. To do this, select the appropriate MIDI channel and output note. For example, to assign a GM/GS/XG sound generator's hi-hat as the metronome click sound, you would select MIDI channel 10 and F#1. You can opt to emphasize the first beat of each bar or assign another sound to the downbeat. Define these settings separately via "High Note" and "Low Note."

Also, activate the option "Precount" and set it to one or two bars. If you activate the metronome option "Record" and deactivate the "Play" option, you'll hear the metronome click while recording but not during playback.

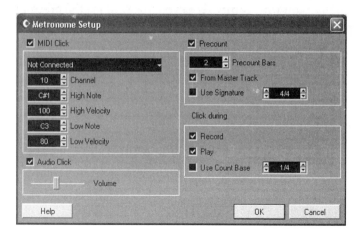

The Metronome Setup window.

3.1.1　The Recording Lamp Is Lit

Now it's time to track. The spotlight here is on procedure rather than results, so we'll dive right in without further guidance on bar length or musical content.

1　Check if the track is in recording mode.

2 Ensure Cycle mode is deactivated. It's switched on and off via the third button from the left in the Transport Panel. If this button lights up yellow, Cycle mode is active.

3 Make sure that the option "Start Record at Left Locator" in the Transport menu is disabled.

4 Set any tempo via the Transport Panel and deactivate the Master button.

5 Press ⬚ [Num] in order to place the cursor at the beginning of the project.

6 Start recording by clicking the Record button in the Transport Panel or pressing ⬚ [Num] on your computer keyboard. Wait for the precount, and then play a random riff.

7 When you're ready to stop recording, click the Stop button in the Transport Panel or press ⬚ [Num] on the computer keyboard.

Once your recording is in "in the can," a bar appears in the Event Display; in Cubase jargon, it's called a "Part." This Part contains the MIDI data that you just recorded.

To audition the track, drag the cursor to the beginning of the recorded MIDI part. You can do this either by clicking the Ruler or the Rewind button in the Transport Panel. Play the track by clicking the Play button in the Transport Panel or pressing ⬚, and listen to the results of your efforts.

Cubase generates a Part for each recording.

You can determine the MIDI part's view. To do this, select PREFERENCES > EVENT DISPLAY > MIDI. If you prefer to see notes displayed in Parts, select "Scores" from the Part Data Mode pop-up menu. Experiment with the different settings. It you click the Apply button, the changes appear immediately in the Project window. This lets you view different settings right away.

3.1.2   Recording in Cycle Mode

When working in Cycle mode, a specific segment consisting of any number of bars is repeated continuously during recording and playback. The positions of the Left and Right Locator define this segment. You'll find these Locators in the Transport Panel. The Left Locator is labeled "L," the Right Locator is labeled "R."

The first step in Cycle mode recording is to position the Locators. There are various ways to do this:

- Click on the values for the Left and Right Locator in the Transport Panel and type the desired values in using the computer keyboard.
- Press and hold [ctrl] while clicking into the Ruler to set the Left Locator. Press and hold [alt] while clicking into the Ruler to set the Right Locator.
- Draw the desired segment into the *upper* Region of the Ruler.

For our recording, we'll use the Locators to define a segment with a length of two bars. To do this, set the Left Locator to the beginning of bar 1 and the Right Locator to the beginning of bar 3. Activate the Cycle button in the Transport Panel so that it lights up yellow. The predefined key command for switching Cycle mode on and off is [/] [Num].

Cycle mode settings.

Generate a MIDI track or select an existing blank MIDI track. Set this track to MIDI channel 10. If you're working with a GM/GS/XG-compatible sound generator, this setting should address a drum set.

There's one matter left for us to clear up before we can begin recording: Cubase SX/SL offers two Cycle modes. These are switched via a mouse click on the "Cycle Rec" lettering on the bottom left of the Transport Panel:

■ When "Mix" is enabled, the new recording is added to previously recorded MIDI data in each pass. This mode is an excellent choice for drum tracks. This lets you record one instrument per cycle. For example, you could begin with the bass drum, then continue with the snare, and so forth.

■ When "Overwrite" is enabled, each take deletes the previous take's MIDI data. In other words, the new take replaces the earlier take.

We'll opt for Mix and get to it. Activate the Click button to hear the metronome, and start recording. Play different drum instruments, recording them in consecutive cycles. Cubase will continue cycling between the two Locators until you stop recording.

3.1.3   Starting and Stopping Recordings Automatically

Cubase SX/SL can switch automatically from playback to recording mode by way of what audio engineers call "punching in." This option is a great choice when you want to replace part of a recording and hear the material preceding the section you want to replace before you start recording.

First, set the Left Locator to the position at which you want to start recording. Then activate the Punch-in button in the Transport Panel. This is the button on the left of the Cycle button. Ensure Cycle mode is deactivated.

Start playback at any position preceding the Left Locator. Recording mode is activated automatically when the cursor reaches the Left Locator.

Punching in is a convenient way to track, but not nearly as convenient as punching in and back out again. You can punch out to switch the recording off automatically when the cursor arrives at the Right Locator. Set the Right Locator to the desired position and activate the Punch-out button in the Transport Panel. This is the button located at the right of the Cycle button. Recording stops automatically when the cursor reaches the Right Locator.

The Punch-in and Punch-out buttons in the Transport Panel.

3.1.4   Quantizing Tracks Automatically

Quantizing squeezes MIDI data into a rhythmic girdle that you can tailor to size. A fundamental function of every sequencer, you're sure to be familiar with the basics of quantizing, so I'll spare you further explanation.

However, Cubase offers a special quantizing option that does bear further examination: MIDI data can be quantized while you're tracking, which is a great help when recording drum parts. Called Auto Quantize, this function is activated and deactivated via the AQ button in the Transport Panel.

To ensure auto quantizing delivers the desired results, you must select a quantizing value. This is done via the Quantize Selector pop-up menu in the Toolbar, or by going MIDI > QUANTIZE SETUP and selecting the desired value in the Grid pop-up menu.

 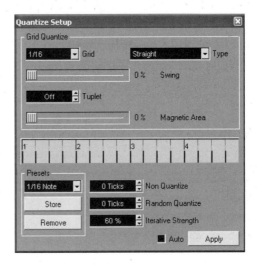

This is where you define the quantizing value.

3.2 Recording Audio

The procedure for recording audio material in Cubase SX/SL is largely the same as for recording MIDI material: create or select a track, press the Record button, and go for it.

But there's a lot more going on under the hood of Cubase's recording engine. Because you're recording audio material, Cubase writes an audio file to your hard disk, specifically, into the given project directory's *Audio* subdirectory. You don't have to worry about where your audio recordings end up on the hard disk of your computer. And, unlike in Cubase VST, you don't have to define destination directories.

Presumably, one thing you will be worried about is the sound of your audio recordings. We'll look at key settings and acquire a few audio engineering skills to ensure they sound as good as they should. Unlike MIDI tracks—which consist merely of data serving to control sound generators—audio recordings capture actual music. For this reason, we'll delve into topics such as signal levels and audio quality.

3.2.1 Choosing the Right Audio Quality

The CD standard calls for 16-bit word width and 44.1kHz sampling rate. An audio CD must adhere to this standard, otherwise it won't play on a CD player.

However, Cubase SX/SL is not limited to 16 bits; it offers far greater word widths of 24 to 32 bits floating and sampling rates up to 96kHz. This gives rise to the question, why work with higher resolutions if the audio material has to be computed back down to 16 bits and 44.1 kHz for the CD?

Let's examine some theory to answer it:

- Word width determines the accuracy of digital/analog conversion as well as the dynamic range. This is why tracks recorded with greater word widths sound cleaner. Furthermore, the noise floor is lower and more headroom is available. The latter is decisive for good recording quality. Tracks recorded at low gain levels are far noisier than tracks recorded at higher levels. Because greater word widths offer more headroom, you can turn signals up to higher levels, and far less noise is introduced to tracks even if they are converted back down later.
- The sampling rate's impact is most prominent in the high frequency range. Higher sampling rates yield a more transparent and natural-sounding sonic image. But even the highest sampling rates are useless for recording and playback if your audio card does not support the given format. In other words, you can't record at 48kHz if your audio card's sampling rate peaks out at 44.1kHz.

Every audio card handles a sampling rate of 44.1kHz, thereby providing satisfactory audio quality. Most recordists are happy to work with this rate. If you import audio material from a CD, the sampling rate is also 44.1kHz, and you can introduce imported files into your song without bother.

If you decide to work with 48kHz, audio data imported from CD has to first be converted to 48 kHz. If your audio card supports 48kHz and you place a premium on natural-sounding tracks, go ahead and record in this format. However, bear in mind that the steps involved in importing CD files or using prerecorded material as found on sampling CDs are more complicated.

Cubase SX/SL handles word widths of 16 bits, 24 bits, and 32 bits floating. As pointed out in the discussion of sampling rate, the audio card must support the selected format. You can only create 24- or 32-bit tracks using an audio card equipped with the necessary converters. The 32-bit floating format is a special case; it also works with 16-bit-cards. This format is available only in Cubase SX. More on this later.

Cubase requires you to enter the settings for the sampling rate and word width just once for the entire Project. This is done under PROJECT > PROJECT SETUP.

By the way, don't worry about how to convert your songs to 16-bit, 44.1kHz CD format when it comes to time to burn them on CD. Cubase automatically computes them down for audio export by way of a process called "dithering." We'll discuss dithering in more detail later in this book.

3.2.2 Choosing the Right Settings

A few preparations are in order before you can record audio in Cubase SX/SL:

■ Define the sampling rate and format (word width) under PROJECT > PROJECT SETUP.

- Go to DEVICES > VST INPUTS and check if the appropriate audio card input is enabled for recording. The VST Inputs window lists all the inputs of your audio hardware. If your audio card offers a stereo input only, that's all you'll find listed there. If you're working with an audio card that offers more than a stereo input, you'll also find the additional inputs in this list. Ensure the input that you want to use is enabled. It's activated via the on/off switch in the Active column. Deactivate all inputs that you don't need because every activated input consumes computing resources.

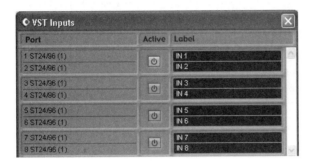

- Eliminate a common source of errors and check the settings in your audio card's control panel: The physical input that is connected to your audio source must be also activated via software to enable recording. For example, if you have connected your mixer to the audio card's line in, you must also activate this line in circuit in your audio card's control panel. If your audio card works with a standard control panel, you can open it by double-clicking the speaker icon in the Windows icon bar.
- Select an audio track for recording by clicking it in the Track List.
- Decide if you want to record in mono or stereo. Do this using the Stereo/Mono button of the track that you have selected for recording. If the button lights up yellow and a two-ring symbol that looks like the Olympics emblem with three rings missing, you're tracking in stereo.

- Open the mixer via DEVICES > MIXER. If you're working with just one track, the mixer shows just one channel strip. If you're working with your template that already contains several tracks, you'll find a dedicated channel for every track in the mixer. The channel for the track that you have selected is automatically enabled in the mixer. The reason for this is that when you select a track in the Track List, it's also selected in the mixer, and vice versa.
  Select the audio input for recording at the top of the mixer channel. Click an entry and a list of inputs activated under DEVICES > VST INPUTS appears. Select the input or the input pair to which your audio source is connected.

- Check the input level. To do this, the Record Enable button must be activated for the track so that it lights up red. Generate an input signal at your audio source. The level meter in the mixer should twitch in response.

3.2.3 The Perfect Level

In terms of recording levels, digital and analog tracks are apples and oranges. When recording analog tracks, savvy engineers sometimes like to slap an input silly with a level that occasionally drives the meter into the red zone. Avoid this at all costs when recording digital tracks. Patching in signal levels that are higher than the system can cleanly handle generates very nasty distortion indeed.

The input signal level makes or breaks audio quality. Always set the output level of your audio source as high as possible without exceeding the 0dB threshold and thereby overloading the input. Keep on eye on the level meter in the mixer channel strip—it tells you when the input is saturated. If it continuously lights up red, the signal is overloading the input. Another helpful indicator is the numeric meter located above the level meter. The value indicated should not exceed 0. You won't be able to actually audition the signal until you have activated the monitor function in Cubase. More on this later.

Bear the following in mind when setting input signal levels:

- You *cannot* set the input level via the channel strip's volume control.

- You can set the input level via your audio card's control panel. Because the control panels of different audio cards are not identical, I am unable to describe exactly how this is done. Please consult your audio card's manual for detailed instructions.

- You *can* set the input level by adjusting the output signal of the audio source that you want record. If it's a keyboard, for example, you can adjust the output signal using its volume control.

- If you work with a mixer that uses subgroups, you can set the input level via the subgroups' volume controls. This is an excellent way to control the recording level. You may recall that I pointed out other advantages of a mixer at the beginning of this book.

3.2.4 Monitoring—Hearing What You're Recording while You're Recording

You must activate the monitor function in Cubase to hear what you're recording as you're recording it. Do this by clicking the Monitor button at the bottom left of the channel strip. The button lights up orange when activated. The input signal is routed through Cubase and patched out its output.

You can select from among various monitoring modes in the VST panel of the PREFERENCES. You'll find the options listed in the "Auto Monitoring" pop-up menu.

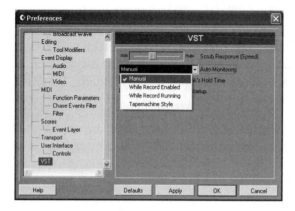

The various monitoring options.

- Manual is the preset. This means you must activate and deactivate monitoring manually as above.

- While Record Enabled: The monitoring function is activated automatically as soon as an audio track is armed.

- While Record Running: You'll hear the monitor signal as soon as recording starts.

- Tapemachine Style: You'll hear the monitor signal during recording and when Cubase is stopped, but not during playback.

If your audio card's latency is high, the original signal and the monitor signal will be audibly out of sync. This is because the monitor signal is delayed by the amount of latency inherent in the card. This can cause tremendous problems. Imagine that you're trying to record vocals and you're hearing your own voice echoed with a perceptive delay. This makes recording all but impossible.

If you're using an external mixer, you can sidestep this problem by monitoring the signal via the mixer's headphones output and disabling the monitor function in Cubase.

Otherwise, the problem can only be solved permanently if you buy a professional audio card that works with an ASIO-2 driver. These cards' latency is very low, and they offer a direct monitoring function. It guarantees latency-free monitoring by routing the input signal directly back out of the audio card without taking the detour that is Cubase. To activate direct monitoring, go to DEVICES > DEVICE SETUP > VST MULTI-TRACK. Activate the "Direct Monitoring" option. This option is not selectable if your audio card doesn't work with an ASIO-2 driver or doesn't support direct monitoring.

For the sake of thoroughness, let me mention that there are audio cards that offer direct monitoring, but don't provide for this option in Cubase for lack of an ASIO driver. In this case, you must activate the function via the card's control panel. Please consult your card's documentation for more on how to do this.

Direct Monitoring has a drawback: If you use Cubase effects such as reverb, chorus or delay during recording rather than adding them later, you won't hear these effects in the monitor signal. The reason is of course that the signal sent to the audio card's input is patched straight to the audio card's output via the direct monitoring circuit. The signal is not sent to Cubase, so it can't lay effects over it. Most recordists can live with this disadvantage. Conventional recording wisdom holds that using effects while tracking is not the best way to go.

3.2.5 Recording

With all preparations out of the way, you can record your first audio track:

1 Place the cursor to the position at which you want to begin recording.

2 Start recording by clicking the Record button in the Transport Panel or pressing ⊡ [Num] on the keyboard.

3 Generate an audio signal, for instance, by playing on a connected keyboard or singing into a connected microphone.

4　Stop recording by clicking the Stop button in the Transport Panel or pressing ⓪ [Num] on the keyboard.

Cubase just created something called an "Audio Event;" it appears as a bar in the Event Display.

Whereas a MIDI recording generates a Part—as does an audio recording in Cubase VST—an audio recording in Cubase SX/SL creates an Event. We'll get to the difference between Events and Parts shortly.

Recording generated an Audio Event.

The Event is automatically labeled with the name of the track, followed by a number. The numbering scheme continues sequentially as you continue to add recorded Events to this track.

If you have used the monitoring function and it's set to manual mode, you must deactivate it if you want to monitor the recorded material.

3.2.6　Recording in Cycle Mode

In Cycle mode, audio tracks are recorded much like MIDI tracks. There are, however, a few differences. Cubase offers three different audio Cycle modes. You can select the desired mode under FILE > PREFERENCES* > AUDIO in the "Cycle Record Mode" pop-up menu.

■　Create Events: The recording process generates a continuous audio file. An Audio Event is generated in each take. This Event marks the recorded section of the audio file. All Events receive the name of the audio file with the extension "Take," followed by a sequential number for each take. The most recent take appears at the top and is played back. To select another take, click it using the right mouse button and activate the command "To Front."

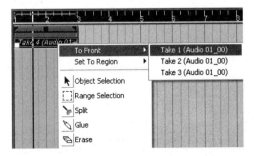

- Create Regions: This option tells Cubase to create Regions rather than events. A Region is a segment within an Event. These Regions are separable, meaning that they can be used individually within a song. As is the case with Events, you can select individual takes of cycled recordings by clicking them using the right mouse button.

- Create Events + Regions: This mode combines the two aforementioned modes. The advantage is that if you cut takes (more on this in the paragraph below), you can restore them because there are still extant as unedited Regions.

Different takes can easily be combined to create a perfect track. To do this, cut the Audio Event at the desired places using the scissors tool. You don't have to cut every take, just the top one. The underlying takes are automatically cut at the same place. Every cut creates a separate section. Once you have cut the Event into different sections, you can select which take you want to use for each section by clicking it via using the right mouse button. Because this is so much faster and easier than tracking until you get the perfect take, you could do things like have your vocalist sing 20 takes. Later, when you're alone and undisturbed, you can select the best bits at leisure and combine them to create a perfect track.

Combine the best bits of different takes to create the ultimate track.

3.2.7 Starting and Stopping Recordings Automatically

Audio tracks also let you punch in and out automatically. The approach is the same as for MIDI tracks. When set to punch-in/out mode, Cubase generates a new audio file. When a new Event is recorded to this file, Cubase layers it over the previously recorded Event. The initial recording is preserved; only it does not play while the segment recorded by punching in/out plays. If you delete the new Event or drag it to another track, you'll hear the initial recording.

3.2.8 Recording with TrueTape (Cubase SX Only)

TrueTape emulates an analog tape machine's tape saturation, adding considerable warmth to your tracks. Though digital tracks have many advantages over analog tape recordings, many musicians and audio engineers hold that they sound clinical. TrueTape is just what the doctor ordered for sterile-sounding tracks.

Looks inconspicuous but delivers great recordings with an analog touch: TrueTape.

Before you try TrueTape, note that:

- TrueTape generates tracks in 32-bit float format.
- Unlike 32 bits, you can use 32-bit float even if your audio hardware's resolution is limited to 16 bits.
- Unlike other VST effects, TrueTape cannot be added to tracks post recording; you must process signals with TrueTape while tracking.

Let's put TrueTape through its paces. Consider yourself fortunate if you own an audio card with low latency. This means you can audition the effect almost without delay and pass judgment on the influence of TrueTape immediately—*almost* because using direct monitoring is not an option. Using it's pointless because you won't hear TrueTape in the monitor signal.

1   Go to DEVICES > DEVICE SETUP > VST MULTITRACK, and deactivate the option "Direct Monitoring."

2   Generate an audio track and activate the monitoring function.

3   Select DEVICES > TRUE TAPE. The TrueTape control panel appears.

4   Switch TrueTape on via the on/off switch at the top left.

5   Play a chord on your keyboard, for our purposes, preferably using an organ sound. Of course, you're free to use any other audio source.

6   Move the Drive control to set the degree of tape saturation. You'll hear immediately how TrueTape works. As the Drive value increases, the sound becomes warmer and fuller. At extreme settings, a touch of warm, even pleasant, distortion is added to the sound.

7   You'll find some presets in the pop-up menu above the Drive control. Try these out too.

If you drag the Drive control to the right, the recording level increases automatically, and the signal may even be saturated. Unlike when making 16-bit recordings, this shouldn't be of concern. TrueTape works with 32 bits floating so it's almost impossible to overload Cubase's input. In our case, Cubase's output or your audio card's input will distort well before Cubase's input is saturated. The former is easily fixed by backing off the channel a touch in the Cubase mixer. To ensure that your audio card's input is not overloading, switch TrueTape off and listen to the monitor signal. If you can hear distortion in the signal, back off the level at the sound source.

If you own Cubase SL and are saddened by you have just read, cheer up. Though TrueTape can enrich the sound of recordings tremendously, the effect is also a matter of taste, genre, and style. For example, if you have a penchant for producing ballads or tend to record lots of vocals and acoustic instruments, you'll find much to love about TrueTape. If slamming' dance productions are your cup of meat, you'll be happy to do without it.

3.3   Importing Audio Material

To reiterate a point made earlier, there is a third way to get music into Cubase next to recording audio and MIDI data. You can import audio material found on sampling CDs, for example, drum loops. The ability to import music also comes in handy when you want to reuse previously recorded tracks in other Cubase projects.

Cubase offers various options for importing audio material. For instance, you can drag audio files directly from the desktop of your computer to an audio track in the Project window.

As soon as you drag the mouse pointer over the audio track, a small window appears showing the current bar position. This lets you drop the audio file at precisely the desired position. When you release the mouse button, the Import Options dialog box opens.

> The dialog box only opens if "Open Options Dialog" is selected in the "On Import Audio Files" pop-up menu found under FILE > PREFERENCES > AUDIO. This is the default setting so you shouldn't have to change anything here.

In the Import Options dialog box, you can tell Cubase to copy the audio file into the project folder. Incidentally, copying doesn't affect the original file. Your best bet is to generate a copy so that all files pertaining to a project are stored in the appropriate project folder.

The dialog box also offers the option of converting the audio file into the current project format. Say you have defined 32 bits as the format for a given project, and then import a 16-bit file. This file will automatically be converted to 32 bits.

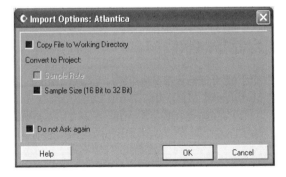

The options menu for importing audio files.

Note: If you load a mono file to a stereo track or a stereo file to a mono track, a message stating "Mono/stereo mismatch" appears in the generated Audio Event. The Event won't play until you change the track status using the Stereo/Mono button.

Audio files can also be imported into Projects from:

- the Pool,
- the Project window of another open project,
- the Audio Part editor of an open project, and
- the Sample Editor of an open project.

I'll acquaint you with all of these importing options as we progress through this book. Cubase SX offers another import function: POOL > AUDIO CD IMPORT lets you load tracks from an audio CD in digital form and insert them into the Cubase project. Remixers, in particular, are sure to be delighted with this function.

Chapter 4

Arranging and Editing Audio Material

Once your first tracks are in the can, we want to take a crack at arranging in the Project window. Of course, you're free to follow along with this chapter's exercises using tracks of your own. However, I urge you to use the material I have prepared for this purpose. That way we'll be speaking the same language at every turn.

The first exercise is to import audio data into an empty project and arrange it there. A few comments before we begin:

- The tempo of the project is 126bpm. Set your project's song tempo to this value.
- I saved intermediate steps to document the work in progress in the *Cubase Projects > Arrangement* directory found on the enclosed CD. There you'll find the various stages of production archived in files named *Arrangement*, followed by a number. As we move along, I'll point out when you can view a production phase as a Cubase project.
- Please follow my example: Save each stage of your production as a project.

4.1   Bringing Audio Material in the Pool

A file is written to the hard disk of your computer whenever you record an audio track. In addition, a link to this file is added to something called the "Pool." Called a "Clip," this link is a copy of an audio file on the hard disk. A Clip enables Cubase to find the required audio data on the hard disk and to play it from there.

The advantage of this working method is that audio data can be archived in separate files rather being stored in Cubase Project files. This means that Cubase Project files are relatively small. In addition, one Project's audio data can easily be used in other Projects because it archived on the hard disk independently of a specific Project.

The Pool rules follow:

- All of a project's audio and video Clips are entered in the Pool.
- Every project comes with a dedicated Pool.

You can open the Pool by clicking the Open Pool button in the Project window. This is the fourth button from the left in the Toolbar. Or you can open the Pool via PROJECT > POOL or the key command $\boxed{ctrl}\boxed{P}$.

The Pool is partitioned into three areas, Audio, Video, and Trash. For now, we'll focus only the Audio box because your Audio Clips are filed there.

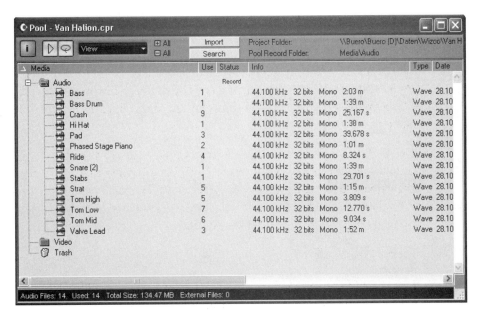

The audio Clips of a project in the Pool.

Here are two general insights to contemplate before you get some hands-on experience with the Pool:

■ If you rename audio files used in Cubase projects, you'll also rename the corresponding Clips in the Pool. Never rename files in Windows Explorer because Cubase will no longer be able to find renamed audio files when you load the given project.

■ Again, store audio files that you're using for a given project in this project's folder. Make a habit of doing this by executing the POOL menu's PREPARE ARCHIVE function before closing a project. Cubase will then copy all audio files used in the project into the project folder.

Tidy up your hard disk by archiving files.

Let's get to it. The first step in our exercise is to generate a new blank project and import the required audio material into the Pool:

1   Start Cubase and select FILE > NEW PROJECT.

2   Select the "Empty" template and click OK.

3   In the Select Directory dialog box, select the *Cubase Projects* folder and click Create.

4   Enter a name for the new project folder to this pop-up dialog box and confirm with OK. Quit the Select Directory dialog by clicking OK.

5   Open the Pool via ⌈ctrl⌉⌈P⌉.

6   Click the Import button in the Pool. A file selection box named "Import Medium" opens. Place the enclosed CD into your CD-ROM drive and locate the folder *Cubase Projects > Arrangement > Audio* on the CD. Open it.

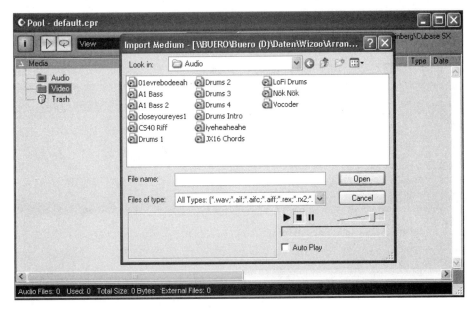

The file selection box for importing audio files.

7 You're looking at a list of audio files. If you want to audition an audio file, select it via mouse click, and then click the playback button at the bottom right of the file selection box. If you click a file when the "Auto Play" option is activated, it will be played automatically.

8 We'll import all audio files at once. Press and hold ⎡shift⎤, click the audio file at the top of the list and then the file at the bottom of the list. This selects all files. Click Open.

9 The Import Options dialog appears. Make sure that the option "Copy File to Working Directory" is activated. Then click OK.

10 The files are copied to the project folder, and the corresponding Clips appear in the Pool.

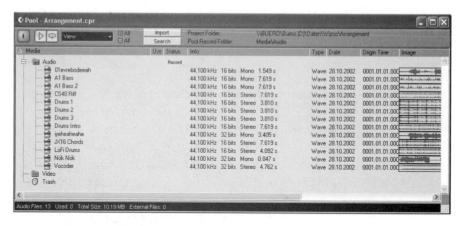

Now the Pool is filled with audio data.

I filed the current status of the project under *Arrangement* in the folder of the same name on CD. If you want to work with my projects, I recommend that you copy the entire folder from CD to your hard disk and open the respective project from there.

4.2 Defining Snap Values

It's worth our while to look at the Snap function before we continue working and begin arranging imported clips. The Snap function is essential. It ensures that operations in the Project window such as dragging, copying, and cutting are carried out accurately, and that the project doesn't degenerate into an arrhythmic mess. Beyond that, the Snap function offers some helpful auxiliary functions that also simplify the process of arranging Audio Events.

Snap settings are entered via the Toolbar, specifically via the:

■ Snap button: Click this button to turn the Snap function on and off. It lights up blue to indicate the Snap function is activated.

■ Snap Mode Selector menu: Select a Snap mode here. Details on the individual Snap modes are discussed below.

■ Grid Selector: You can determine the resolution of the Snap function here if you have selected "Grid" mode in the Snap Mode Selector menu. Your options are Bar, Beat, and Use Quantize. If you select "Bar," you'll move through the Event Display in steps consisting of a full bar. If you select "Beat," the Snap function is contingent upon the number of beats in the underlying time signature. If, for example, it's a 4/4 beat, the Snap grid is made up of quarter notes. The "Use Quantize" setting sets the Snap function to the value defined in the Quantize Selector menu.

■ Quantize Selector menu: This menu's principle purpose is defining MIDI quantizing. In connection with the Snap function, it serves another purpose: If you select the Use Quantize option in the Grid Selector, the note value defined in the Quantize Selector menu determines the Snap grid.

The four options for defining the Snap function are ordered hierarchically from left to right. The further to the right a menu, the more it depends on the preceding menu's settings. Consequently, the Quantize Selector menu is only enabled when the Use Quantize option has been selected in the Grid Selector. Both menus are enabled only when the Snap function is activated via the Snap button.

4.2.1   The Snap Modes

You'll find seven entries in the Snap Mode Selector menu. These signify the following:

■ Grid: The settings in the Grid Selector and Quantize Selector menus define the Snap function. This is the Snap preset. It ensures that you find the desired positions swiftly and surely when dragging, copying and cutting.

- Events: If you move objects when this mode is enabled, they snap into place when you drag them close to the beginning or end of other objects.

- Shuffle is a good choice if you want to rearrange tracks quickly because it changes the sequence of objects: If you drag an object over another object, the two trade places.

- Magnetic Cursor: If you drag an event into the proximity of the cursor, it snaps into place at the cursor position.

- Grid + Cursor: This mode is very similar to the aforementioned mode. The difference is that you'll move through the Event Display according to the specifications of the Grid Selector and Quantize Selector menus.

- Events + Cursor: This mode combines the Magnetic Cursor and Events modes.

- Events + Grid + Cursor* combines the Events, Grid and Magnetic Cursor modes.

4.2.2   The Snap Point in Audio Events

An event's Snap Point rather than its starting point determines its position in the Snap grid. Though the Snap Point by default marks the beginning of an Audio Event, it can be reassigned to any position within the event. For instance, if you move the Snap Point to the middle of an the event, the event will snap into position so that its center point rather than its starting point is aligned with the Snap Point.

This explains the idea behind the Snap Point—to mark the place within an event for purposes of alignment. Case in point: Say you have recorded a vocal line in which a specific word marks the beginning of a bar. However, this word doesn't coincide perfectly with the beginning of the event. In this case, you can set the Snap Point to this key position and the event will be aligned to it.

In order to adjust the Snap Point of an Audio Event, proceed as follows:

1   Double-click the Audio Event. It opens in the Sample Editor.

2   Right-click into the waveform view in the Sample Editor to open the Quick menu and ensure that ELEMENTS > AUDIO EVENT is enabled.

3   If "Audio Event" is activated, in the waveform view you'll see markers designating the event's beginning, end, and Snap Point. The "S" marks the Snap Point.

4   Click on the "S" flag and drag the Snap Point to the desired position while holding the mouse button down.

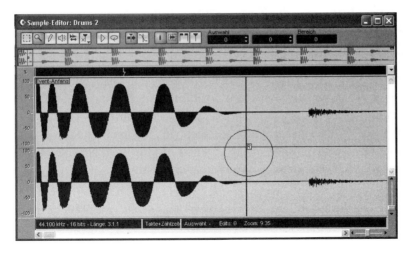

The Snap Point in an Audio Event.

We'll work with the Snap function in the following exercises. You'll discover how the right Snap settings can make arranging so much easier.

4.3   Loading Audio Material from the Pool to a Track

Open the Pool via PROJECT > POOL or by pressing `ctrl``P`. You can see the audio files that we imported earlier "swimming" in the Pool. If you didn't do this, you can catch up to the current project status by loading *Arrangement*.

In the Pool, you'll also find the Clips *Drums 1, Drums 2, Drums 3,* and *Drums Intro.* Listen to them. To do this, select a clip and click the Play button at the top left of the Pool window. Alternatively, you can click into the Clip's waveform view. Note, however, that in this case the Clip always plays from the position at which you clicked in the waveform view.

The first track of our arrangement will be a drum track. Position the two Clips *Drums 1* and *Drums 2* in the Event Display. You can do this in two ways:

- Grab a clip with the mouse, drag it into the Event Display, and release the mouse button at the desired position. A small window next to the mouse pointer helps you zero in on the desired position.
  To make it easier to locate the correct bar position, enable the Snap function, set Snap Mode to "Grid" and Grid to "Bar". Now you'll step through the Event Display in increments of bars.

- Right-click a clip and select INSERT INTO PROJECT > AT CURSOR in the Quick menu. This inserts an event at the current song position. The song position for the first Clip is 1.01.01.000, so set it to the beginning of the first bar. The Snap function doesn't do this for you, you must select the song position via the Transport Panel or Ruler.

Let's get to work:

1 Insert *Drums 1* into the Event Display at the beginning of the first bar.

2 Insert *Drums 2* so that it follows *Drums 1* in the event display, that is, at the beginning of bar 3.

Your Project window should now look something like the screenshot below.

As you can see, Cubase SX/SL automatically generates an appropriate track when Events are inserted. In our case, this is an audio track in stereo format because the source materials are stereo recordings.

To avoid chaos and confusion as you develop your arrangement, it's essential that added tracks are easily identified. So, let's give your first track a meaningful name. To do this, double-click the track name in the Track List ("Audio 01") and type in "Drums."

Now listen to the results of your efforts. Set the Left Locator to the beginning of bar 1, the Right Locator to the beginning of bar 5, and activate the Cycle button in the Transport Panel. Deactivate the Master button in the Transport Panel, and set the song tempo to 126bpm. Click the Play button.

Admittedly, you're probably not bowled over by the rich sonic experience, but bear in mind that we've barely scratched the surface.

4.4 Moving and Copying Events

We'll use the Move and Copy functions to embellish the drum track. At this point, your project should consist of an audio track with the Events *Drums 1* and *Drums 2*. Note that you'll also find the current status of the project on CD filed under *Arrangement 1*.

Let's look at the rules for moving and copying events using the mouse:

- Events can be moved in the Event Display by grabbing them with the mouse and dragging them to another position. A tiny window next to the mouse pointer shows the current song position and helps you place events with precision.

- If you want to copy an event, press and hold [alt] and drag the event to the desired position. A copy is generated at the given song position when you release the mouse button.

- You can also move/copy several events at same time. To do this, select the events one after other while pressing [shift] or drawing a frame around the desired events using the mouse. The rest of the procedure is the same as for dragging or copying individual events.

- Events can be moved vertically as well as horizontally. Cubase automatically generates new tracks when you drag events vertically.

You can restrict this move function to one direction. This prevents errors, for example, accidentally dragging events along the vertical axis so that they are dropped into other tracks. To do this, carefully move the selected events a short distance in the desired direction, press [ctrl], and drag the events to the desired position while holding [ctrl] down.

When moving and copying events, an info box indicates the exact song position.

Let's get some practice doing this and extend our drum arrangement while we're at it:

1 Press and hold the [shift] key and click the events *Drums 1* and *Drums 2*. This selects both. Release [shift].

2   Press and hold the ⟨alt⟩ key and drag the selected events to song posi-
    tion 5.1.1. Cubase copies both events and inserts the copied events at
    the target position. Presto—the arrangement has been extended to
    eight bars.

3   Select all events of this track and drag them four bars to the right to
    song position 5.1.1. You now have four bars space at the beginning of
    the track.

4   Open the Pool and insert the *Drums Intro* clip into the audio track at
    the beginning of bar 1.

The arrangement has been lengthened to twelve bars and consists of
three different events.

Cubase offers alternative copying options using the mouse. These will get
the job done quicker in some situations:

■   EDIT > DUPLICATE and ⟨ctrl⟩⟨D⟩ create a copy of an event that is
    inserted directly after the original. If you select several events, they are
    copied as a unit.

■   EDIT > REPEAT and ⟨ctrl⟩⟨K⟩ open a dialog box in which you can indicate
    any number of copies. This option also lets you copy one or more
    events.

■   EDIT > FILL LOOP creates copies between the Left and Right Locator.
    The last copy is cut off if it extends beyond the Right Locator.

4.5   Cutting Events

You're now familiar with dragging and copying and know how to use the
Snap function. In the next step, we'll develop our arrangement by cutting
events.

First, we'll invite some company over to join the Audio Events in the Event
Display. For this purpose, open the Pool and drag the *Drums 3* clip to the
beginning of bar 13 on the audio track. You'll also find this project status
on CD, where it's archived as *Arrangement 2*.

Let's look at the options Cubase puts at your fingertips for cutting events:

- The Split tool (scissors icon): This tool can be selected either via the Quick menu (right mouse button), or from the Toolbar. If you want to cut an event, simply click it at the desired position using the Split tool. The event is lopped off at this position.

- The function EDIT > SPLIT AT CURSOR (key command ⸤alt⸥⸤X⸥) cuts the selected events at the cursor. If you have not selected any particular events, all events on all tracks are cut at this position.

- The function EDIT > SPLIT LOOP cuts events at the Left and Right Locator on all tracks. This function is only selectable when you have defined a loop, but you don't have to enable Cycle mode to use it.

Using the Split tool.

Let's get back to work on our arrangement. First, we'll use the Split tool, and then edit Audio Events. Proceed as follows:

1 Ensure that the Snap function is enabled: Snap Mode Selector is set to "Grid" and the "Bar" option is selected in the Grid Selector.

2 Cut the *Drums1* Event beginning at bar 5 right down the middle, that is, at bar 6. This event is a two-bar drum pattern that repeats after the first bar, with the difference that the first bar starts with a crash cymbal and the second bar doesn't. Halving the event yields two parts; one with, the other without a crash cymbal.

3 Drag the events starting at bar 7 forward to the beginning of bar 13.

4 Select the second half of the event that we just cut and select EDIT > REPEAT. Enter a value of 5 in the dialog box under "Count" and confirm with OK. Cubase copies the event and inserts the copies at bar 7. Bar 12 remains blank for the time being.

Let's whip up a fill for bar 12:

1   Select "Use Quantize" in the Grid Selector, and then select "1/8 Note" in the Quantize Selector.

2   Cut the *Drums 1* event beginning at song position 15 right behind the first eighth note beat. Ensure the info box next to the mouse shows the position 15.1.3 when you cut the event.

3   Drag the event at bar 15 to the beginning of bar 12 while pressing [alt]. A copy of this event appears.

4   Select the event bat 12 and select EDIT > REPEAT. Enter a value of 7 in the dialog box under "Count" and confirm with OK. Bar 12 is filled.

4.5.1   How to Eliminate Pops at Split Points

When events are cut, oftentimes pops are audible at the point of incision. This problem is swiftly and easily solved in Cubase:

1   Select the event that you want to edit.

2   Choose the Zoom tool (the magnifying glass icon) from the Quick menu or Toolbar.

3   Frame the event using the Zoom tool. The event is zoomed to a much larger view.

4   At the very top of the event view, you'll find one small blue triangle each at the beginning and end of the event. Select the Object Selection tool and nudge the blue triangle a short distance towards the center from the beginning or end of the event depending on where the pop occurs.

Be sure to move the triangle just a hair, otherwise you will not only eliminate the pop but also create an audible fade-in or fade-out. Though this can be a hip effect, that's not what we want to do at this point.

4.6   Using Editing Functions Creatively

Now that you have mastered the skills of moving, copying, and cutting events, as well as setting the Snap function to best effect, I want to encourage you to piece together a drum track on your own. Use the drum track that we just created as your source material. You'll find the current project status filed under *Arrangement 3* on CD.

I'll leave the remaining steps to your imagination, bar a few tips and suggestions:

- Select all events in the drum track that we created and drag them downwards a ways while pressing [alt]. When you release the mouse button, Cubase automatically generates a new track and loads the copied events to it. You can experiment to your heart's content in the copied version. The source material is preserved on your original track.

- Switch on the Solo function for the new track by clicking the "S" button. It lights up red when the Solo function is activated. From now on, you'll hear only the currently selected track. This makes selecting easier, and allows you to audition your arrangement at any time.

- Continue adding to your collection of material by cutting events while using resolutions that are finer than a bar.
- Play around with different Snap modes. For example, you can quickly change the sequence of specific events in Shuffle mode.

You'll find filed on CD under *Arrangement 4* an example of a drum track created from the material of our drum track. Track 2 contains this new version.

4.7 Using Audio Parts

Up to this point, we have worked exclusively at the Event level. But Audio Events can also be grouped in Audio Parts.

An Audio Part is a container for Audio Events. It's especially useful when you want to handle several Events as a unit, for example, when copying. When Events are contained in a Part, you can simply copy the Part rather than copy each Event separately.

You have several options for creating an Audio Part:

- Select one Event or several Events on the same track; then select AUDIO > EVENTS TO PART.
- Paste together two or more Audio Events on the same track using the Glue tool.
- Draw in a part using the Draw tool (pencil).
- Double-click in an audio track at a position between the Left and Right Locator.

The last two methods create an empty Audio Parts that you can add events to.

When you double-click an Audio Part, the Audio Part editor rather then the Sample Editor opens. It shows the events contained in the part and allows them to be edited, for instance, in terms of size and position within the part. The Sample Editor opens when you double-click an event in the Audio Part editor.

Audio parts can broken back down into individual events at any time by choosing AUDIO > DISSOLVE PART.

4.8 Using Regions

Please open the Pool and examine the "Use" column. It indicates how often each clip is used in a project. That's nice, but not tremendously helpful in practice. Let's see why using a simple example.

Say you dragged a clip into the Event Display, thereby creating an Audio Event. Then you cut this Audio Event, creating two Audio Events from the one. The Use column in the Pool reads "2" for this clip because the clip is actually used twice.

Then you decide to delete one of the two surgically contrived Audio Events, perhaps because it doesn't sound good at this position. Logically enough, the Use column shows a value of "1" for the clip and the deleted Audio Event is lost forever in the digital ether. If you reconsider and want to hear it at another position, so you must repeat the entire song and dance—restore the original event, cut it again, and so forth. Though this doesn't seem so dramatic in our simple example, confusion is guaranteed in elaborate arrangements.

There is a way to get around this problem using so-called "Regions." Let's convert the events of our drum track into Regions, in the process illustrating the benefits of Regions to you. First save your work, and then reload the project *Arrangement 3*.

Then proceed as follows:

1 Select all events of the drum track.

2 Select AUDIO > EVENT AS REGION.

This converts all selected events into Regions, affording us greater handling and editing convenience:

■ In the Pool's Audio folder, you'll find a plus sign next to the drum Clips. Clicking it opens a list of this Clip's individual Regions. You can now drag these Regions as often as you like to any position in the Event Display.

■ When you click an Audio Event using the right mouse button, you'll see the option "SET TO REGION" at the very top of the Quick menu. If you select it, a submenu opens listing all of the event's Regions. These are easily selected by clicking them once. This lets you swap Regions quickly and speedily rearrange your song.

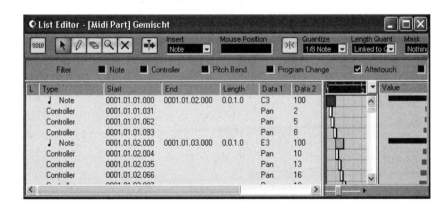

When working with Regions, be sure to give them meaningful names for better orientation. You can easily rename a Region, for example, by selecting it in the Pool, clicking the name box, and typing in the desired name.

4.9 Adjusting the Tempo and Length of Events

Up to this point, we had no trouble arranging the material I had prepared because all Audio Events shared the same tempo and were cut precisely at the appropriate song positions.

But what if you want to use a specific audio file in your arrangement and find that its tempo is different, or perhaps that it hasn't been cut cleanly? Let's find out: I created such a scenario for you and stored it as *Arrangement 6*.

Track 1 is the reference track. The tempo is 126bpm. The Audio Event *LoFi Drums* is on track 2. Not only is the event's tempo different, it's also too long. This means it's out of sync with track 1. Our goal is to edit the event *LoFi Drums* so that it's exactly two bars long with a tempo of 126bpm. Let's begin by trimming the Audio Event to the proper length.

1   Double-click the event *LoFi Drums*. The Sample Editor opens.

2   Select the entire event in the Sample Editor via ⌈ctrl⌋⌈A⌋.

3   Activate the Loop button in the Sample Editor to activate loop mode. Click the Play button in the Sample Editor to play the event.

4   As you hear the event play, note that it's out of step; the pattern is too long by two eighth notes. To size the selection down to exactly two bars, grab its right edge and, while the event is playing, drag it to the left until it sounds as if it's in sync.

5   It takes a close-up to bring it into exact position. Press ⌈H⌋ repeatedly to zoom closer to the waveform. Press the ⌈→⌋ to jump to the end of the selection. Drag its right edge precisely to the beginning of the next beat, which should now be very easy to see.

6   Stop playback in the Sample Editor by clicking the Play button.

7   Select AUDIO > BOUNCE SELECTION. This stores the edited event as a new audio file. Cubase automatically adds a new clip named *LoFi Drums* (2) to the Pool.

Now let's adjust the drum loop's tempo to match the 126bpm song tempo.

1   Delete the *LoFi Drums* event in the Event Display and replace it with the clip *Drums LoFi (2)*.

2   Click on the Object Selection button in the Toolbar and select the option "Resizing Applies Time Stretch" from the menu. This selects the Stretch tool.

3   Use this tool to extend the *LoFi Drums (2)* event to a length of exactly two bars. The Snap grid helps you zero in on the bar borderline.

4   This prompts Cubase to run its trusty time-stretch algorithm and convert the event's tempo to 126bpm.

You have another option for adapting the tempo of events to the song tempo alongside time stretching; it's called "slicing." Put in simple terms, the event is chopped up into small segments and these segments are played sequentially in the given song tempo. The advantage of slicing over stretching is that a sliced event automatically changes its tempo when you change the song tempo. If you have recorded a song at a specific tempo and later decide that art would be better served by a slower or faster tempo, all you have to do is enter the desired tempo and the events are automatically adapted to it.

Let's see how this works by slicing up the event *LoFi Drums (2)*. To make it easier for you to check out its effect, we'll cancel the tempo change brought on by time stretching. To do this, select EDIT > UNDO SIZE. This resets *LoFi Drums (2)* to the "wrong" tempo.

Proceed as follows:

1   Select the *LoFi Drums (2)* event.

2   Select TRANSPORT > LOCATORS TO SELECTION or enter the key command [P].

3   Double-click the *LoFi Drums (2)* event. The Sample Editor opens.

4   Drag the horizontal zoom slider at the bottom right of the Sample Editor to the left until the entire event is shown in the Sample Editor. This lets you keep an eye on what's happening during the following steps.

5   Activate the Hitpoint Mode button in the Sample Editor. This is the button at the far right in the Sample Editor's toolbar.

6   You can now see in the Sample Editor's waveform view a series of perpendicular lines called Hitpoints. The event is cut at these positions. You can adjust the number of Hitpoints using the Hitpoint Sensitivity slider. The default setting will do for the purpose of our example.

7   A few more adjustments require our attention. Go to the Use pop-up menu and select Sensitivity, and enter "2" for Bars (because the event is two bars long). Set Beats to 0 (because the event is *exactly* two bars long), and Signature to "4/4" (the event is in 4/4 time). The Original Tempo box at the top right of the Sample Editor should now show a value of about 131bpm.

8   Select AUDIO > HITPOINTS > CREATE AUDIO SLICES. The Sample Editor closes and an Audio Part named *LoFi Drums (2) Sliced* appears in the Event Display in place of *LoFi Drums (2)*. This Audio Part contains all the pieces of the sliced Audio Event.

9   Play the event. Presto—the event runs at the right tempo.

Again, sliced events always adapt to the song tempo automatically. Let's confirm that rule:

1   Activate the solo button ("S") for the audio track with the *LoFi Drums (2) Sliced* part.

2   Turn the metronome on by activating the Click button in the Transport Panel.

3. Type "120" into the tempo display of the Transport Panel and confirm via ⌜return⌟. This changes the song tempo to 120bpm.

4. Play the track. The drum loop marches perfectly in step with the metronome.

4.10 Adapting Song Tempo to Events

In the preceding section, you learned how to adapt Events to a song tempo. It's likely that at some point you'll encounter the reverse case, finding it necessary adjust a song tempo to the tempo of an Event, say a drum loop.

This is also easily done in Cubase, as the following example will demonstrate:

1. Select FILE > NEW PROJECT.

2. Select the Empty template and click OK.

3. Click OK in the Select Directory dialog box. A new blank Project window appears.

4. Select FILE > IMPORT > AUDIO FILE.

5. Go to the *Cubase Projects > Arrangement > Audio* folder on the CD and open it. Select the *Drums 1.wav* file and click Open. A dialog box appears. Ensure the option "Copy File to Working Directory" is activated and confirm with OK.

Cubase generates an audio track and loads the Audio Event *Drums 1* to it. As you can clearly see even without zooming it up, this event is not exactly two bars long, but a little shorter. This is a first indication that the tempo of the event and the tempo of the song don't tally.

Activate the Click button in the Transport Panel and deactivate the Master button. Play the track. Now you can also hear that the metronome click and the drum loop don't share the same tempo. Let's change that now:

1 Select the event *Drums 1*.

2 Select PROJECT > BEAT CALCULATOR.

3 Set the value "8" in the Beats pop-up window because the loop has a length of two bars, which is equal to eight quarter notes.

4 "126.000" appears in the BPM box. This means the tempo of the loop is 126bpm.

5 Type"126" into the Transport Panel's tempo display and confirm via ⟨return⟩.

Now when you audition the drum loop along with the metronome click, you'll hear that they are perfectly in step. You'll see that the drum loop is now exactly two bars long in the event display. Ergo, we succeeded in adapting the song tempo.

4.11   How to Create a More Complex Arrangement

The following section challenges you to create a more complex arrangement using a variety of audio material.

Recall that we had filled the Pool with plenty of material to do this at the beginning of this chapter. If you want to restore this starting point, load the project *Arrangement*. In it, you'll find a full Pool and an empty Project window.

If you don't want to lose all the editing you have done to the drums thus far, you can also use your project.

I also got the ball rolling in *Arrangement 5*; feel free to use it as a head start and continue working from there.

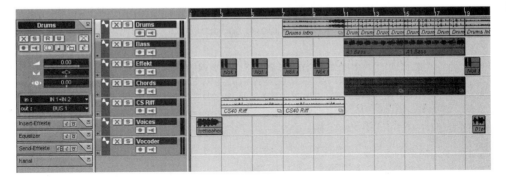

A more complex arrangement could look like this.

A few general pointers that will help you with your arrangement:

- If you're starting from scratch, your best bet is to first create a simple drum track to provide a basic groove. Don't try to perfect it now. All you need for the time being is a solid rhythmic backbone for the other tracks to lean on.

- For your second step, I suggest that you generate a bass track.

- Drag, copy, and cut as you please. For purposes of speed and accuracy, make a habit of using the Snap function. Recall that you can drag and copy several events simultaneously, and that these shortcuts may save you tons of time.

- Use the two Clips *CS 40 Riff* and *JX 16 Chords*. Try manipulating them by cutting at selected positions.

- The *Vocoder* Clip offers a series of different vocal lines. You must cut these into individual segments in order to be able to use them. You may find that you have to assign Snap Points to align the material.

- Label all tracks with meaningful names. You can also assign different colors to tracks via the Color Selector pop-up menu to distinguish them better.

- Arrange the tracks in whatever order seems clearest to you. To move a track, grab it in the Track List with the mouse and drag it to the desired position. For example, you could start with drum tracks at the top, followed by the bass track, and so forth in descending order.

4.11.1   A First Glimpse of the Mixer

We don't want to delve into the details of mixing just yet, though we'll examine this topic in great depth later in this book. However, we want to be able to adjust the volume of individual tracks, so you're about to get your first glimpse of the Cubase mixer. So, open the mixer via DEVICES > MIXER or the key command 〔F3〕.

The mixer offers a channel strip for every track. Every channel strip is labeled with the name of the given track. This makes your job much easier because you can immediately see which track you're editing.

The channel strips' big faders adjust volume levels. The best way to set volume levels is to place the Left Locator to the song's beginning and the Right Locator to its end. Activate Cycle mode and play the track. You'll hear clearly how changing the volume of individual channels affects the mix.

Here's another little secret that you may want to take to heart: Volume controls are a two-way street. They also turn levels down. In other words, often a song is better served by backing off the volume of specific tracks a hair to make other tracks come through louder and stand out better in the mix. If you tend to turn everything up, you'll soon run out of headroom and saturate the output.

Chapter 5

Arranging and Editing MIDI Material

After learning how to arrange and edit audio material in the previous chapter, we shall now turn our attention to MIDI tracks.

To help you to a better understanding of how this is done, we'll work our way through some exercises with MIDI tracks. I recommend that you follow along with them. To do this, load the project named *MIDI*. You'll find it in the *Cubase Projects > MIDI Examples* directory on the book CD. When you load this project, a message reading "Pending Connections" may appear on your screen. If so, this is attributable to the MIDI interfaces—yours and mine are probably not the same and Cubase can't find yours. You can fix this problem by selecting your MIDI output in the right column of this dialog box.

Please use a GM-enabled sound generator for this project. To this end, select the MIDI port that connects a GM sound generator to your system. This could also be the sound generator of your audio card if it works with GM. Store the project after you have configured these settings so that you're not confronted with this message again next time you load it.

The program change commands for this project are set to the following GM sounds: Track 1 uses the GM sound *Synth Bass 1* (PRG: 39), track 2 the GM sound *Lead 2 (Sawtooth)* (PRG: 82). If you don't own a GM-compatible sound generator, select any bass sound for the bass track and a synth brass sound for the chords.

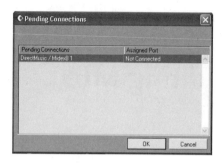

5.1 MIDI vs. Audio: Contrasts in Working Methods

■ When working with MIDI in Cubase, the focus is always on "Parts." Unlike audio material, where Events are broken down into Parts, no distinction is made between Events and Parts.

■ All cutting, copying and moving techniques that you have learned so far can be applied to MIDI Parts. However, there are two things to bear in mind:

For one, copying a MIDI part doesn't always yield virtual copies. If you copy using _alt_, Cubase generates an independent copy that can be edited separately. You must use the key combination _alt_ _shift_ to generate a virtual copy. You'll recognize virtual copies by their italic lettering and by the small icon at the bottom right of the part. If you edit the content of a virtual copy, this affects all other virtual copies of this part.

For the other, consider this when cutting MIDI: If you cut a MIDI part at a position where one or several MIDI notes extend beyond the point of incision, the results will depend on the following program setting: FILE > PREFERENCES > MIDI > FUNCTION PARAMETERS > SPLIT MIDI EVENTS. If this option is enabled, notes are cut and new notes are generated at the beginning of the new part. If this option is disabled, the notes remain in the first part but extend in full length beyond the end of that part.

■ The Snap function works for MIDI Parts in much the same way as for Audio Events. The only difference is that MIDI Parts—unlike Audio

Events—don't have a Snap Point. The part beginning and/or part end are always used for purposes of aligning parts and arranging songs.

Another important distinction between MIDI and audio is that adjusting the tempo of MIDI material is a miracle in effortlessness. The value in the Transport Panel or tempo track always dictates the tempo.

5.2   Using the Inspector

The Inspector has been revamped from the bottom up, and in SX/SL now offers many functions that allow no-nonsense editing right there in the Inspector. Particularly the MIDI effects that replace the classic VST modules now offer unheard-of possibilities. If you're a seasoned VST veteran, you'll do well to invest some time getting to know the new Inspector functions. If SX/SL is your introduction to the wonderful world of sequencing, you'll want to get acquainted with old and new functions. Though the section below doesn't provide an encyclopedic description of the Inspector, I'll point out some options that will help you refine your MIDI tracks.

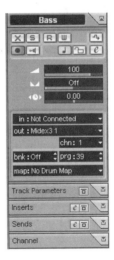

As a rule, the content of the Inspector hinges upon the track type. For MIDI tracks, the Inspector offers five different panels that you can show and hide as required. Use the down arrows at the right of the panels to do this. When you open another panel, the currently opened panel closes automatically. If you press and hold *ctrl* while opening panels, several panels can remain open at the same time. Press and hold *alt* to open and close all panels at the same time. Please note that all parameter settings in the different panels are effective even when the panels are hidden.

The Inspector panels.

Let's take a closer look at the various panels. All panels have one thing in common: Whenever you edit parameters, add effects to tracks, or change program change commands and volume levels,

MIDI events are converted or processed in real time or before they are sent to the MIDI output. The actual MIDI data of a track doesn't change, so every change can be undone at any time. This facilitates experimentation with parameters of the different panels. On the other hand, the edited settings are not shown in the Cubase MIDI editors because MIDI data doesn't actually change. If you want to change a track's data permanently via the Inspector parameters, you must execute the function MIDI > MERGE MIDI IN LOOP, which we'll examine in detail later.

5.2.1   General Track Settings

The top panel displays the selected MIDI track's general settings, which can also be edited in this panel. Use the example song to hear the effects of editing. All you have to do is play one of the two tracks. Enable the SOLO function and activate Cycle mode for a four-bar segment.

If you have not done so already, open the General Track Settings panel now. Some buttons and menus should be familiar to you from the chapter on MIDI recording. Let's scrutinize some of the key functions offered there.

You'll find three faders. The Volume fader sends MIDI Controller 7, which controls—you guessed it—the volume of your sound generator. This fader is linked to the corresponding volume control in the Cubase mixer. If you adjust it, the mixer control changes right along with it, and vice versa.

The same applies to the second fader labeled Pan. It sends MIDI Controller 10, which determines a sound's stereo position.

Go ahead; try these two faders. To do this, simply start playback and manipulate them. Changes should be audible immediately. If this is not the case, check if your sound generator receives and processes MIDI Controllers 7 and 10.

The third fader is called Delay. It lets you delay MIDI output by setting positive values or accelerate it by setting negative values. A simple experiment explains this function best: Play both tracks of the example song and change the delay setting for one of the two tracks. Though drastic changes in the delay value throw off the timing of the playback, they vividly illustrate the influence of this parameter. In real-world applications, subtle changes in the delay value can introduce a human feel, for example, to make a drum track play a little behind or ahead of the beat. Extreme settings can even create delay effects. To do this, simply copy a track several times and set different delay values for the various copies.

You're already acquainted with the remaining boxes for selecting MIDI channels and switching sounds. Bear in mind that entering appropriate instrument settings to the MIDI Device Manager makes it much easier to switch the sounds of your sound generator.

5.2.2 Track Parameters

Track parameters influence a track's MIDI data, specifically, values that determine transposition, velocity, and length, as well as a random function.

The button that opens and closes the panel turns green as soon as track parameters are activated. This gives you a visual indication if track parameters are influencing data. The same holds true for the insert and send effects panels, with the difference that these buttons light up blue when effects are activated.

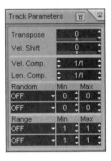

The track parameters.

You'll find the Bypass Parameters button to the left of the button that hides and shows the panel. When you activate it, the track parameter settings are disabled and you can A/B or compare your settings with the unedited material. The panel button lights up yellow when the bypass button is activated.

The first four parameters in the track parameters are easily explained, but you'll get a better idea by playing a MIDI track in Cycle mode, trying out the parameters described below, and hearing their effects.

- Transpose: This parameter transposes the notes on the track in semitone steps.

- Vel. Shift: This parameter changes the dynamics of a track. The value entered here is added to or subtracted from the velocity of the individual notes.

- Vel. Comp. (velocity compression): The value entered here serves as a velocity multiplier. For example, say the note you want to edit has a velocity of 100 and you enter a value of "1/2" for this parameter. In this case, the note is rendered with a velocity value of 50.
  This parameter is great for smoothing out the velocity of recordings. To do this, simply define values lower than 1. Though this decreases overall velocity, you can compensate for this by redefining the velocity parameter. Case in point: Take three notes with velocity values of 50, 80 and 120 and say you set their velocity compression to "1/2". This yields values of 25, 40, and 60. Now if you increase velocity by a value of 60, the notes are played at velocities of 85, 100 and 120. This irons out velocity peaks without flattening the dynamic range.

- Len. Comp. (length compression): This parameter influences the length of notes. Its value also consists of a numerator and a denominator. For instance, a value of "2/1" doubles all note lengths, while a value of "1/2" halves them. Try this out using the Chords track of the example song. A setting of "1/2" yields a far more percussive sounding track.

5.2.3 Experimenting at Random

It's all in the name—the Random function generates random values. Subtle variations as well as drastic modifications of source material can be achieved. Each MIDI track offers two random generators that can be adjusted separately.

You'll come to understand the workings of the random generators best by experimenting with them a bit. In the Random menu, select the parameter that you want to modify. The two Min and Max boxes let you determine the extent of the random function's influence. If you limit its range, random settings affect only values that lie between the left and right box. Please note that the left box cannot be set to a higher value than the right box.

It's tip time again:

- Working with Random > Pitch yields what may best be called experimental results. Modifying the pitch of notes bends tracks way out of shape.
- You can breathe more life into a MIDI track by processing it using Velocity and Length while limiting the range via Min and Max.
- "Position" influences the chronological position of MIDI data. This can also loosen up an unnaturally tight a track. Proceed with caution: Value ranges that are too great throw the track's rhythm completely off.

5.2.4 Experiment with the Range Function

The Range function lets you define pitch and velocity to adjust all notes within this range to the parameter settings or filter them out completely. Let's check out a couple of examples:

All velocity values outside the range staked out by Min and Max change when you select Range > Vel. Limit. Values that lie below the Min value are set to the Min value; values above the Max value are set to the Max value. You can simulate the workings of a limiter with this feature. When you select Range > Vel. Filter, notes below the Min value and above the Max value are not rendered.

"Note Limit" is also a very hip option. It transposes notes that lie outside a specific range by octaves so that they end up with pitches within this range. This lets you eliminate big octave jumps. If the range is too small so that notes can't be transposed by an octave, the pitch is set to the center of the range. This, of course, results in some very blue notes.

For purposes of clarification, try this little experiment:

1   Select the part on the bass track and activate the Solo function.

2   Open this part in the Key Editor by selecting MIDI > OPEN KEY EDITOR.

3   Activate the Infoline via the first button from the left in the Key Editor. It's labeled "i".

4   Select the second note bar from the left.

5   Raise the pitch by an octave either by dragging the note bar up with the mouse or typing E3 as the new note under "Pitch" in the Infoline.

6   Play the track and listen to the result.

Let's fix this intentional wrong note using the Range function:

1   Go to Range and select Note Limit.

2   Set the Max value to a note below E3, for example, to C3. In this case, the most practical way to enter values is via keyboard. All you have to do is click the box and type in the value.

Everything sounds the same as it did originally. This little example illustrates how the Range function works and it confirms that Inspector parameters merely influence MIDI note output rather than actually changing a track's data. You can hear that the Bass track sounds right yet see the "wrong" pitch in the Key Editor.

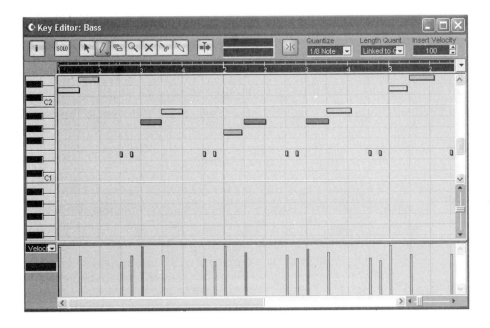

Cancel all changes by simply reloading the example song.

Let's try another experiment to examine the workings of the Note Filter function:

1 Select the part on the bass track and set it to Solo.

2 Play the track.

3 Go to Range and select Note Filter.

4 Enter "F1" for the Min value and "G8" for the Max value.

This filters out all notes below F1, thereby creating a variation on the bass track.

5.3   Using MIDI Effects

You'll find two panels named Inserts and Sends in the Inspector. You may have already deduced that they let you use MIDI effects. Rather than try your patience with a long-winded monograph describing all effects, I'll refer you to the Cubase manual. You'll be acquainted with two effects further below by way of hands-on exercises.

5.3.1   How Do MIDI Effects Work?

There is a fundamental difference between MIDI and audio effects (the latter will be addressed later in the book). Unlike an audio effect, which processes a sound, a MIDI effect processes MIDI data, that is, the information that controls your sound generators. As discussed in the section on Inspector parameters, this is done in real time while data is being sent.

Up to four insert and send effects each can be used per MIDI track. MIDI data is routed through effects from top to the bottom. This lets you come up with interesting combinations of effects.

5.3.2   The Difference between Insert and Send Effects

MIDI effects can be patched into the virtual signal bus in two ways, as an insert and as a send effect. The selection of MIDI effects is the same in both panels.

The panels for the insert and send effects.

Join me in contemplating the difference between insert and send effects:

- When you use an insert effect, MIDI data is routed through the effect. It's processed there, and the result is sent to the MIDI output. This means that you'll hear the effect signal rather than the data on the original track.

- When you use a send effect, data is routed to the MIDI output and sent through the effect at the same time. You'll hear both the original (or dry) and processed (or wet) data. The wet effect signal can also be sent via another MIDI output and another MIDI channel. The Sends panel lets you define a MIDI output and a MIDI channel below every effect for this purpose.

Here's a practical example to demonstrate the difference between the two:

1 Select the *Chords* track in the example song. Set the track to Solo and activate Cycle mode. Play the track.

2 Open the Inserts panel.

3 Click "No Effect" in the top effect slot and select "AutoPan" in the pop-up menu.

4 A window opens that lets you define AutoPan settings.

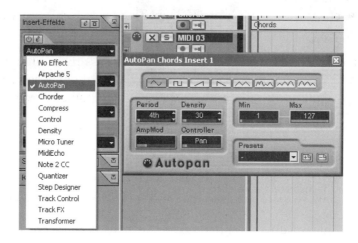

5 Select the Presets menu option "Pan > Pan Hacker" in the effect window. This prompts the sound's stereo position to bounce back and forth between the left and right sides.

6 Switch the insert effect off by clicking the blue on/off switch located above the effect slot.

7 Open the Sends panel.

8 Click "No Effect" in the top effect slot and select "AutoPan" in the pop-up menu.

9 A window opens that lets you define AutoPan settings.

10 Click the designation "Not Connected" in the first effect slot. Select a MIDI output from the pop-up menu, and a MIDI channel from the pop-up menu on the right. Don't select the same output and MIDI channel as the original track; at the very least, enter a different MIDI channel. The program change command in the original track's parameters is automatically relayed to the new output so that you hear the effect signal and the original signal rendered using the same sound.

The tonal differences between insert and send effects are readily apparent. Used as an insert effect, Pan Hacker butchers the sound, as a send effect, it dices and slices with more finesse and the panning is audible as a kind of reverb.

5.3.3 Experiment with Different MIDI Effects

The fastest way to learn how the different MIDI effects work is to try them out. Insert them so that you'll hear the wet effect signal only. This makes it easier to gauge the effect. As mentioned above, the following section introduces two effects.

5.3.4 AutoPan

You'll recall that we used this effect to modulate the stereo position, so you're vaguely familiar with it. AutoPan can do more than this, though. Activate AutoPan as an insert effect for the *Chords* track and play the track in Cycle mode.

Consider first the different presets. These are divided into areas called Expression, Filter, and Pan. This tells you that sending panorama values is only one of AutoPan's functions: In fact, AutoPan can send any MIDI controller with the most diverse settings to your sound generator.

Select the different presets and cast a glance at the Controller parameter in AutoPan. It indicates the controller that is currently being sent to your sound generator. However, this will only invite a response if your sound generator is able to process the given MIDI controller. If in doubt, consult your device's operating manual; it lists all usable controllers. Virtually every sound generator interprets Expression data, so go ahead and select the preset "Expression > Off Rhythmn." It's sending volume commands to mute notes, thereby chopping up your MIDI data.

Try combining this preset with the "Hacker Pan" preset that we used above. To do this, open another AutoPan in the second insert slot and select this preset. I stored these settings for you as a project. You'll find it on the book CD in the *Cubase Examples > MIDI Examples* directory under *AutoPan*.

5.3.5   Arpache 5

This is an imaginative name for an arpeggiator. An arpeggiator breaks down chords, rendering them note by note. You can define the sequence in and tempo at which notes are rendered using various parameters.

We need a chord track to put Arpache 5 to the test, so let's create one using our example song. We'll work in the Key Editor, entering notes step by step using the mouse. You get twice the mileage out of this dual-purpose exercise because it also lets you practice working with the Key Editor. If you're anxious to get to it, feel free to simply play and record a chord track. To do this, generate a new MIDI track and simply record the chords as illustrated in the picture below.

Here's how to go about creating the chord track in the Key Editor.

1   Ensure that the original version of the *MIDI* project is loaded. If necessary, reload the project.

2   Generate a new MIDI track below the two existing tracks.

3   Select the Draw tool from the mouse's Quick menu or Toolbar.

4   Draw an empty part into the new track in the Event Display. It must have the same length and position as the two existing parts. In other words, it should lie exactly below them.

5   Select MIDI > OPEN KEY EDITOR.

The area in which the Key Editor shows MIDI notes is called the Note Display. It consists of a graph depicting MIDI notes as horizontal bars. To the left of the Note Display is a virtual keyboard indicating notes.

The Key Editor features a dedicated Toolbar. Select the pencil tool from it.

We want the first three bars of our chord track to comprise whole notes, so set the Quantize box in the Toolbar to the value "1/1 Note." Set the Length Quant. box (length quantizing) to "Linked to Quantize."

Explanation: The quantize option lets you define the grid by which you navigate through the Note Display. This affects the view of grid lines. The setting in the Length Quant. box determines the note value that is created when you click with the mouse to enter notes. If you hold the mouse button down while entering notes, you can drag the mouse to generate any note value regardless of the defined length quantize setting. However, the quantize setting still determines the grid in which these notes are inserted.

Use the pencil tool to move through the grid and watch the two displays for the note and song position in the middle of the Toolbar. You can also view the notes on the virtual keyboard.

Now let's create notes for the chord track:

1   Click into the Note Display at the note C3 and song position 1.1.1.
    Cubase generates a MIDI note with a length of one bar. It appears in
    the Note Display as a horizontal bar.

2   Click into the Note Display at the note E3 and song position 1.1.1. Then
    click into the Note Display at the note G3 and song position 1.1.1.
    Presto—the first bar is finished.

3   Generate the notes B2, D3, G3 at song position 2.1.1 for the second bar,
    and the notes C3, E3, and A3 at song position three for the third bar.
    Create whole notes only.

4   For the last bar, set Quantize to "1/2 Note," and generate the notes B2,
    E3, and A3 at song position 4.1.1 and the notes B2, E3 and G3 at song
    position 4.3.1. That's all there is to it!

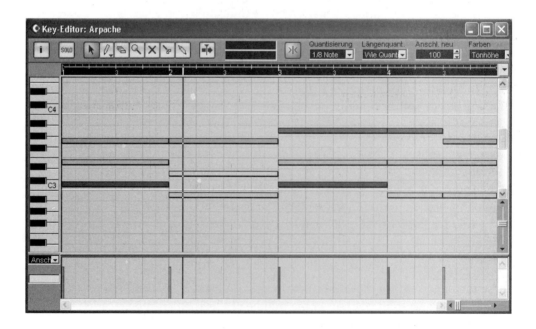

Hope you enjoyed our little excursion to the Key Editor. Now we have a
chord track and can turn our attention to Arpache 5.

Select the chord track, set it to Solo, and play the track in Cycle mode. Open the Inserts panel and select "Arpache 5" in the top effect slot. An effect window opens automatically; enter your settings to it.

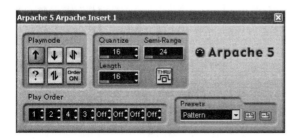

You'll find the Presets box at the bottom right of Arpache 5. Select the "Simple up-down" preset from the pop-up menu. We'll use this preset to poke & probe a couple of Arpache 5's parameters.

> When adjusting settings while the sequence is playing, give Arpache 5 some time to adopt the edited values. Often it won't render changes properly until a new cycle begins.

The Quantize parameter serves to determine the speed of the arpeggio. It's defined in note values. Try it out.

The Length parameter also works with note values. As its name would suggest, it changes note lengths.

The Semi-Range parameter determines the arpeggio's range. Values are entered in increments of semitones. Experiment with this parameter by changing the value in steps of 12 semitones. This corresponds to an octave, and is perfect for discerning the effects of this parameter.

The buttons in the Playmode box determine the sequence in which arpeggio notes are played. Next to ascending and descending cascades and a combination of these two modes, there is also a random function called Play Order.

Activating the Order button enables the underlying Play Order function. It lets you define a sequence in which the chord's notes are played. Every position corresponds to a position in the arpeggio. The sequence of played notes is determined from left to right; entering an appropriate number selects the desired note. The numbers correspond to the keys that have been pressed beginning with the lowest note. In our example, the first chord consists of the notes C, E, and G. The numbers in this chord are 1 = C, 2 = E and 3 = G. The formula for the second chord in our example is 1 = B, 2 = D and 3 = G.

Now let's improve on the arpeggio. Select AutoPan for your second insert effect and in it, the preset "Pan > Wide Pan." Now the arpeggio's stereo position slowly sweeps from left to right. You'll also find this result on CD in the *MIDI Examples* folder under *Arpache*.

5.4   Editing MIDI Data

To recap an essential point, the Inspector's parameters affect MIDI output in real time rather than actually change MIDI data. In some situations, though, you want to be able to access the information that you're hearing in the MIDI Part. This sounds unlikely, but it's not. For example, you may want to manipulate the individual MIDI notes of our arpeggio track in an editor.

For this type of scenario, Cubase offers the MERGE MIDI IN LOOP command in the MIDI menu. This command not only changes the MIDI data according to the Inspector's parameter settings, it can also mix different tracks' data. It processes data between the Left and Right Locator of tracks that have not been muted.

Let's use MERGE MIDI IN LOOP to transform the notes of our arpeggio track into real MIDI notes.

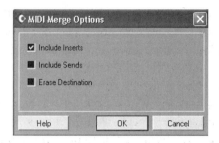

1   Load the *Arpache* project from the *MIDI Examples* folder on CD.

2   Ensure the Left Locator is placed at the beginning of bar 1 and the Right Locator at the beginning of bar 5. This defines the section that you aim to process. In our example, this is the entire part.

3   Generate a new MIDI track below the *Arpache* track.

4   Mute the *Bass* and *Chords* tracks by activating their *X* buttons.

5   Select the newly generated MIDI track.

6   Select MIDI > MERGE MIDI IN LOOP. A dialog box called "MIDI Merge Options" opens. Ensure the "Include Inserts" option is activated. Leave the "Include Sends" and "Erase Destination" options switched off.

7   Quit the dialog box by clicking OK.

Cubase created a new part in the newly generated track. Audition it. You'll note that Cubase didn't factor the parameters from the general track settings, and that this track is not played back with the usual sound. This is why you must define the desired program change command for the new track. Then you can delete the original track.

In closing, we'll view the new part in two MIDI editors.

1   Select the new part.

2   Select MIDI > OPEN SCORE EDITOR or enter the key command [ctrl][R]. This opens the part in the Score Editor. You can clearly see that the original chords have been transformed into arpeggios.

3   Close the Score Editor.

4   Select MIDI > OPEN LIST EDITOR or enter the key command [ctrl][G]. This opens the part in the List Editor. The MIDI events that were generated by AutoPan and determine the stereo position are readily visible. In the List Editor, these are provided with the designation PAN in the VALUE 1 column.

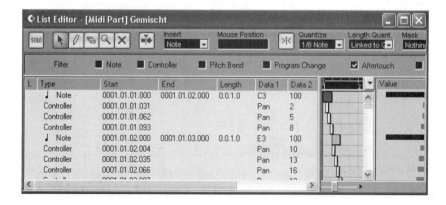

You'll find the results of these processing efforts filed under *MIDI In Loop* in the *Cubase Projects > MIDI Examples* folder on CD.

5.5 Creating and Editing MIDI Drums

Now that you're on a first-name basis with many MIDI editing options, we'll examine how to create and edit MIDI drums in Cubase. To this end, I extended our example song's latest version with a drum part. You'll find this version filed under *MIDI Arrangement* in the *MIDI Examples* folder on the CD. Load this project into Cubase.

In the section below, we'll edit the drum part in the Drum Editor and create a few variations on this part.

1 Click the *Drums* part and drag it to the beginning of bar 5 while pressing [alt]. This generates an independent copy of the part.

2 Select the first *Drums* part, and then select MIDI > OPEN DRUM EDITOR. This opens the part in the Drum Editor.

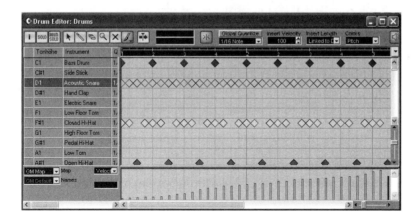

In the Drum Editor grid, all drum events appear in the form of rhombuses. A column listing instrument names and the corresponding notes is at the left of the grid. The contents of the list should reflect the GM assignment because this is how the part was recorded. The option "GM Map" must be selected in the Map pop-up menu below the list of drum sounds to ensure that the list tallies with the GM assignment. Check this by clicking individual events in the grid using the mouse. The sound you hear should be the sound indicated in the list.

Time to explore the Drum Editor:

1   Set the zoom slider at the bottom right of the editor so that all events in the part are visible.

2   Select all events for *Bass Drum* and *Acoustic Snare* by framing them using the mouse. Press ⌐del⌐ to delete the events. The part should now consist of just hi-hat cymbals, which will work fine for an intro.

Now we'll add instruments to a part. To do this, first close the Drum Editor, and then generate a copy of the second drum part. Open this part in the Drum Editor via MIDI > OPEN DRUM EDITOR. Proceed as follows in the Drum Editor:

1   Select the Drumstick tool from the Toolbar.

2   Place a crash cymbal (Crash Cymbal 1) at the first hit of the part. To do this, click this position in the grid using the drumstick tool. To make it easier to find the right spot, keep your eye on the display, watching for the note and song position in the Toolbar.

3   Continue spicing up the part by adding some hits and deleting others. The best tool for deleting individual hits is the Eraser.

The Drum Editor lets you create new drum parts as well as edit existing parts. Try your hand at doing this by creating a snare roll:

1   Use the pencil to draw a new empty part with a length of one bar in the drum track, and then open this part in the Drum Editor.

2   Select the Drumstick tool from the Toolbar.

3   Select the value "1/32 Note" in the Quantize pop-up menu.

4   Click into the *Acoustic Snare* column at the beginning of the part using the Drumstick tool, hold the mouse button down, and drag the mouse to the right until the entire part is filled with snare hits.

So far, so good, but we're not finished yet. Though we have obtained the desired notes, they all have the same velocity, and that doesn't sound much like a drum roll. For a more realistic effect, we must change the velocity of individual events:

1   Ensure that the *Acoustic Snare* column is still selected. The light gray coloring indicates that this is the case.

2   Find the Controller Display below the grid in the Drum Editor. A small pop-up menu is located to the left of it. Select the option Velocity in this menu.

3   Miniature vertical bars appear in the Controller Display. These represent the velocities of the individual snare hits.

4   Click in the Toolbar on the small triangle for the Draw tool (brush icon) and select "Line" from the menu.

5   Draw a line in the Controller Display running from the bottom left to the top right. This creates a typical snare role, which is characterized by rising intensity.

This proves my point—you can indeed edit existing parts and create new parts in the Drum Editor. Let your imagination run wild, using the Drum Editor to create variations of our drum parts as well as new drum parts.

5.6   MIDI Tracks in the Mixer

We'll put in some serious time with the Cubase mixer later in the book. For now though, the mixer will sidetrack us just long enough to learn how it serves to handle MIDI tracks.

Unlike Cubase VST, Cubase SX/SL doesn't offer a separate MIDI mixer. Instead, Cubase SX/SL shows all mixer channels—be they audio, VST Instrument, or MIDI—in a single panel.

The mixer provides access to MIDI tracks' volume and panorama settings. When you tweak these control features, MIDI commands are sent to the corresponding control features on the sound generator.

Cubase grants you access to key functions throughout the program, so you'll recognize many of the buttons found here from your experiences with the Track List and the Inspector—the arming and solo buttons, to name just two.

Please load the project named *MIDI Arrangement* from the *Cubase Projects > MIDI Examples* folder on CD now. Select DEVICES > MIXER or press [F3] on the computer keyboard. The mixer opens. You should be looking at as many channels as there are MIDI tracks, in our case, four.

The mixer in Cubase SX offers an extra large view. The top of the mixer is extended and, in the case of MIDI tracks, can show send or insert effects.

Cubase SL doesn't offer this view. This doesn't mean that SL users have to do without this functionality, though. Every channel strip in Cubase SX and SL is furnished with an editing button labeled with a cursive "e." The channel settings window opens when you click this button. This window provides a detailed view of a channel, presenting all parameters, including insert and send effects.

If you're running Cubase SL and want to configure these effects directly in the mixer, you can use the channel settings window. Of course, the insert and send effects are also available for your tweaking pleasure in the Inspector. Which of the two you choose to make changes in is immaterial —the settings are always loaded to every panel in the program.

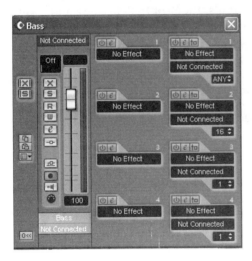

The channel settings window.

A final good-to-know fact: You can also call up a track's mixer channel while in the Inspector. Use the Channel panel to do this.

5.7   Converting MIDI into Audio

After you have recorded and edited MIDI tracks, you can convert them into audio data. This makes good audio engineering sense in some situations, for example, when you're preparing to burn your music on CD and want to create the necessary master file directly in Cubase. MIDI data is not music—you must transform it into audio data first. The procedure is quite simple.

1   Generate a stereo audio track in Cubase and arm this track.

2   Connect your sound generator's audio output to your audio card's input. If you're working with several sound generators, you're sure to have connected these via a mixer. In this case, connect the mixer's output to the audio card's input.

3   Set the input signal level and start recording.

Cubase now plays the MIDI tracks and simultaneously records the output signal of your MIDI sound generator to the audio track. By the time your song runs its course, MIDI has been converted into audio.

A few observations on converting MIDI to audio:

■   Recording all MIDI tracks at the same time is not always the best solution. Though it's the fastest option, it has a major drawback: Recording different tracks at once limits your options when it comes time to mix. The best, if not speediest, approach is to convert each MIDI track into an audio track individually. To do this, repeat the process on separate audio tracks until all MIDI tracks have been recorded.

■   Never delete the original MIDI tracks, not even after recording them as audio tracks. Recordists tend to suffer from a curious recurring malady—the irresistible urge to perfect tracks. Editing is no longer possible once the original track has been deleted. If you save the original track, you can make changes months or years from now. Then all you have to do is convert it into an audio track. So, get into the habit of muting rather than deleting converted MIDI tracks.

- Transforming MIDI into audio tracks brings with it another benefit: you can process the new audio tracks via Cubase's audio effects. This is why you should record MIDI tracks dry whenever possible, that is, disable your sound generator's onboard effects.

- If you're running Cubase SX, consider recording with TrueTape. It can work sonic magic on instruments such as organs, basses, and string pads.

Chapter 6

VST Instruments

VST Instruments are software-based sound generators such as synthesizers, drum computers, samplers, and the like. In Cubase, these instruments are addressed via MIDI tracks in exactly the same way as external sound generators. However, their audio signals appear in the Cubase mixer's channels and can be shaped there. The sounds of VST Instruments can be edited, and these manipulations can even be recorded in real time.

In recent years, the sound quality and possibilities of VST Instruments have attained such an amazing standard of quality that I wouldn't think twice about using them in productions. And this holds true for the VST Instruments that ship with Cubase SX/SL as well as separately available instruments, for example the *HALion* sampler, *The Grand* concert piano, or every keyboardist's fave steel-string slinger, *Virtual Guitarist*.

6.1   Things to Watch for when Using VST Instruments

A word to the wise before we gain some hands-on experience with VST Instruments: Read the following general observations on how these sound generators work. Think of this information as preventive medicine—take it now to avoid pains later on.

- VST Instruments generate audio signals that are patched out via your audio card. If the audio output isn't enabled or doesn't work, you can't use VST Instruments.

- VST Instruments have a healthy appetite for computing resources. For this reason, your computer's performance capabilities dictate the number of VST Instruments that can be used simultaneously. But no matter how powerful your rig, it's not possible to use an unlimited number of VST Instruments. When your computer is pushed to the limits of its performance, playback may begin stuttering or be marred by clearly audible background noise.

- Though the processor determines computer performance, it also hinges on the size of the main memory (RAM). Some VST Instruments require lots of RAM because they work with samples. These samples are loaded into the main memory, some in full others in part. If you want to work in relative comfort with VST Instruments, experience teaches that your computer should be furnished with at least 512MB RAM.

- The latency of your audio card is critical to enjoying the use of VST Instruments. The difference between pleasure and pain when using these sound generators is an audio card with an ASIO driver and low latency, particularly if you want to play VST Instruments via a MIDI keyboard in real time. If your audio card's latency is high, the lag between the striking of a key and the sounding of the note will be clearly audible. If you play MIDI tracks in Cubase with a VST Instrument, this delay is not a problem because Cubase is able to compensate for it. The rule thumb for latency is that the fun starts at values below 10 milliseconds.

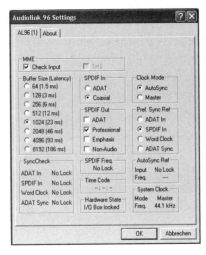

The control panel of a professional audio card: Latency is adjusted at the top left.

- If latency is extremely low, you'll get a real kick out of playing VST Instruments in real time. Your computer, however, may not share your enthusiasm. Even very fast computers can be stymied by latency as low two milliseconds and may give voice to its distress by stuttering or issuing ugly popping noises. I recommend that you determine a basic latency that is a good compromise for all or at least most situations, or adjust latency to suit the application. If you decide to play VST Instruments, select a lower latency. If you're ready to mix in Cubase or edit audio material, set a higher latency. To this end, professional audio cards that let you change latency on the fly without restarting Cubase are certainly the groovier choice.

6.2   Activating VST Instruments

Time to play some VST Instruments in Cubase: First, we'll resort to pre-recorded MIDI tracks and have VST Instruments play them. We'll enlist the services of the A1 virtual analog synthesizer and the LM-7 drum machine to do this. Both are standard appointments of the basic Cubase SX/SL versions.

We'll resurrect an example song from the preceding chapter for purposes of experimentation. Load the project named *MIDI Arrangement* from the *Cubase Projects > MIDI Examples* folder in Cubase. Though the tracks of this project address external GM sound generators, we're about to change that.

The first step is to activate the required VST Instruments:

1   Select DEVICES > VST INSTRUMENTS. A rack offering different slots opens. In Cubase SX, up to 32 slots can be assigned to VST Instruments. The total number in Cubase SL is 16.

2   Click "No VST Instrument" in the first slot. A list of all VST Instruments installed on your system opens.

3   Select LM-7 from the list or via DRUMS > LM-7. This assigns and activates the LM-7 drum machine.

4   Click "No VST Instrument" in the second slot.

5   Select A1 from the list or via SYNTHS > A1. This assigns and activates the A1 synthesizer.

LM-7 and A1 are standing by and ready to run.

The rack offers four buttons and two menus for every instrument:

■ At the top left, you'll find a button that switches the VST Instrument on and off. The button lights up blue to indicate the instrument is enabled.

■ Click the button labeled with the cursive "e" to access the parameters of a VST Instrument. It opens the VST Instrument's control panel in a separate window.

■ The two buttons with the arrow symbols serve to change the sounds of the given instrument. This is even easier using the menu to the right of these buttons: Click the arrow pointing down to open a list of available sounds. The contents of the list vary according to the VST Instrument.

■ At the top right, you'll see a menu labeled "File." This menu lets you save and load individual sounds as well as entire sound banks.

Cubase automatically inserts a channel strip into the mixer when you activate a VST Instrument. The VST Instrument's output determines the channel's configuration. If the output is mono, Cubase inserts a mono channel. The same goes for stereo. A1 and LM-7 have stereo outputs, so you'll find two new stereo channel strips in the Cubase mixer. Check this by opening the mixer via DEVICES > MIXER or via the key command *F3*.

Note that both instruments' channel strips have green backgrounds to distinguish them visually from the other channel strips.

6.3   Assigning VST Instruments

Let's see what the two instruments LM-7 and A1 do in our example song. We'll begin by addressing a drum track to the LM-7 drum machine.

1   Select the drum track in the Track List.

2   Open the Inspector's top panel for the drum track if it has not already open.

3   Click on the label "Not Connected" located at the right of "out:" in the Inspector. A list of physical MIDI outputs and activated VST Instruments appears.

4   Select LM-7.

Start playback. The drum track is played by the LM-7 using a sound set called "Compressor." Change this sound set to the set named "909." Do this in the instrument rack, on the LM-7's control panel, or in the Inspector; simply click the box next to "prg:" and select "909."

> Don't be surprised if it takes the LM-7 a while to swap sounds. It works with samples that have to be loaded for each sound set, and that takes time.

When you audition the song, perhaps the first thing that strikes you is that the track routed through the LM-7 is in time and runs in sync with the pure MIDI tracks—even if your audio card's latency is high. Cubase compensates for the latency of the audio card to ensure perfect timing.

We'll use the A1 for the remaining three tracks. It's not multi-timbral, meaning that it can't play different sounds on several MIDI channels simultaneously. We need three A1s, so let's activate two more of these beasts in the instrument rack:

1   Select DEVICES > VST INSTRUMENTS.

2   Select A1 or SYNTHS > A1 for the third slot.

3   Repeat step 2 for the fourth panel.

Three entries for this instrument are added to the Inspector's Out directory—A1, A1 2 and A1 3. Configure them as follows:

1   Assign the A1 output to the *Bass* track.

2   In the Inspector, click next to the "prg:" box and select the sound "Bass > Smackdabass WMF" from the list.

3   Assign the A1 2 output to the *Chords* track. Select the sound "Lead > Nice'n Fine JH" for A1 2.

4   Assign the A1 3 output to the *Arpache* track. Select the sound "Percussion > 1/16 Sequencer JH" for A1 3.

This selection of sounds is merely a suggestion. I urge you to try out the different sounds of the A1. Feel free to do this in real time while playing tracks. A1 is able to swap sounds immediately because it's actually the parameters that are being changed.

You'll find the results filed under the project name *Instruments* in the *Cubase Projects > VST Instruments* folder on the CD.

6.4   Playing VST Instruments in Real Time

Now that you know how to address VST Instruments using existing MIDI tracks, let's learn how they can be played using a connected MIDI keyboard. Of course, anything you play can be recorded to a MIDI track.

To belabor the point, if you want to play VST Instruments in real time, your audio card's latency must be low. Otherwise, the delay between the striking of a key and the rendering of the sound is too great for comfort.

Proceed as follows to play a VST Instrument via your connected MIDI keyboard:

1   Activate any VST Instrument via DEVICES > VST INSTRUMENTS.

2   Generate a MIDI track.

3   Go to the general track settings of the Inspector; assign the VST Instrument as an output to this track.

4   Check to confirm that your recording keyboard is selected as a MIDI input in the Inspector.

5   In the mixer, check the volume controls of the given instrument channel strip and the master channel to ensure they are turned up.

Play your recording keyboard; you should hear the selected VST Instrument. If you want to record what you're playing, simply proceed as you would for any other MIDI recording.

6.5   Processing VST Instruments in the Mixer

In the Cubase mixer, two channel strips are assigned to every VST Instrument, one for the assigned MIDI track, and one for rendering the VST Instrument's audio signals. These VST Instrument channel strips offer the same setting options as audio channel strips.

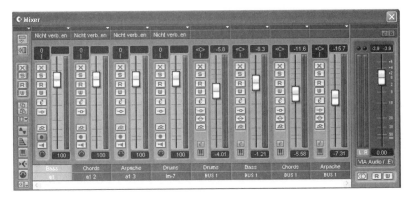

MIDI channel strips on the left, VST Instrument channel strips on the right.

Please heed the following general guidelines when working with the mixer:

- Adjust the volume and panorama for VST Instruments on their instrument channel strips rather than their MIDI channel strips. Set neutral values for the MIDI channel strip, that is, set panorama to the center position and the volume control to a value of 100. Pressing ⌜ctrl⌝ while clicking the channel strip's volume and panorama control is the fastest way to do this.

- For less clutter and more clarity, you can banish the MIDI channel strips from the mixer by hiding them. Use the "Show/Hide MIDI Channels" button at the bottom left of the mixer to do this.

The names of the tracks in the Track List are loaded to the corresponding MIDI channel strips in the mixer but not to the VST Instrument channel strips. Each strip is labeled with the name of the selected VST Instrument only. For the sake of clarity, you should label the instrument channel strips manually.

The name of the selected VST Instrument appears below the respective VST Instrument channel strip. Double-click it and enter the given track name in its stead.

Please note that the instrument channel strips are not selected automatically when you select the corresponding track in the Project window. Instead, the program always selects the corresponding MIDI channel strip when you select a track.

In the following section, you'll learn how to process VST Instruments with effects. For purposes of example, we'll lavish some reverb on a track of an example song. Please load the project named *Instruments* from the *Cubase Projects* > *VST Instruments* folder to ensure you'll work under the described conditions.

Our goal is to treat the Arpache track to a helping of reverb. To this end, we'll use Reverb A as a send effect.

1 Select DEVICES > VST SEND EFFECTS or enter the key command [F6]. The VST Send Effects window opens.

2 Click "No Effect" in the top slot of the VST Send Effects window. A list of all installed effects opens. Select REVERB > REVERB A.

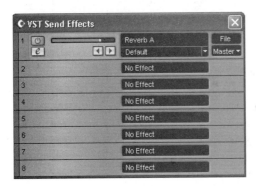

3 Reverb A is activated automatically, and the effect's control panel opens automatically. Close the control panel for the time being.

4 Select DEVICES > MIXER or press [F3] to open the mixer.

5 Find the instrument channel strip for *Arpache* and click the Edit VST Channel button in this strip. This is the fifth button from the top on the left of the volume control. It's labeled with a cursive "e."

6 The channel settings window opens.

In the channel settings window, you'll see arrayed from the right to left a copy of the mixer channel strip, the insert effects, an equalizer, and the send effect. Reverb A appears at the top right of the send effects.

1   Click the small on/off switch located above "Reverb A."

2   A small horizontal fader is visible below the designation "Reverb A." It controls the amount of effects signal or dry/wet balance. Center the fader by dragging it to the right via the mouse.

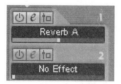

3   Set the track to Solo via the "S" button and play the track. Listen to the results of your efforts.

Cubase SX affords you a large view of the mixer. The panel is extended upwards, providing additional space in which the send effects can be edited. To this end, activate the "Show All Sends" button in the extended view.

You'll find the results of the effects processing exercise stored as a project named *Reverb A* in the *Cubase Projects > VST Instruments* folder on the CD.

6.6 Recording VST Instrument Parameter Changes

As you get the hang of working with VST Instruments such as the A1, you may soon wish to record parameter changes. You're probably aware that you can sweeten even the hippest analog sound by shaping it in real time, for instance, by sweeping a filter or varying a modulation via an LFO (low frequency oscillator). Analog synthesizers and dynamic parameter changes go together hand in glove, and some musical styles wouldn't be what they are without the two.

The good news is that recording parameter changes is possible for all VST Instruments. Even better, this is easily done. Let's learn how by using the *Reverb A* project for the A1.

Load the *Reverb A* project from the *Cubase Projects > VST Instruments* folder on CD. Then proceed as follows:

1   Select the *Chords* track in the Track List.

2   Click the button with the cursive "e" in the general settings of the Inspector (top panel). The A1 control panel opens.

3 Play the track.

4 Grab the Cutoff knob in the Filter box with the mouse and twist it to about the center or 12 o'clock position. You can hear how the sound changes.

5 Stop playback.

Now we'll record a control movement:

1 Activate the "W" button at the top left of the A1 window. It should light up red. This enables write mode so that parameter changes can be recorded.

2 Deactivate Cycle mode in the Transport Panel.

3 Play the track, go to the A1 panel, and slowly turn the CUTOFF knob from the center position to the right.

4 Stop playback after running through the *Chords* part.

5 Deactivate the "W" button in the A1.

6 Activate the "R" button in the A1. If should light up green. This enables read mode so that the program can read the recorded parameter changes.

7 Reactivate Cycle mode and play the track from the beginning of the project. Note how the sound changes in the course of the part. Note also how the Cutoff knob in the A1 control panel moves.

8 Stop playback and close the A1 control panel.

A glance at the Project window reveals that Cubase added a new track to our project. Named "VST Instrument Automation," this track is sort of a collective repository for VST Instruments' automation data.

This track folder contains the track "A1 2." If you click the small "+" symbol at its lower left corner, another subordinate track named "Cutoff" opens. It contains recorded automation data, which is shown in the form of a curve in the Event Display. You can see points along this curve called automation events.

Automation events can be edited in the Event Display. To do this, first enlarge the automation data view by framing it with the Zoom tool (the magnifying glass) from the Toolbar.

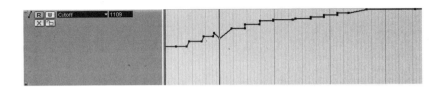

A few tips on editing automation data:

- If you want to move an automation event, click it using the arrow tool, hold the mouse button down, and drag the event to the desired position.

- If you want to create another automation event, click the desired position in the automation curve using the arrow tool.

- If you want to delete an automation event, click it using the arrow tool and press 〔del〕. You can also use the Erase tool (the eraser symbol). If you want to delete several events at the same time, frame these using the arrow tool, and then press 〔del〕.

- If you want to delete all data in an automation track, click its name in the Track List and select "Remove Parameter" from the pop-up menu.

The Draw tool (pencil) offers further editing options. It works in different modes. In order to select a mode, click the small arrow in the button for the Draw tool. A list offering the different modes opens.

- "Draw" mode lets you draw in automation events. Click into the curve, and an event is inserted at this position. You can draw curves if you hold the mouse button down.

- In "Line" mode, the cursor turns into a set of cross hairs. It draws a line when you use it to click into an automation track in the Event Display and drag the mouse while holding the mouse button down. Give it a shot: Try to smooth out our recorded automation curve using the Line tool, and you'll soon grasp the principle. You'll see what a smoothed curve looks like in the Cutoff project in the Cubase Projects > VST Instruments folder on the CD.

- Try out the other modes out too. You'll find that they let you edit automation data in Cubase SX/SL flexibly, purposefully, and swiftly.

6.6.1 Tips on Automating the A1

In the following section, I will share a few tips on automating the A1 synthesizer that we used in the preceding exercise.

The following steps can be applied to many other VST Instruments, provided that like the A1, they can be automated using automation data as well as via MIDI controllers. Every parameter on the A1 can be addressed via a separate controller. In combination with MIDI effects, this affords you jaw-dropping sound-sculpting possibilities.

Do you recall using AutoPan in the preceding chapter? We used it and MIDI Controller 10 to modify a MIDI track's panorama position and discovered that this MIDI effect can send any other controller command. Let's take advantage of this opportunity using the A1:

1   Load the *Instruments* project from the *Cubase Projects > VST Instruments* folder on the CD.

1   Select the *Arpache* track in the Track List and click the button with the cursive "e" located at the top of the Inspector. The A1 control panel opens.

2   Drag the mouse pointer over the A1's knobs and watch the small black display at the center of the A1's control panel. It shows information on the given parameter. The number of the MIDI controller assigned to the given parameter appears at the far right above "Ctrl."

3   Drag the mouse arrow to the Cutoff knob in the Filter box. You can see that it's controlled via MIDI Controller 74.

4   Open the Inserts panel for the *Arpache* track.

5 Assign AutoPan to the top slot as the insert effect for the *Arpache* track. AutoPan's control panel opens automatically.

6 Select PAN > WIDE PAN in AutoPan's Presets pop-up menu.

7 Click the designation "Pan" in the "Controller" box displayed in the AutoPan control panel. Enter a value of "74" and confirm via ⟨return⟩. The designation "Brightness" appears in the box; this is the name for Controller 74.

8 Play the track and listen to the result. Open the AI control panel and observe the Cutoff knob.

Experiment with different presets in AutoPan. Remember to enter a value of "74" to the Controller box.

Seek out more AI controllers and put them to good use. For example, Controller 71 controls Filter Resonance. Give AutoPan a real workout: Use several AutoPan entities as insert effects and assign different controllers to the different versions. I assure you that you'll come up with very interesting results very fast. You'll find an example of what is possible in the *Filter* project located in the *Cubase Projects* > *VST Instruments* folder on the CD.

6.7 Converting VST Instrument Tracks into Audio Tracks

As mentioned earlier, VST Instruments burden your computer's CPU. Frankly, even with fire-breathing computers, the 32 VST Instrument interfaces offered by Cubase SX are closer to utopian fancy than practical reality. In real-world applications, you'll hardly manage to use 32 instruments simultaneously. There is a limit to every computer's performance. Depending on your rig, it may come sooner or later but you can be sure it will arrive. You'll know that this is the case when playback stutters or the play button obstinately refuses to respond.

Check how much computing power the *Cutoff* project requires from your system. To do this, load the *Cutoff* project from the *Cubase Projects > VST Instruments* folder on CD. Select DEVICES > VST PERFORMANCE or press F12. The VST Performance window opens. Play the track.

The top level meter in VST Performance indicates CPU load. The display twitches a certain distance to the right—how far depends on your computer.

Mute all tracks of the song. You can see that the load is lightened somewhat, but it doesn't drop down to zero.

You can lower the CPU load even further by switching VST Instruments completely off via DEVICES > VST INSTRUMENTS. This little exercise illustrates that simply activating a VST Instrument burdens your CPU.

There is a solution to this problem called "Audio Mixdown." It mixes tracks played by VST Instruments down to one or several audio files, including all mixer settings and automation data. Replacing the original VST Instrument tracks with the newly generated audio tracks spares considerable CPU power. VST Instrument tracks' appetite for computing resources is far greater than that of audio tracks.

Bear the following rules in mind when you mix down to audio:

- Everything that is audible during playback is recorded to the audio track. If you want to convert specific tracks only, you must solo these or mute the other tracks. It's advisable to convert every VST Instrument track into a separate audio track. This facilitates mixing later down the line.

- Only the section of the project located between by the two Locators is exported to the audio file.

- You can determine whether or not insert or send effects are recorded to the audio file.

- For the mixed down audio files, define the same resolution and sample rate that you defined in the project settings for the current project.

- Unlike when converting MIDI tracks to audio tracks as described in the preceding chapter, you're not required to record VST Instrument tracks in real time. Cubase mixes these tracks down automatically; all it takes is a little CPU time.

6.7.1   Audio Mixdown

Let's put the audio mixdown function through its paces using the *Cutoff* project. We'll export every track separately and work down the Track List from top to bottom.

1   Set the Left and Right Locators to mark the segment that you want to export. In our case, set the left Locator to the beginning of bar 1 and the Right Locator to the beginning of bar 5.

2   Set the bass track to Solo (the "S" button light ups red).

3   Select FILE > EXPORT > AUDIO MIXDOWN. The "Export Audio Mixdown in" dialog box opens.

1 Use "Look in" to select the target directory, that is, the destination to which you want to export the file. Generally, it will be the *Audio* folder within the given project folder.

2 Type in a meaningful file name, in our example something like "Bass A1."

3 The default resolution is 16 bit. You can select it by passive consent: Leave it and the sample rate 44.100kHz unchanged.

4 Go to "Channels" and select "Mono." Our bass generates a monaural signal only. We did not use stereo effects or the like, so the bass track can readily be exported as a mono file.

5 The "Import to" box lets you determine if the exported audio file is loaded automatically into the Pool and a new audio track is generated for the exported audio file. Note that the "Audio Track" setting hinges on the "Pool" setting: there cannot be a track without a Pool. The default setting will do, so leave both options activated.

6 Export the track by clicking OK.

It will take a moment to mix the track down depending on the length of the track and speed of your computer. The new audio track is added to your project as soon as it has been computed. It contains an Audio Event that plays the A1 bass. You'll find the corresponding Clip in the Pool, and the corresponding audio file has been written to your hard disk.

Follow the same audio mixdown procedure for the other three tracks. When you do this, please bear the following details in mind:

- We used automation data in the Chords track. This means that the option "Include > Automation" must be activated in the "Export Audio Mixdown in" dialog box. This track can also be exported as a mono file.

- Export the two Arpache and Drums tracks as stereo interleaved files. Arpache has been processed with stereo effects that we created using the AutoPan MIDI effect, and the LM-7 has generated drums in stereo.

After all instrument tracks have been exported and are now available as audio tracks, select DEVICES > VST INSTRUMENTS and switch off all VST Instruments.

Select DEVICES > VST SEND EFFECTS and switch the Reverb A effect off.

Now open the VST Performance display via DEVICES > VST PERFORMANCE or F12 and play the track. The CPU load indicator is at low ebb; your computer has plenty of reserves and is ready to rise to new challenges.

You'll find the results of the audio mixdown in the *Audiomix* file in the *Cubase Projects* > *VST Instrument* folder on the CD.

6.7.2   A Few Tips on the Subject of Audio Mixdown

■ Don't delete every VST Instrument track that you export immediately. That way you still have the option of editing the original track and exporting it again.

■ Once you have exported a VST Instrument track, don't forget to switch this instrument off. Otherwise, you won't conserve much performance capacity. Ensure that you don't switch off instruments required for other tracks. In addition, switch off insert and send effects that are not being used for other tracks.

■ Always select the correct channel setting in the "Export Audio Mixdown in" dialog box. Stereo files require twice the storage capacity of mono files. Export in stereo only when necessary.

■ Don't generate unnecessary data. Case in point: Say that your song has 100 bars and a VST Instrument track plays different parts for 20 bars. In this case, don't export all 100 bars in one go. Instead, proceed selectively, exporting only segments containing recorded data. Mark each part using the Left and Right Locator and export it, then mark and export the next part, and so on. When exporting tracks, audio data is written even for passages where an instrument doesn't play notes, and this data takes up storage space.

Part 2

Basics of Mixing and Mastering

Chapter 7

Introduction to Mixing

You've written your song, recorded your parts, and did a few fixes with overdubs. You like what you're hearing from the monitors, and now you're ready for the next step: mixing and, ultimately, mastering the fruits of your creativity.

For those who are impatient and don't want to take the time to read the rest of this book, here's the complete story on mixing:

"Adjust the levels, tonal balance, stereo or surround placement, and add effects as needed so that the music sounds really, really great."

Okay, I guess we can all go home now ... but wait! It's not quite that simple. That description is like saying "To play the piano, hit a combination of white and black keys with your fingers until you come up with a combination of notes that sounds wonderful." The hard part, of course, is knowing which notes to hit, when to hit them, and to have the physical and mental ability to do both without errors.

Mixing is similar: you have to make a huge number of value judgements. Which instrument should be most prominent at any given time? Do you want to mute some sections that seem redundant? Do you want a raw, in-your-face sound, or a smooth, well-produced sound? Do you want a massive guitar sound, or something that shares its space with other instruments? Who is your target audience?

How successfully you answer these sorts of questions determines the success of your mix. Mixing is a combination of art—you have to be able to judge what sounds good—and science, where you need to know what technologies and processes will produce the sounds you want. As a result, this portion of the book will include aspects of both art and science.

7.1   The Mindset: Producer, Engineer, Musician

In professional situations, the musician is part of a team of (hopefully) experienced and musically intelligent people. Two of the people who play an important role on this team are the producer and the engineer. In a home or project studio environment, the musician doesn't necessarily have access to these high-powered talents and has to perform those roles from within. Although this may seem difficult at first, this experience is probably one of the greatest teachers you can have in learning how to be objective about your playing, your style, and your sounds.

During the mixing process, it helps to be aware of the ideal role of each of the three participants (musician, producer, engineer) so that you can assume those roles at will:

- The *producer* oversees the process and rides herd on the arrangement, the overall emotional impact, and makes artistic judgements about what does and does not work. To fulfill the function of a producer, you need to see each piece as part of a whole and each track as part of a final composition. If you know where you are going, it's a lot easier to get there; the job of the producer is to figure out where you are going.

- The *musician* participates in the mix on any one of several levels, from simply observing the producer to making sure the production remains true to the original intent of the music.

- The *engineer* is the one at the session who doesn't drink, smoke, talk much, or complain, and is responsible for translating the producer's needs into a technological solution. If the producer says the vocals need more "presence," it's up to the engineer to decide which tweaks will result in that particular effect. Of course, this is a stereotype and no stereotype is accurate, but every engineer I ever worked with respected the job and took it seriously. It can be helpful to adopt an engineer's attitude when mixing; forget about whether you could have done a better solo and simply work with what you have.

By becoming familiar with these roles, you can apply their differing outlooks to your music and obtain a more balanced perspective. Above all, don't just mix the music—*produce* it. Turn the collection of tracks into a cohesive statement.

A common mistake among beginning producers is to overproduce. Sometimes tracks are best left unprocessed, and sometimes parts should be removed to create space for other parts. Don't fall in love with the elements that make up a particular piece of music; keep your focus on the final result. Sure, that may have been a great guitar lick—but does it support the song, or just show that the guitarist can play lots of notes in a very short period of time?

7.2   Left-brain vs. Right-brain Activity

The human brain is a dual processing system. The left hemisphere is involved in more analytical tasks, such as math, decoding directions, reading, and so on. The right hemisphere is more involved with creative tasks and emotional responses; it's the part that "feels" rather than "thinks." This is not some weird new age philosophy; it's possible to hook up electrodes to people's heads and see which hemisphere of the brain is working during a particular task.

So what does this have to do with mixing? *Everything*—here's why.

In general, it is difficult for people to switch back and forth between the two hemispheres. Every musician knows what I'm talking about: suppose you're in a right-brain groove, generating an idea a minute, when all of a sudden there's a technical glitch. Now you have to switch over to left-brain mode and begin the troubleshooting process. When you start playing music again, the groove is gone, because your brain became stuck in left-brain mode.

In a conventional recording studio situation, the engineer gets to stay in left-brain mode, the artist gets to stay in right-brain (e. g., doesn't have to worry about level-setting and such because the engineer takes care of that), while the producer has the difficult job of trying to integrate the two. If you're trying to perform all these functions at once by yourself, you'll find it's not all that easy. This is why it's always great if you can have associates to help during the mixing process.

However, if you're flying solo, there are still ways to reconcile the right brain/left brain dichotomy. The most important thing is to make sure you don't have to think about left-brain activities, so you can stay in right-brain mode. If working with Cubase becomes second-nature, it will be that much easier to stay in right-brain mode. Here are some tips on how to do this:

■ Learn the keyboard equivalents for various operations. Once memorized, it takes less effort to just hit a couple of keys than to locate a specific part on the screen, move your mouse to it, go down a menu, select an item, etc. Cubase makes it easy to create your own set of Key Commands, as well as display a list of commands. It's also possible to create Macros, which allow individual keystrokes to trigger a chain of commands (e.g., use a keystroke to remove DC offset from an audio file, then normalize it).

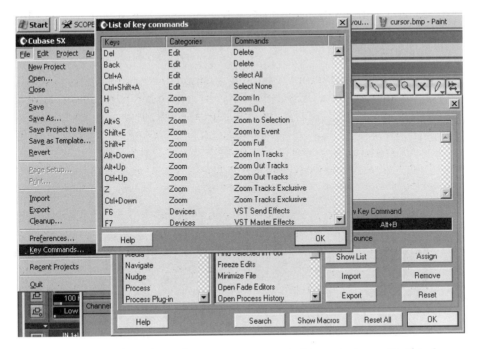

Go FILE > KEY COMMANDS, and you can create new key commands, see the list of existing commands, create Macros, and even export your key commands for use in other Cubase studios.

- Use Window layouts to organize specific combinations of windows for certain tasks, like mixing, overdubbing, working with VST instruments, setting up send effects, etc. This requires much less thought than opening windows and dragging them around.

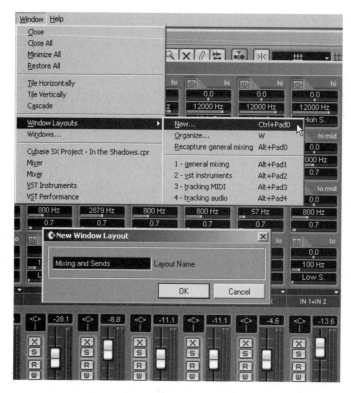

You can save a particular layout of windows at any time by going WINDOW > WINDOW LAYOUTS > NEW, then typing in a name for the layout and clicking OK. For more information on Window Layouts, see Chapter 9.

■ The use of color and graphics goes well with right-brain thinking, as your brain can decode colors more easily than words. This is why it's important to customize Cubase for the way that works best for you. For example, in Cubase SX, you have the option of seeing EQ settings as knob positions or lines. I find it easier to scan the lines to see what's happening compared to taking a look at the knobs (and I would find it even easier if the lines changed color depending on their setting, like the way Cubase handles velocity indications in the MIDI piano roll editor). You may prefer the knobs, though—use what works best for you.

7.2.1   Feel vs. Perfection

Some older albums, recorded under technically primitive conditions, still conveyed a joyousness and enthusiasm—a "feel"—that made for great music. And some newer albums are so perfect, so automated and equalized, that the sound is sterile and somehow mechanical. There are some producers who believe that the feel is all important; if a musician does a great part but blows a couple of phrases, that's all right if the feel was good. Other producers insist on doing a part over and over and over until it's technically perfect. Both approaches have their advantages and pitfalls, so try to strike a balance. Don't fall into the trap of being so self-critical that you never complete anything, but also don't get so loose that everything sounds "great" and you lose the ability to evaluate.

One of the wonderful aspects of computer-based recording is you can save your mixes as you go along. You may find out that it was the first or second mixes, not the last ones, that had a certain quality. You might also find that combining different parts of different mixes can do wonders for a tune—maybe you were really inspired when doing the intro to one mix, but nailed the middle of a different mix. Although most people do this kind of editing in a two-track digital audio editor, you can import your final mixes into Cubase, get out the scissors tool, cut and move, then export the edited version.

7.3   Challenges Facing the Solo Artist

There's more to being a solo artist than just dealing with the right/left brain dichotomy. The fact that one person can write, play, produce, record, master, and even duplicate music is unique to modern times. But just because we *can*, does that mean we *should*? There's much to recommend human interaction, and the reality check that comes from a trusted associate who can give honest, objective feedback (and in the case of a producer or engineer, offload some of the left-brain activities).

Many readers are fortunate enough to work with friends and associates, while others, for any number of reasons, tend to work solo. Is this an inherently flawed concept? Not necessarily, because doing all the tasks yourself is highly educational. Programming drum parts made me a better bass player. Producing myself forced me to be more objective, and engineering—well, I learned that mostly from working with some really fine engineers and have tried to continue on from there. Over the years, I've gotten reasonably skilled at these arts. Sure, I'd rather have Sheila E. do my drum parts, but you can't have everything.

The key to pulling off the difficult task of being a solo musician is *not to fall in love with your music.* Distance yourself from what you do, so you can make the kind of objective decisions normally reserved for the producer. Following are some tips on how to create "better music through detachment."

7.3.1   The Radio Factor

A song's intro is crucial. If a radio station or A&R person doesn't like the first ten seconds, you're through. They *might* listen to ten seconds of your next cut, but don't count on it.

Here's a test for intros. Picture an office party filled with a variety of people, from the new mailroom guy to upper management. They're all a bit tipsy and chatting away, while the radio (whose quality is nowhere near as good as the monitors in your studio) provides background music. A commercial comes on, followed by an announcer saying the station logo—"K-TONE, where the music still matters"—then they lead into your song. Picture this scene as vividly as you can in your imagination.

Try to put yourself in the position of one of the partygoers, then "look" around you. How do the people react? Do they stop talking and listen? Do they listen for the first few bars, then go back to conversing? Do they ignore it entirely? Is there something in the first few seconds to grab their attention and keep it? For your tune to be played on the radio, think of it in the context of radio play. It has to be able to segue from anything to anything, appeal to short attention spans, and be different. Doing this exercise can help clarify what needs to be done to make the song stand out more.

The bottom line: Every mix should, if at all possible, do something to grab people's attention in the first ten seconds.

7.3.2   Got Live if You Want It

My preferred way to test a song is to play it in front of an audience (preferably non-musicians). It's the quickest way to find out what connects and what doesn't. Then you can apply that feedback to improving the song. But if you can't do that, to simulate the effect of playing a piece one-on-one to an audience, I go back to square one, pick up a single guitar or keyboard, and re-arrange the song for playing as a solo performer in real time.

Something good happens every time I try this. For example, in one song I had what I thought was a nifty little instrumental figure between the verse and chorus. It was not possible to duplicate with solo guitar, so I substituted an alternate chord pattern—which ended up being more compelling than the original, and as a side benefit, could be played live.

Remember, songs used to be honed on the road and captured in the studio. Now songs are often created in the studio and re-created on the road. As you mix a tune, always imagine an audience is listening. It will make a difference in how the song develops.

7.3.3   The Cleverness Factor

For me, the paramount lesson from doing years of studio work behind songs was that *everything* supports the lead singer. Your licks are there *only* to make the lead vocal more effective.

Many years ago, I came up with a lyrical, melodic bass part for a verse. It was composed in isolation, while waiting for the engineer to get a good snare drum sound, and I fell in love with the part. But played behind the vocal, it was too distracting. The producer told me to simplify the part, and I ended up playing something that any moron who had just picked up a bass could play. It was hard to let my clever bass part go, but the simpler version made a far greater contribution to the tune.

When mixing, many times it's what you *mute* that makes the song work, not what you leave in. If you recorded 30 tracks, don't feel you have to use them all. The less there is going on, the more important the remaining parts become. The mixing process is your last chance to be brutally honest: if something doesn't work quite right, get rid of it, regardless of how clever it is or how good it sounds on its own.

7.3.4   What Are Your Real Goals?

Of course, all this advice assumes that you *want* to connect with an audience. But I don't necessarily advocate that. Creating music is, in the larger sense, about self-discovery, and that's the magical part. Even if I was told that I'd never sell another CD in my life, I'd still make music.

I feel there are only two ways to be successful. One is to be totally true to yourself and hope that the music you create strikes a chord in others as well. This usually creates the brightest stars with the longest careers, because there is no artifice. And if it doesn't "fit" with a mass audience, at least what you have is honest, and your friends will probably love it.

The other option is to carefully study past hits, cool chord progressions, pick lyrical subjects with wide appeal, etc., and do mixes that are designed to appeal to specific audiences. I've known songwriters who take this approach, and while there is always a kernel of soul in what they do, they approach writing more as a business than as art. That's fine too and can lead to a comfortable, well-paying, career without the drawbacks of fame. In that case, you really need to study mixes so your tunes can fit in with what's "commercially acceptable." And you may need to add a lot more compression when mastering because "everyone else does it," not because you necessarily think it's appropriate.

I think combining the two approaches yields the best results. Let the artist in you create, then let the hard-headed, objective part of you produce, mix, and master. While this section has concentrated on what it takes to become more objective, I don't mean to trivialize the creative factor. As in so many aspects of life, it's the synthesis of opposites that creates the best results. Go ahead, love your music—but don't be *in* love with it if you want to remain objective.

Okay, enough opinions ... let's get technical.

7.4   About Frequency Response and Hearing

One goal of mixing and mastering is to produce a balanced, even sound. It should have a full, satisfying bass without "muddiness," a well-defined midrange, and sparkly (not screechy) highs. To achieve this, as well as use equalization properly, we need to understand frequency response.

Frequency response defines how a system records or reproduces the spectrum of audible frequencies, which stretches from 20Hz to 20,000Hz. (Hz, short for Hertz, measures the number of cycles per second in a wave; 1kHz or kiloHertz equals 1000 Hz.) This is usually shown on a graph. The Y-axis (vertical) shows level, and the X-axis (horizontal) indicates frequency.

Here, the graph shows a straight line from 0 to 20kHz. This is called a *flat* response, which means that no range of frequencies is accented or diminished.

The audible range is further divided into bands. These are not precisely defined, but here's a rough guide:

- **Bass:** Lowest frequencies, typically below 200Hz
- **Lower midrange:** 200 to 800Hz
- **Midrange:** 800Hz to 2.5kHz
- **Upper midrange:** 2.5kHz to 8kHz
- **Treble:** 8kHz and higher

While these guidelines are approximate, they are still useful as references. For example, bass guitar and kick drum occupy the bass range. Vocals are in the midrange and lower midrange. Percussion instruments like tambourine have lots of energy in the treble region.

Although electronic devices like hi-fi amplifiers often have a flat frequency response, no mechanical device does. A speaker's response falls off at high and low frequencies. Guitar pickup response falls off at high frequencies, which is why guitar amps often boost the upper midrange.

Loud, extended mixing sessions are very tough on the ears. Mixing at low levels keeps your ears "fresher" and minimizes ear fatigue; you'll also be able to discriminate better between subtle level variations. Loud mixes may get you hyped up, but they'll also trip your ear's built-in "limiting" (ears don't hear in a linear fashion).

However, because the ear's frequency response changes depending on level, if you mix or master at *too* low a level, you might boost the bass and treble too much. Mix at a comfortable listening level—neither too loud nor too soft. Then check at both high and low levels to find a good average setting.

7.5 Monitoring and Acoustics

All the effort you put into recording, overdubbing, and mixing is for nothing if your monitoring system isn't honest about the sounds you hear. The issue isn't simply the speakers; the process of monitoring is deceptively complex, as it involves your ears, the acoustics of the room in which you monitor, the amp and cables that drive your monitors, and the speakers themselves.

All of these elements work together to determine the accuracy of what you hear, and therefore, how you mix and master.

If you've ever done a mix that sounded great on your system but fell apart when played elsewhere, you've experienced firsthand what can go wrong with the monitoring process.

7.5.1 The Problem with Ears

For starters, your ears—the most crucial and important components of your monitoring system—aren't perfect. Even healthy, young ears aren't perfect, thanks to a phenomenon called the Fletcher-Munson curve. Simply stated, the ear has a midrange peak and does not respond as well to low and high frequencies, particularly at lower volumes. The response comes closest to flat response at relatively high levels. The "loudness" control on hi-fi amps attempts to compensate for this by boosting the highs and lows at lower levels, then flattening out the response as you turn up the volume.

Another limitation is that a variety of factors can damage your ears—not just loud music, but excessive alcohol intake, deep sea diving, and just plain aging. I've noticed that flying temporarily affects my high frequency response, so I wait at least 24 hours after getting off a plane before doing anything like mixing that involves critical listening. The few times I've broken that rule, mixes that seemed perfectly fine at the time played back too bright the next day. Also note that professional audio engineers often exhibit a dip in the all-important midrange frequencies from too much day-in, day-out exposure to louder-than-average sounds.

You've heard it before, but believe me: Take care of your hearing so at least your ears aren't the biggest detriment to monitoring accuracy! Back in my touring days when I'd often play 200 days out of the year, I wore cotton in my ears. While not as effective as present-day, high-tech earplugs, I feel it really saved my hearing. These days, I often carry the cylindrical foam ear plugs you can buy at sporting good stores. I wear them while walking city streets, at clubs, when hammering or using power tools (the impulse noise of a hammer hitting a nail is major!), or anywhere my ears are going to get more abuse than someone talking at a conversational level. I make my living with my ears, and taking care of them is a priority. Good hearing should be your priority too.

7.5.2   Other Variables

The room in which you monitor will also influence how you mix. For a real ear-opener, set up an audio level meter (e.g., the kind made by Radio Shack for monitoring workplace noise levels), sit with it in the middle of your room, run a sine wave test tone oscillator through the speakers, and watch the meter. Unless you have great monitors and an acoustically-tuned room, that meter will fluctuate like a leaf in a tornado. Speakers by themselves do not have perfectly flat responses, but they look like a ruler compared to the average untreated room.

You don't even need a level meter to conduct this test: play a steady tone around 5 kHz or so, then move your head around. You'll hear obvious volume fluctuations. (If you can't hear the 5kHz tone, then perhaps it's time to look for a different line of work.)

These variations occur because as sound bounces around off walls, the reflections become part of the overall sound, creating cancellations and additions.

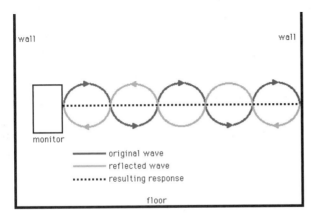

This illustration shows a "standing-wave" condition, where a wave reflects back from a wall out of phase, thus canceling the original waveform. At other frequencies, the reflection can just as easily reinforce the original waveform. These frequency response anomalies affect how you hear the music as you mix.

Another example of how acoustics affects sound is when you place a speaker against a wall, which seems to increase bass. Here's why: Any sounds emanating from the rear of the speaker, or leaking from the front (bass frequencies are very non-directional), bounce off the wall. Because a bass note's wavelength is so long, the reflection will tend to reinforce the main wave. This is a greatly simplified explanation, but it gets the principle across.

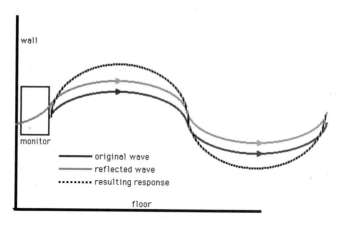

Placing a speaker with its back against the wall often gives an apparent increase in bass; placing it in a corner accentuates the bass even more.

As the walls, floors, and ceilings all interact with speakers, it's important that any speakers be placed symmetrically within a room. Otherwise, if (for example) one speaker is three feet from a wall and another ten feet from a wall, any reflections will be wildly different and affect the response.

The subject of acoustically treating a room deserves a book in itself; we are just touching on the basics here to provide background on an important element of the mixing process. If you have the money, hiring a professional consultant to "tune" your room with bass traps and similar mechanical devices (this is different from room-tuning with graphic EQ) could be the best investment you ever make in your music. I can't really give specific advice here for your situation, because every room is different.

Some people try to compensate for room anomalies by inserting a graphic equalizer just before their power amp and "tune" the equalization to adjust for room anomalies. While this sounds good in theory, if you deviate at all from the "sweet spot" where the microphone was, the frequency response will be off. Also, heavily equalizing a poor acoustical space simply gives you a heavily-equalized poor acoustical space. Like noise reduction, which works best on signals that don't have a lot of noise, room tuning works best on rooms that don't have serious response problems.

7.5.3   Near-field Monitors

Traditional studios have large monitors mounted at a considerable distance (six to ten feet or so) from the mixer, with the front flush to the wall, and an acoustically-treated control room to minimize response variations. The "sweet spot"—the place where room acoustics are most favorable—is designed to be where the mixing engineer sits at the console.

In smaller project studios, near-field monitors have become the standard way to monitor. With this technique, small speakers sit around three to six feet from the mixer's ears, with the head and speakers forming a triangle.

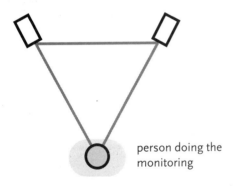

person doing the
monitoring

the "sweet spot"

When using near-field monitors, the speakers should point toward the ears and be at ear level. If slightly above ear level, they should point downward toward the ears.

Near-field monitors reduce (but do not at all eliminate) the impact of room acoustics on the overall sound, as the speakers' direct sound is far greater than the reflections coming off the room surfaces. As a side benefit, because of their proximity to your ears, near-field monitors do not have to produce a lot of power. This also relaxes the requirements for the amps feeding them.

However, placement in the room is still an issue. If placed too close to the walls, there will be a bass build-up. Although you can compensate for this with EQ (or possibly controls on the speakers themselves), the build-up will be different at different frequencies. High frequencies are not as affected because they are more directional. If the speakers are free-standing and placed away from the wall, back reflections from the speakers bouncing off the wall could cause cancellations and additions for the reasons mentioned earlier.

You're pretty safe if the speakers are more than six feet away from the wall in a fairly large listening space (this places the first frequency null point below the normally audible range), but not everyone has that much room. My solution, crude as it is, has been to mount the speakers a bit away from the wall on the same table holding the mixer, and pad the walls behind the speakers with as much sound-deadening material as possible.

Nor are room reflections the only problem; if placed on top of a console, reflections from the console itself can cause inaccuracies. To get around this, in my studio the near-fields fit to the side of the mixer, and are slightly elevated. This makes as direct a path as possible from speaker to eardrum.

7.5.4 Anatomy of a Near-field Monitor

There are lots of near-field monitors available, in a variety of sizes and at numerous price points. Most are two-way designs, with (typically) a 6" or 8" woofer and smaller tweeter. While a 3-way design that adds a separate midrange driver might seem like a good idea, adding another crossover and speaker can complicate matters. A well-designed two-way system will beat a so-so 3-way system.

There are two main monitor types, *active* and *passive*. Passive monitors consist of only the speakers and crossovers and require outboard amplifiers. Active monitors incorporate any power amplification needed to drive the speakers from a line level signal. I generally prefer powered monitors because the engineers have (hopefully!) tweaked the power amp and speaker into a smooth, efficient team. Issues such as speaker cable resistance become moot, and protection can be built into the amp to prevent blowouts. Powered monitors are often *bi-amped* (e.g., a separate amp for the woofer and tweeter), which minimizes intermodulation distortion and allows for tailoring the crossover points and frequency response for the speakers being used.

However, there's of course nothing wrong with hooking up passive monitors (which are less expensive than active equivalents) to your own amps. Just make sure your amp has adequate headroom. Any clipping that occurs in the amp generates lots of high-frequency harmonics (ask any guitarist who uses distortion), and sustained clipping can burn out tweeters.

7.5.5   Is There a "Best" Monitor?

On net bulletin boards, you'll see endless discussions on which near-fields are best. In truth, the answer may rest more on which near-field works best with your listening space and imperfect hearing response. How many times have you seen a review of a speaker where the person notes with amazement that some new speaker "revealed sounds not heard before with other speakers"? This is to be expected. The frequency response of even the best speakers is sufficiently uneven that some speakers will indeed emphasize different frequencies compared to other speakers, essentially creating a different mix.

Although it's a cliché that you should audition several speakers and choose the model you like best, I believe you can't choose the perfect speaker, because such a thing doesn't exist. Instead, you choose the one that colors the sound the way you prefer.

Choosing a speaker is an art. I've been fortunate enough to hear my music over some hugely expensive, very-close-to-perfect systems in mastering labs and high-end studios, so I know exactly what it should sound like. My criterion for choosing a speaker is simple: whatever makes my "test" CD sound the most like it did over the high-end speakers wins.

If you haven't had the same kind of listening experiences, book 30 minutes or so at some really good studio and bring along one of your favorite CDs (you can probably get a price break because you're not asking to use a lot of the facilities). Listen to the CD and get to know what it should sound like, then compare any speakers you audition to that standard. For example, if the piano on your mix sounds a little understated on the expensive speakers, choose speakers where the piano is equally understated.

One caution: if you're A-B comparing a set of speakers and one set is slightly louder than the other (even $\frac{1}{10}$ of a dB can make a difference), you'll likely choose the louder one as sounding better. Make sure the speaker levels are matched as closely as possible in order to make a valid comparison.

A final point worth mentioning is that speakers have magnets which, if placed close to monitors, can distort the monitor's display. If you plan to place a monitor near the speakers (e.g., audio for video work), go for magnetically-shielded speakers as they do not exhibit this problem.

7.5.6   Learning Your Speaker and Room

Ultimately, because your own listening situation is imperfect, you need to "learn" your system's response. For example, suppose you mix something in your studio that sounds fine, but in a high-end studio with accurate monitoring, the sound is bass-heavy. That means your monitoring environment is shy on the bass, so you boosted the bass to compensate (this is a common problem in project studios with small rooms). In future mixes, you'll know to mix the bass lighter than normal in order to have it come out okay.

Compare midrange and treble as well. If vocals jump out of your system but lay back in others, then your speakers might be "midrangey." Again, compensate by mixing midrange-heavy parts back a little bit.

You also have to decide on a standardized listening level. I believe in monitoring at low levels when mixing, not just to save my ears, but also because if something sounds good at low volume, it will sound great when really cranked up. However, this also means that the bass and treble might be mixed up a bit more than they should be to compensate for the Fletcher-Munson curve. So, before signing off on a mix, I check the sound at a variety of levels. If at loud levels it sounds just a hair too bright and boomy, and if at low levels it sounds just a bit bass- and treble-light, that's about right.

7.5.7 Headphones, Hi-Fi Speakers, and Satellite Systems

Musicians on a budget often wonder about mixing over headphones, as $100 will buy you a great set of headphones, but not much in the way of speakers. Although mixing exclusively on headphones is not a good idea, I highly recommend keeping a good set of headphones around as a reality check (not the open-air type that sits on your ear, but the kind that totally surrounds your ear). Sometimes you can get a more accurate bass reading using headphones than you can with near-fields. Careful, though: it's easy to blast your ears with headphones and not know it. Watch those volume levels (and be real careful about accidentally setting up a feedback loop— a loud enough squeal could cause permanent damage).

As to hi-fi speakers, here's a brief story. For almost 15 years, I mixed over a set of trusted bookshelf speakers in my home studio. These were some of the least sexy-sounding and most boring speakers in the world. But they were neutral and flat, and more importantly, I had "learned" them during the process of taking my mixes to many pro studios for tweaking or mastering. In fact, when listening over expensive speakers, the sound was almost always exactly what I expected, with one exception: signals below about 50Hz simply vanished on my speakers. Therefore, with instruments like orchestral kick drums, I had to mix visually by checking the meters, then verifying the mix at another facility. Thankfully, I've since upgraded to "real" near-field monitors that can hear signals down to about 30 Hz.

So yes, you can use hi-fi speakers if you absolutely must, assuming they're relatively flat and unbiased (watch out; some consumer-oriented speakers "hype" the high and low ends). However, they often aren't meant to take a lot of power, so be careful not to blow them out. One other tip: unless the manufacturer states otherwise, I recommend placing bookshelf speakers horizontally, with the tweeters on the outside. This gives better stereo separation than mounting the speakers vertically.

Lately, "satellite" systems have appeared where the near-fields are physically very small—in fact, too small to produce adequate bass (some would argue that no 6" or 8" speaker can really produce adequate bass, but sometimes we need to reconcile finances and space with the laws of physics). To compensate, a third element, the "subwoofer," adds a fairly large speaker, and is crossed over at a very low frequency so that it reproduces only bass notes. This speaker usually mounts on the floor, against a wall; in some respects placement isn't too critical because bass frequencies are relatively non-directional.

Can you use satellite-based systems to make your computer audio sound great? Yes. If you're living space is tight, is this a good way to make your hi-fi setup less intrusive? Yes. Would you mix your major label project over them? Well, I wouldn't. Perhaps you could learn these systems over time as well, but I personally have difficulty with the disembodied bass when it comes to critical mixes.

7.5.8   Testing on Multiple Delivery Systems

I'm distrustful enough of speakers that before signing off on a mix, I'll run off a CD or two and listen through anything I can—car stereo speakers, hi-fi bookshelf speakers, big-bucks studio speakers, boom boxes, headphones, etc. This gives me an idea of how well the mix will translate over a variety of systems. If the mix works, great—mission accomplished. But if it sounds overly bright on five out of eight systems, I'll pull back the brightness just a bit. Of course, some of this can be compensated for during the mastering process, but ideally, you want any project to require the least amount of mastering possible.

Many "pro" studios will have their big speakers mounted in the wall, a pair of near-fields for reality testing, and some "junk" speakers sitting around to check what something will sound like over a lo-fi consumer system (such as the average TV). Switching back and forth among the various systems can help "zero in" on the ultimate mix that translates well over any system.

7.5.9   The Learning Curve

If all of the above sounds like there's a learning curve ahead of you, that's true. Pay attention to your hearing first, then the room acoustics, then the monitor. Once you've found a good location for the speakers that is unlikely to change, get to know the sound so you can mentally compensate for any response anomalies.

The more you monitor, the more educated your ears will become. Also, the more dependent they will become on the speakers you use (some producers carry their favorite monitor speakers to sessions so they can compare the studio's speakers to speakers they already know well). But the good side of all this is that even if you can't afford the ultimate monitoring setup, with a bit of practice you can learn your system well enough to produce a good-sounding mix that translates well over a variety of systems—and that's much of what mixing is all about.

7.6   Plug-ins: Tools for Mixing and Mastering

Steinberg invented the VST (Virtual Studio Technology) concept where signal processors, mixers, and other elements of the studio became "native" parts of the computer environment. The VST plug-in format is cross-platform (i.e., compatible with both Mac and Windows), however on the PC, Cubase also accepts the Microsoft DirectX plug-in format.

There are two main types of plug-in technology: *host-based* (also called *native*) and *hardware-based*. Hardware-based plug-ins run only with certain specialized hardware computer cards designed for digital signal processing, such as the UAD-1 series from Universal Audio/Mackie, the PowerCore plug-ins from TC Works, and CreamWare's Pulsar XTC effects and soft synths. Host-based plug-ins use the computer's microprocessor to do any needed digital signal processing, and therefore require no specialized hardware.

Native plug-ins require a certain amount of CPU power, so the more plug-ins you run (especially software synthesizers), the harder the CPU has to work. As a result, there are limits as to how many plug-ins you can use with a software program. If you want to run more plug-ins, the two main solutions are to use a faster CPU (e.g., 2GHz instead of 500MHz) or increase the system latency (the time required for the system to process signals). Increasing latency means the CPU doesn't have to work as hard, but it increases the response time when moving faders, playing soft synths, etc.

7.7 The Mixing Process

Mixing is not only an art, it's the ultimate arbiter of how your music sounds. A good mix can bring out the best in your music, while a bad mix can obscure it.

An effective mix spotlights a composition's most important elements, adds a few surprises to excite the listener, and sounds good on any system—from a transistor radio to an audiophile's dream setup. Translating a collection of tracks into a cohesive song isn't easy; mixing requires the same level of creativity and experience as any part of the musical process.

To understand why mixing is so tricky, we need to examine some of the problems involved in trying to make a good mix. But first, let's decide what's going to hold our final mix.

7.8 Mixdown Options

There are several ways to create a mixed file in Cubase SX/SL. Following are the most common options.

7.8.1 Exporting a Mixed File from within Cubase ("Rendering to Disk")

The easiest way to create a final stereo mix in Cubase is to adjust all the settings exactly as you want (EQ, levels, etc.), including any automation you want to use. When the mix is perfect, you can then go FILE > EXPORT > AUDIO MIXDOWN and "render" the file in any one of several formats, with sample rates up to 96 kHz, and bit resolution up to 32-bit floating point. There are two main "families" of file types:

- WAV, AIFF, and Broadcast WAV format files can be imported by CD-burning and digital audio editing programs.

- MP3, Ogg Vorbis, RealAudio, and Windows Media Audio format files use *data compression* (which can degrade the sound) so they don't need as much data, allowing them to stream more easily over the web or be used in multimedia productions. For example, a tune that requires 40MB as a WAV file, when compressed by 10:1, ends up as a svelte 4MB file.

  Do not confuse data compression, which reduces the amount of data a song requires, and audio compression, which restricts a signal's dynamic range. Also, note that the data-compressed file formats available to Cubase use "lossy" compression. In other words, you cannot "uncompress" the data and end up with the original; data that is discarded to create a smaller file size cannot be retrieved.

7.8.2   Mixing to Analog Tape

Analog tape is a signal processor that some engineers feel "warms up" the sound, due to inherent distortions within the tape medium itself. These people sometimes prefer mixing to analog tape as an alternative to staying in the digital domain.

Of course, this is easy to do with Cubase: assign its master output to two channels of your audio interface's analog outputs (or digital outs, followed by a digital-to-analog converter), and patch these into the recorder's analog inputs. Pros generally prefer mixing to the widest tape possible at the fastest possible speed (e.g., ½-inch tape at 30 inches per second). Although there's always controversy about analog vs. digital, the bottom line is that 30 ips tapes can sound great. Add Dolby SR noise reduction, and you have sound quality that need make no excuses to digital systems.

7.8.3   Mixing Direct to Digital

In this case, you connect your audio interface's digital output (usually either SPDIF or AES/EBU) to the digital input of a stand-alone CD recorder, DAT machine, Minidisc, or another computer.

> SPDIF is considered a "consumer" standard, but is used a lot in pro circles as well. It has two variations: a wire-based version that terminates in RCA phono jacks, and an optical version that uses TOSLINK optical connectors. AES/EBU interfaces are balanced digital lines rather than unbalanced, allowing them to cover a greater distance without signal degradation. Although AES/EBU can be either optical or wired, it is usually carried over balanced lines terminating in XLR connectors.

Be careful to observe two important points:

- The sample rate of the Cubase project, audio interface, and mixdown device must all be the same. For CDs, the standard sample rate is 44.1kHz; broadcast generally uses 32kHz, and video runs at 48kHz. Surround sound and other "high-resolution" audio may use sample rates up to 96 or even 192kHz. However, as the most common delivery medium at present is the CD, 44.1kHz is currently the most common sample rate.

■ The mixdown device should be set to slave to the clock signal coming out of the audio interface. This insures that the mixdown device will synchronize properly to a digital control signal (called *word clock*) that is carried by the digital out. Lack of sync, which can be caused by setting both devices as clock sync masters, usually leads to (at the very least) pops and clicks in the audio, and in extreme cases can cause "tearing" sounds and drop outs. Your mixdown device's manual should include information on how to set it as a slave to a master clock source.

7.8.4   Mixing to a Digital Recorder via Analog Connections

Digital offers perfect transfers, but some prefer patching in analog mastering tools between the computer's output and the mixdown device's input. This includes units like Dolby's famous Model 740 Spectral Processor, "vintage" gear like the Pultec equalizer, and so on; you'll need an audio interface with analog outputs and a mixdown device with analog inputs. Otherwise, you may need to add a stage of conversion (e. g., an analog-to-digital converter if your mixdown device has only digital inputs).

7.8.5   Mixing Back into Cubase via a Digital or Analog Mixer

An often-overlooked option is sending multiple busses from Cubase into the inputs of a digital or analog mixer, and simultaneously recording the mixer's output in two Cubase tracks. There are some good reasons for doing this:

■ You can patch analog effects into the mixer (like a really high quality hardware reverb) or patch the mixer output through analog mastering tools.

■ You can use the mixer's onboard EQs instead of Cubase's to lighten the host processor's load.

- You can move faders and twist knobs on the mixer in real time when mixing, thus having some of the advantages of a "control surface."
- When you save the Cubase project, you save not only the source tracks, but the final mix as well.

For more information on sending Cubase outputs to a physical mixer, see Chapter 26.

7.9 Before You Mix

Preparation for the mix begins the moment you start recording, and part of that involves recording the cleanest possible signal. Eliminate as many active stages as possible between source and recorder; many times, devices set to "bypass" may not be adding any effect but are still in the signal path, which can add some slight noise or signal degradation.

How many times do line level signals go through preamps due to lazy engineering? If possible, send sounds directly into your audio interface—bypass any mixer or preamp altogether. For mic signals, use an ultra-high quality outboard preamp and patch that directly into the audio interface rather than use a mixer with onboard preamps.

Always record with the highest possible fidelity. Although you may not hear much of a difference when monitoring a single instrument, with multiple tracks the cumulative effect of stripping the signal path to its essentials can make a significant difference in the sound's clarity.

7.9.1 The Arrangement

Before you even think about turning any knobs, scrutinize the arrangement. Solo projects are particulary prone to "clutter" because as you lay down the early tracks, there's a tendency to overplay to fill up all that empty space. As the arrangement progresses, there's not a lot of space for overdubs.

Here are a couple of suggestions when tracking that will make it much easier to create a good mix:

- Once the arrangement is fleshed out, go back and recut any overly-busy tracks that you cut earlier on. Try to play these tracks as sparsely as possible to leave room for the overdubs you've added. Sometimes I've found it very helpful to recut a song from scratch as soon as I've finished mixing it, or have played it live numerous times. Like many others, I write in the studio, and often the song will have a slightly tentative feel because of that. Recutting always seem to both simplify and improve the song.

- With vocal-based songs, try building a song around the vocalist instead of completing the rhythm section and then laying down the vocals. I often find it better to record simple "placemarkers" for the rhythm section, then immediately get to work cutting the best possible vocal. Then I go back and re-record the rhythm section. When you recut the rhythm section for real, you'll be a lot more sensitive to the vocal nuances.

7.10 Mixing: The 12-step Program

You "build" a mix over time by making a variety of adjustments. There are (at least!) twelve major steps involved in creating a mix, but what makes mixing so difficult is that these steps interact. Change a track's equalization (tone quality), and you also change the level because you're boosting or cutting some element of the sound. Alter a sound's stereo location, and you may need to shift the ambience or equalization. In fact, you can think of a mix as an "audio combination lock" since when all the elements hit the right combination, you end up with a good mix.

Let's look at these twelve steps, but remember, this is just one person's way of mixing—you might discover a totally different approach that works better for you.

7.10.1   Step 1: Mental Preparation and Organization

Mixing requires a tremendous amount of concentration and can be extremely tedious, so set up your workspace as efficiently as possible. Cubase's Window Layouts options are particularly helpful in this regard, as you can switch with a couple mouse clicks among different mixer views, sets of channels, and so on.

To save a particular window layout:

1   Set up your windows exactly as desired, for example, as a mixing environment.

2   Go WINDOW > WINDOW LAYOUTS > NEW.

3   Name the layout, such as "Mixer with VST Performance."

4   Click on OK.

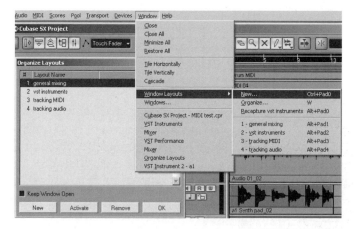

You can create a new window layout by going to the Window menu, or by keeping the Organize Layouts window open (check the "Keep Window Open" box) and clicking on the New button. The Organize Layouts window is also where you can activate or remove window layouts.

To recall a particular window layout, go WINDOW > WINDOW LAY-OUTS and select the desired layout. You can also select "Organize," where you can activate particular layouts, as well as remove or create new ones.

> Layouts remember only which windows are open and their spatial relationship. You cannot, for example, save one mixer view that shows EQs and another mixer view that shows Inserts.

In any event, no matter how efficiently you work, for best results take a break periodically (every hour or so is a good interval) to "rest" your ears and gain a fresher outlook on your return. Even a couple minutes of off time can restore your objectivity and, paradoxically, complete a mix much faster.

7.10.2   Step 2: Review the Tracks

Listen at low volume and familiarize yourself with the tracks. Make sure all tracks are named, note which tracks have active plug-ins that may need to be adjusted, and the like. Group sounds logically, such as having all the drum sounds on consecutive channels.

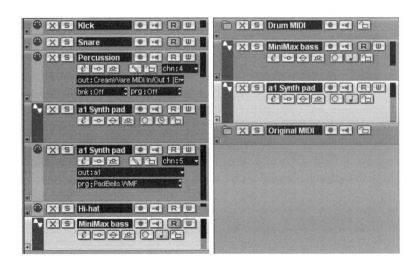

The messy view on the left shows four MIDI drum tracks for kick, snare, percussion, and hi-hat. The hi-hat was recorded after the bass and pad parts, so it shows up below them rather than with the other drum parts. Also, the a1 Synth pad part has been converted into audio, but the original MIDI track driving it has been retained in case it needs to be edited later on.

The view on the right shows what happens after cleaning this up: all the MIDI drum tracks have been placed in a folder track; a folder track has also been created for the original MIDI parts that drove synths, but placed below everything else so it's out of the way. This layout also creates a more logical mixer channel arrangement as well.

7.10.3 Step 3: Put On Headphones and Listen For Glitches

Fixing glitches is a "left brain" activity, as opposed to the "right brain" creativity involved in doing a mix. Switching back and forth between these two modes can hamper creativity, so do as much cleaning up as possible—erase glitches, bad notes, scratch tracks, and the like—before you get involved in the mix.

I highly recommended using the Solo button to solo each track and listen to it from beginning to end. With MIDI tracks, check for duplicate notes that "flam" or create chorusing-type effects and avoid overlapping notes on single-note lines (such as bass and horn parts).

With audio tracks, listen for any spurious noises just before or after audio appears (mic handling sounds if the vocalist likes using a hand-held mic, vibrating string on a guitar, hum from a bass amp, etc.). It's amazing how many little noises you'll hear on vocal tracks, like clicks from someone moving their tongue prior to singing. These low-level glitches may not seem that audible, but multiply them by a couple dozen tracks and they can definitely muddy things up.

It's easy to edit audio with Cubase, which now provides detailed audio editing. Double-click on a piece of audio, and a sample editing window appears with the audio. You can even zoom in far enough to draw out clicks with a pencil tool, as well asselect a region and apply an audio process (silence, fade in, fade out, normalize, etc.) as accessed via AUDIO > PROCESS. Fades are particularly useful if the audio has been cut and has a click at the beginning or end. This is something you'll hear when soloed, but if the click occurs on the beat, you might not notice it with other tracks playing.

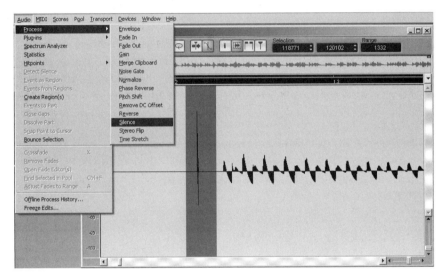

It's easy to get rid of stray clicks: open your audio in the sample editor, select the region you want to remove, and click on AUDIO > PROCESS > SILENCE.

7.10.4 Step 4: Render Soft Synths as Audio Tracks

If you're sequencing VSTi devices via MIDI, consider converting them to hard disk tracks. This will free up DSP processing power for any effects you want to use during mixdown, or perhaps allow you to replace a not-so-great-sounding reverb with one that requires more CPU power. Also, these audio tracks will be saved in a Project folder, making the sound more "transportable" because the person receiving the project files doesn't need to have the soft synth itself resident within Cubase. For more information, see Chapter 23 on Mixing and MIDI.

7.10.5   Step 5: Set Up a Relative Level Balance between the Tracks

Now that our preparations are out of the way, it's time to get into mixing itself.

Do not add any processing for now. Concentrate on the overall effect of hearing the tracks by themselves and work on the overall sound; don't get distracted by detail work. With a good mix, the tracks sound good by themselves—but sound even better when interacting with the other tracks.

I suggest settings levels in mono at first, because if the instruments sound distinct and separate in mono, they'll only open up more in stereo. Also, you may not notice parts "fighting" with other if you start off in stereo.

7.10.6   Step 6: Adjust Equalization (EQ)

This can help dramatize differences between instruments and create a more balanced overall sound. Work on the most important song elements first (vocals, drums, and bass), and once these all "lock" together, deal with the more supportive parts. We'll talk about EQ in far more detail in the chapter "About Equalization" on page 193.

The audio spectrum has only so much space, and you need to make sure that each sound occupies its own turf without fighting with other parts. Processing added to one track may affect other tracks; for example, if you boost a guitar part's midrange, it may interfere with vocals, piano, or other midrange instruments. If you add more treble to a bass part so that it cuts better on little speakers, make sure it doesn't start fighting with the low end of a rhythm guitar part. Sometimes boosting a frequency for one instrument implies cutting the same region in another instrument to make room.

One common mistake I hear with tapes done by singer/songwriters it that they (naturally) feature themselves in the mix and worry about "details" like the drums later. However, as drums cover so much of the audio spectrum (from the low frequency thud of the kick to the high frequency sheen of the cymbals) and as drums tend to be so upfront in today's mixes, it's sometimes best to mix the drums first, then find "holes" in which you can place the other instruments. For example, if the kick drum is very prominent, it may not leave enough room for the bass. So, boost the bass around 800 to 1,000Hz to bring up some of the pick noise and brightness. This is mostly out of the range of the kick drum, so the two don't interfere as much.

Try to think of the song as a spectrum and decide where you want the various parts to sit and their prominence.

7.10.7 Step 7: Add Any Essential Signal Processing

By essential, I don't mean "sweetening," but processing that is an integral part of the sound (such an echo that falls on the beat and therefore changes the rhythmic characteristics of a part, distortion that alters the timbre in a radical way, vocoding, etc.). As this sound will presumably be a part of the mix unless you change your mind later, you want to take it into account when mixing the other instruments.

7.10.8 Step 8: Create a Stereo Soundstage

Now use the pan controls to place your instruments within the stereo field. Your approach might be traditional (i.e., the goal is to re-create the feel of a live performance) or imaginary. Pan mono instruments to a particular location, but avoid panning signals to the *extreme* left or right; they just don't sound quite as substantial as signals that are a little bit in from the extremes.

Note that you can access the pan control for wide mixer channels, but not narrow ones. You can also find the pan control in the Inspector for audio channels, under the Channel tab.

Because bass frequencies are less directional than highs, most engineers place the kick drum and bass toward the center, unless the bass is a synth type and is in stereo. Also consider timbral balance; for example, if you've panned the hi-hat (which has a lot of high frequencies) to the right, pan a tambourine, shaker, or other high-frequency sound somewhat to the left. The same technique applies to midrange instruments as well.

Another spreading technique involves EQ. Copy a signal so it's in two channels, but equalize them differently (for example, if you have a stereo graphic equalizer plug-in, use it to cut the even-numbered bands with one channel, and the odd-numbered bands with the other channel).

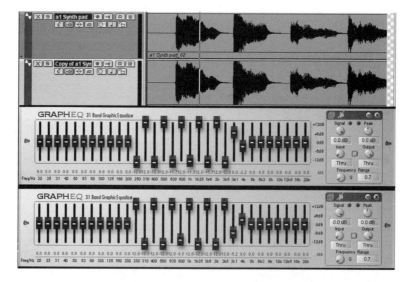

Here a track has been copied. Each has a graphic EQ plug-in from CreamWare's XTC card of VST and VSTi devices. The EQs are set so the midrange boosts and cuts are equal and opposite, which adds a bit of stereo spread to mono signals. Don't forget to use the pan controls to spread these two channels.

This won't work successfully on instruments with limited ranges, like voice or a lead synth part. But if you're exercising all the keys on your 88-note controller, or using a drum machine, this technique can give a very unusual type of stereo imaging.

Stereo placement can significantly alter how we perceive a sound. Consider a doubled vocal line, where a singer sings a part and then doubles it as closely as possible. Try putting both voices in opposite channels; then put both voices together in the center. The center position gives a somewhat smoother sound, which is good for weaker vocalists. The opposite-channel vocals give a more defined, sharp sound, that can really help accent a good singer.

7.10.9 Step 9: Make Any Final Changes in the Arrangement

Remember that, as with so many things in life, less is more—minimize the number of competing parts to keep the listener focused on the tune and avoid "clutter." Get rid of anything that doesn't serve the song. Conversely, if you find that a song needs some extra element, this is your final opportunity to add an overdub or two.

You can also use mixing creatively by selectively dropping out and adding specific tracks. This type of mixing is the foundation for a lot of dance music, where you have looped tracks that play continuously, and the mixer sculpts the arrangement by muting parts and doing radical level changes.

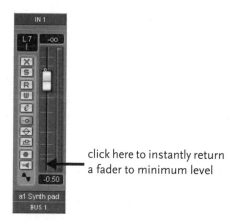

click here to instantly return
a fader to minimum level

Although Cubase can automate the Mute function, you can also mute rapidly with fader automation by simply clicking at the bottom of the fader travel (just above the level indicator).

7.10.10 Step 10: The Audio Architect

Start building your space by adding reverberation and delay to give the normally flat soundstage some acoustic depth. This is also the time for more signal processing—sort of the equivalent of adding spices during the cooking process.

Generally, you'll want an overall reverb to create a particular type of space (club, concert hall, auditorium, etc.) but you may also want to use a second reverb to add effects, such as a particular "splash" on a snare drum hit or gated reverb on toms.

In the early days of recording, the general procedure was to add just enough reverb to be noticeable and simulate the effect of playing in an acoustical environment. Nowadays, reverb devices have become so sophisticated they can create effects in their own right that become as much a part of a tune as any instrumental line. However, don't drown a part in reverb. If a part is of questionable enough quality that it needs a lot of reverb, redo the part. A bad part is a bad part, no matter how much reverb you put on it.

7.10.11 Step 11: Tweak, Tweak, and Retweak

Now that the mix is on its way, it's time for fine tuning. If you're into auto-mation, start programming your mixing moves. Remember that all of the above steps interact, so go back and forth between EQ, levels, stereo place-ment, and effects until you get the sound you want. Listen as critically as possible; if you don't fix something that bothers you, it will forever bother you every time you hear the mix.

7.10.12 Step 12: Check Your Mix over Different Systems

Before you sign off on a mix, check it over a variety of systems. If the mix sounds good under all these situations, your mission is accomplished.

With a home studio, you have the luxury of leaving a mix and coming back to it the next day when you're fresh, and after you've had a chance to listen over several different systems and decide what tweaks you want to make. This is one reason why automation is so wonderful—if everything was perfect about a mix except one little thing that bothers you, you can edit the automation to fix the one problem.

I can't emphasize enough that you should mix until you're satisfied. There's nothing worse than hearing one of your tunes six months later and kicking yourself because of some flaw you didn't take the time to cor-rect, or didn't notice because you were in too much of a hurry to complete the mix.

However, you must be equally careful not to beat a mix to death. Once I interviewed Quincy Jones and he offered the opinion that recording with synthesizers and sequencing was like "painting a 747 with Q-Tips." A mix is a performance, and if you overdo it, you'll lose the spontaneity that can add excitement. A mix that isn't perfect but conveys passion will always be more fun to listen to than one that's perfect to the point of sterility. As insurance, don't always re-record over your mixes—when you listen back to them the next day, you might find that an earlier mix was the "keeper."

In fact, you may not even be able to tell too much difference among all the mixes. A record producer once told me about mixing literally dozens of takes of the same song, because he keep hearing small changes which seemed really important at the time. A couple of weeks later he went over the mixes, and couldn't tell any difference between most of the versions. Be careful not to waste time making changes that no one, even you, will care about a couple days later.

One important tip is that once you've captured your ultimate mix, you should also run a couple extra mixes, such as an instrumental-only mix or a mix without the solo instrument. These additional mixes can really come in handy at a later time, if you have a chance to re-use your music for a film or video score, or need to create extended dance mixes. Be prepared!

Part 3

Equalization, Dynamics, and Reverberation

Chapter 8

About Equalization

A lot of what makes a world class studio is good equalization, dynamics control, and reverb. So, in this part, each of these merits its own chapter.

Equalization (abbreviated EQ) is probably the most-used tool in the engineer's arsenal of sound shapers. One of the goals of mixing and mastering is to create a balanced, even response—equalization can help this to happen.

Equalization is crucial to the mixing process so that each instrument can stake out its own part of the audible frequency spectrum. One common example of how to use EQ is when the bass and kick drum interfere with each other. A classic solution is to trim the low end a little bit on the kick to make room for the bass, but then also boost the kick's high frequencies so that the "clack" of the beater hitting the drum becomes very prominent. This allows the ear to "fill in" the kick sound because where it hits is well-defined. In some cases, you might try the reverse—trimming some low end from the bass and boosting its highs.

There are no rules—only what sounds good. However, we will present some guidelines here to get you started in the right direction. First, we'll cover how to view and adjust Cubase's EQ, then present a series of tips on applying EQ.

8.1   Cubase's EQ Section

One of Cubase's best features is that four stages of very flexible EQ are available for every VST audio channel. Even better, the equalization parameters are automatable, so you can manipulate the frequency response in real time and have the program "remember" your moves.

Here's one example of how automation is useful: suppose you have a singer accompanied by guitar. During vocals, you can cut the guitar's midrange just a tiny bit in the vocal frequencies so that the voice stands more by itself. When the singer isn't singing, the midrange can come up a bit to emphasize the guitar.

8.1.1   Viewing EQ

There are two main ways to view a channel's equalization section. In the Expanded main mixer view (available only in Cubase SX), you can choose to view the EQ either as knobs or as a "linear" interface that presents data as strips. To select one or the other on a global basis, use the Global Strip icons toward the left of the mixer.

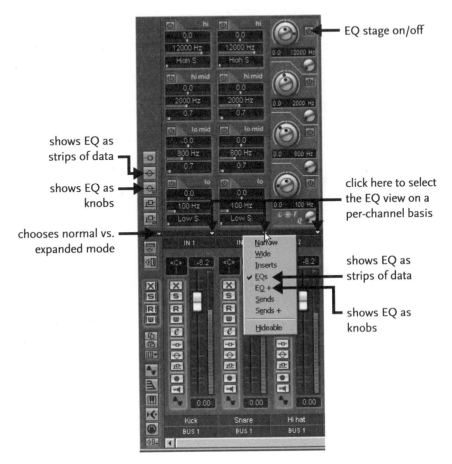

Cubase SX allows several ways to look at EQ: globally or on a per-channel basis.

To select the EQ interface on a per-channel basis, click on the small arrow above the fader and choose "EQs" (strips) or "EQ+" (knobs).

You can also see a channel's EQ in detail (knob settings and frequency response curve) by looking at the VST Channel Settings. To select this, click on the Edit ("e") button to the left of the fader (or above the fader if the channel is in narrow mode). This works with both Cubase SX and SL.

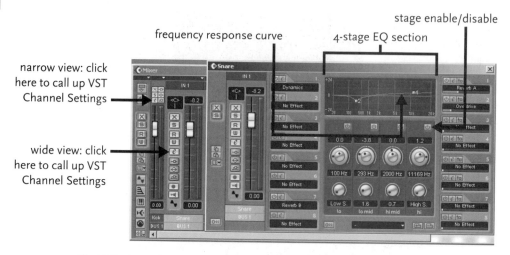

frequency response curve

4-stage EQ section

stage enable/disable

narrow view: click here to call up VST Channel Settings

wide view: click here to call up VST Channel Settings

The VST Channel Settings view shows the EQ section in detail. The frequency response curve shows the results of the knob settings.

8.1.2 Parametric EQ basics

The four stages (also called "bands") of EQ are called *parametric* stages (the Lo and Hi stages allow other responses, described later). A parametric equalizer is an exceptionally versatile way to adjust frequency response. Each band can boost (make more prominent) or cut (make less prominent) a specific part of the frequency spectrum.

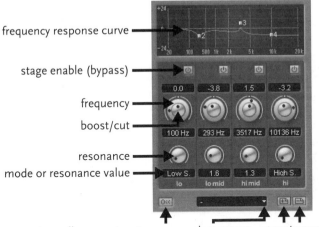

frequency response curve

stage enable (bypass)

frequency

boost/cut

resonance

mode or resonance value

return all parameters to zero   select preset   store/remove preset

The EQ view in the VST Channel Settings window lets you see the EQ settings in detail as well as store, remove, and select presets. Having a library of presets available is very handy if you have favorite settings for a particular vocalist, guitar, snare drum, etc.

Each stage has three controls:

- **Frequency** (the outer knob of the two concentric controls in the middle of the module) determines where the boosting or cutting takes place. Example: if the high frequencies need boosting, you would dial in a high frequency. Note that the number below the knob shows the exact frequency chosen by the knob. You can also click on this and type in a precise value if desired.

- **Boost/cut** (the middle knob of the two concentric controls) changes the response. Boosting increases the level in the chosen frequency range. Cutting decreases the level. The number above the knobs shows the precise amount of boost or cut, specified in deciBels (dB). A change of 6dB doubles the level (−6dB halves it), which is a considerable amount. Changes of no more than 1 or 2dB are common when mixing and mastering. Even changes of a few tenths of a dB can make a difference. Like the frequency parameter, you can also type in a specific value.

A "decibel" is an audio unit of measurement that represents the smallest change in level the untrained ear can discern when compared to a reference signal.

■ **Bandwidth** (also called Resonance or Q) sets the range of frequencies affected by the boost or cut, from broad to narrow. Broader settings are gentler and used for general tone shaping. Narrow settings generally help solve specific response problems. Example: suppose there is some 60 Hz hum on a recording; setting a very narrow cut at 60Hz will get rid of the hum, without affecting other frequencies.

8.1.3 Other Responses

The most common parametric EQ response, bandpass, boosts or cuts a band of frequencies as we've just described. However, there are other possible response options.

Low Shelf response, set to cut low frequency response.

Turning the EQ section's Lo stage resonance parameter fully counter-clockwise shows its value as Low S (low shelf). A shelving response starts boosting or cutting at the selected frequency, but this boost or cut extends outward toward the extremes of the audio spectrum. Past a certain point the response hits a "shelf" equal to the maximum amount of cut.

High pass response, set to gently cut low frequency response.

If you turn the Lo stage resonance parameter fully clockwise, its value shows High P (high pass). This response progressively reduces response below a certain frequency—the lower the frequency, the greater the reduction. This is sometimes used to remove subsonic (very low frequency) energy. It is not possible to boost response in High Pass mode; however, the boost/cut control determins the *slope* of the response reduction. Turning the boost/cut control counterclockwise gives a gentler slope, while clockwise gives a sharper slope.

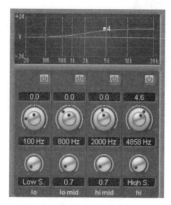

High Shelf response, set to boost high frequency response.

Turning the Hi stage resonance parameter fully counterclockwise shows its value as High S (high shelf). The response is similar to the low shelf, but affects the high frequencies.

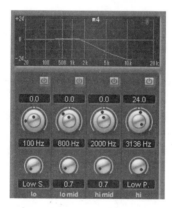

Low pass response, set to sharply cut high frequency response.

If you turn the Hi stage resonance parameter fully clockwise, its value shows Low P (low pass). This response progressively reduces response above a certain frequency. The reduction in response is greater toward the spectrum's higher frequencies. A typical application is removing hiss.

CD tracks 01—09 show a variety of equalization effects applied to audio. Track 1 is the original waveform, track 2 does a 6 dB bandpass boost at 1 kHz with a 1-octave bandwidth, track 3 is the same but has a 6dB cut, track 4 is a highpass filter starting at 1kHz, track 5 is a high shelf filter that's boosting 6dB starting at 1kHz, track 6 is a high shelf filter that cuts by 6dB starting at 1kHz, track 7 is a lowpass filter starting at 1kHz, track 8 is a low shelf filter that's boosting 6dB starting at 1kHz, and track 9 is a low shelf filter that cuts by 6dB starting at 1kHz.

8.2 Equalization Tips and Techniques

Too many people adjust equalization with their eyes, not their ears. For example, after doing a mix, I noticed the client writing down all the EQ settings I had made. When I asked why, he said it was because he liked the EQ and wanted to use the same settings on the instruments in future mixes.

But that's the wrong attitude. EQ is a *part* of the mixing process. Just as levels, panning, and reverb are different for each mix, EQ should be custom tailored for each mix as well. But to do that, you need to understand how to find the magic EQ frequencies for particular types of musical material, as well as what tool to use for what application.

There are four main applications for EQ:

- Problem-solving.
- Emphasizing or de-emphasizing an instrument in a mix.
- Altering a sound's personality.
- Changing the stereo image.

Each application requires specialized techniques and approaches. But note that equalization is very powerful—use it sparingly. When you make a change that sounds right, cut it in half. In other words, if boosting a signal by 2dB at 4kHz seems to improve the tune's sound, pull back the boost to 1dB and live with the sound for a while. It's easy to get stuck in a spiral where if you boost the treble, the bass then lacks prominence ... so you boost the bass, but now the midrange seems weak, so you boost that, and now you're back to where you started.

8.2.1 Problem-solving

EQ can fix some obvious problems. Examples: Slicing a sharp notch at 60Hz (50Hz in Europe) can knock hum out of a signal; trimming the high frequencies can remove hiss. Generally, problems occur in specific frequency ranges, which is why the parametric is ideal for problem-solving.

Another common problem is an instrument with a resonance or peak that interferes with other instruments or causes level-setting difficulties.

Here's a real-world example that shows how to take care of this situation.

I often work with classical guitarist Linda Cohen, who has a beautiful nylon-string guitar. It has a full, rich sound that projects very well on stage, thanks to a strong body resonance in the lower midrange that causes a major level peak. However, recording is a different matter from playing live. Setting levels so the peaky, low frequency notes don't distort cause the higher guitar notes to sound weak by comparison.

Although compression/limiting is one possible solution, it alters the guitar's attack. While this effect might not be noticeable in an ensemble, it sticks out with a solo instrument. A more natural-sounding answer is to use EQ to apply a frequency cut *equal and opposite* to the natural boost, thus leveling out the response. But there's a trick to finding problem frequencies so you can alter them; here's the procedure.

1   Turn down the monitor volume—things might get nasty and distorted during the following steps.

2   Set the EQ for lots of boost (10—12dB) and fairly narrow bandwidth (a resonance setting of around 10).

3   As the instrument plays, slowly sweep the frequency control. Any peaks will jump out due to the boosting and narrow bandwidth. Some peaks may even distort.

4   Find the loudest peak and cut the amplitude until the peak falls into balance with the rest of the instrument sound. You may need to widen the bandwidth a bit if the peak is broad, or use narrow bandwidth if the resonance is particularly sharp.

This technique of "boost—find the peak—cut" can help eliminate midrange "honking," reduce strident resonances in wind instruments, and much more. Of course, sometimes you want to preserve these resonances so the instrument stands out, but many times applying EQ to reduce peaks allows instruments to sit more gracefully in the track.

This type of problem-solving also underscores a key principle of EQ: It's often better to cut than boost. Boosting uses up headroom; cutting opens up headroom. With Linda's guitar, cutting the peak allowed for bringing up the overall gain to record at a higher overall level.

8.2.2   Emphasizing Instruments

The same technique of finding and cutting specific frequencies can also eliminate "fighting" between competing instruments. For example, when mixing a Spencer Brewer track for Narada records, there were two woodwind parts with resonant peaks around the same frequency. When playing *en ensemble* they would load up that part of the frequency spectrum, which also made them difficult to differentiate. Here's a way to work around this:

1   Find, then reduce, the peak on one of the instruments (as described above with the classical guitar example) to create a more even sound.

2 Note the amount of cut and bandwidth that was applied to reduce the peak.

3 Using a second stage of EQ, apply a roughly equal and opposite boost at either a slightly higher or slightly lower frequency than the natural peak.

Both instruments will now sound very articulated, and because each peaks in a different part of the spectrum, they will tend not to step on each other.

8.2.3   New Sonic Personalities

EQ can also change a sound's character—for example, turn a brash rock piano sound into something more classical. This type of application requires relatively gentle EQ, possibly at several different points in the audio spectrum.

Musicians often summarize an instrument's character with various subjective terms. Let's correlate these terms to various parts of the frequency spectrum (this is, of course, a very subjective interpretation).

This graph gives a rough idea of which frequency ranges translate into particular musical terms.

For example, to add warmth, apply a gentle boost (3dB or so) somewhere in the 200 to 500Hz range. However, as in the previous case, remember that if possible, cutting is preferable to boosting—for example, if you need more brightness and bottom, try cutting the midrange rather than boosting the high and low ends.

8.2.4   Changing Stereo Position

Although the traditional way to change stereo position is with panning, another less-used, but occasionally useful, method involves EQ. This can be particularly useful when you need to impart stereo imaging to monaural signals.

With mono, duplicate the track so that you now have two tracks of identical material. Pan one channel left and one channel right, then edit the EQ to create more of a spread. For example, if you use a high shelf filter to boost 4dB starting at 2kHz in the right channel, cut the left channel by 4dB at 2kHz, using the same type of filter. As mentioned elsewhere, highs are more directional than lows, which will definitely tilt the channel toward the right of the stereo image. For a more extreme image, cut the bass in the right channel and boost it by an equivalent amount in the left channel. This will "push" the image further into both the right and left channels.

With stereo signals, the same general concept applies. This won't work successfully on instruments with limited ranges, like voice or a lead synth part. But if you're exercising all the keys on your 88-note controller, or using a drum machine, this technique can give a very unusual type of stereo imaging.

8.2.5   Other Equalization Tips

■ Problem-solving and character-altering EQ should be applied early on in the mixing process as they will influence how the mix develops. But wait to apply most EQ until the process of setting levels begins. Remember: EQ is all about changing levels—albeit in specific frequency ranges. Any EQ changes you make will alter the overall balance of instruments.

■ Instruments EQed in isolation to sound great may not sound all that wonderful when combined. If every track is equalized to leap out at you, there's no room left for a track to "breathe." Also, you will probably want to alter EQ on some instruments so that they take on more supportive roles. For example, during vocals consider cutting the midrange a bit on supporting instruments (e.g., piano) to open up more space in the audio spectrum for vocals.

- One of your best "reality checks" is the equalizer's bypass switch. Use it often to make sure you haven't lost control of the original sound. One of the great things about Cubase's EQs is that you can enable or bypass *each* stage to determine how it changes the sound.

- Subsonic energy can't be heard, but uses up dynamic range and should be eliminated if possible. The High P mode may be useful if there is subsonic energy in a tune; set it to pass only frequencies above 20 to 100Hz, depending on the instrument being equalized. Turn the boost control up as much as possible for the steepest possible slope, consistent with the sound retaining a natural quality.

- Shelving filter responses are good for a general lift in the bass and/or treble regions. They can also tame bass and/or treble regions that are too prominent.

- The ear is most sensitive in the midrange and upper midrange. Be wary of harshness when boosting in this region.

- Oddly enough, some digital filter algorithms may cause distortion if you *cut* levels. After doing an operation, always listen to a processed file and check that the waveform isn't clipping. If there's a problem, you can always undo the operation or if necessary, use Cubase's history option.

- An instrument's EQ has to be factored in to the level-setting process. For example, suppose a relatively bright synth sound needs to fit into a track. It can be mixed at a lower level and still have presence, because our ears are most sensitive in the upper midrange area (around 3.5kHz). A similar situation occurs with strummed acoustic guitars, which cover a lot of bandwidth. Even at relatively low levels, acoustic guitars can take over a mix (sometimes a good thing, sometimes not). So, many engineers greatly accentuate the high end, but turn the overall level way down. Thus, the guitars still add some percussive propulsion, but don't interfere with the rest of what's going on in the midrange.

■ 400Hz is often considered the "mud" frequency because a lot of instruments have energy in that frequency range, and that energy adds together into a bit of a sonic blob. A piano may sound perfect when mixed at a certain level by itself, but sound indistinct when other instruments are mixed in. Try cutting either the piano or the other instruments a bit at 400Hz or so, as that will open up more space for the instrument that isn't being cut. Both should come through clearly in the mix as separate entities.

Chapter 9

About Dynamics

Next to equalization, dynamics control is one of the most important elements of mixing. Before getting into how dynamics control works and how to apply it to your mixes, let's get a little background.

9.1   Basics of Dynamics

Dynamic range is the difference between a recording's loudest and softest sections. Live music has an extremely wide dynamic range; prior to the CD, it was impossible to capture this range on tape (or vinyl). So, being able to restrict the dynamic range—soft enough not to overload the tape, but loud enough to rise above the tape hiss—was essential.

With the advent of 24-bit and 32-bit floating point digital audio, the medium's dynamic range is no longer a significant issue; given quality input and output electronics, we can pretty much record the highest and lowest levels. But dynamics control remains a crucial part of mixing and mastering. Part of this is due to habit—our ears are used to compressed sound—and part of this is an artistic effect, which if used correctly, can make sounds "jump out" more and give more punch to a production.

Another use for compression is to cover up for mistakes or players who lack a good "touch." For example, a really good singer knows how to use mic technique to move the mic closer or further away to keep relatively constant levels. But an inexperienced singer might not have that kind of technique, leading to level variations that, unlike level changes designed to enhance the music, instead cause some words to drop out or passages to be uneven.

Bassists often use compression because the ear is less sensitive in the bass range, so subtle dynamics tend to be wasted. Evening out the bass's dynamic range provides a full low end to music, thus making it easier to hear the bass part. Compression also helps bring music above the background noise of everyday life, particularly when listening in cars, where the road noise is significant. Finally, compression is used a lot in commercials to make the perceived loudness as high as humanly possible, in soundtracks to keep music from competing too much with dialog, and in broadcasting to prevent overmodulation (distortion).

How much compression to use is controversial. Many listeners think "louder is better," so pop music records are compressed—sometimes to the point of destroying dynamic range—to sound "hotter." DJs prefer highly-compressed dance music to minimize level variations, thus giving them more control over level via the DJ mixer's faders. Classical and jazz recordings use little compression.

9.2 Types of Dynamic Control

There are several types of dynamic control. Here are the basics of each type, we'll get into the details later.

9.2.1 Manual Gain-riding

Initially engineers adjusted the gain manually while recording—turning down on peaks, turning up during quiet parts—to restrict dynamic range. But it's hard to do this fast and consistently, so having a machine to do dynamic range restriction was a big improvement. Still, many engineers still ride gain as a sort of "preliminary compression."

9.2.2 Normalization

Normalization is a very basic type of dynamics control. It doesn't restrict the signal's dynamic range, but instead moves the signal within the overall dynamic range so that the signal's peaks reach the maximum available headroom.

A signal should also not peak too low below the available headroom, as that throws away dynamic range. The normalization process calculates the difference between a recording's highest peak and the maximum available level, then increases the recording's overall level so that its highest peak reaches the maximum level.

You don't always have to normalize to the maximum level. You could normalize a signal to, for example, −3dB below maximum.

9.2.3 Limiting

A limiter is like a governor on a motor: signals will not exceed a user-settable threshold. Limiting leaves signals below the threshold untouched, making it a useful processor for digital recording, where you do not want signals to exceed 0dB. By simply setting the threshold to a level very slightly below 0 (like −0.1), a limiter can insure that distortion doesn't happen.

However, two cautions are in order:

- Excessive limiting will result in distortion, because you can only squash a signal so much before audible artifacts occur.
- The type of limiter that exerts dictatorial control over level is called a "brickwall" limiter—so-called because when the signal hits the threshold, it hits a "brick wall." A "soft" limiter will give a gentler limiting effect, but may allow overloads to occur.

9.2.4   Compression

A compressor evens out variations in dynamic range by amplifying soft signals to make them louder and attenuating loud signals to make them softer. The net result is much less level difference between soft and loud signals, which evens out level variations and increases the sustain of percussive instruments. Depending on its control settings, the effect of compression can be more drastic than a limiter because it affects signals below the threshold as well as above them.

> There are also multi-band compressors, which split the signal into different bands, then compress them individually. For more information on these, see the section on Mastering.

9.2.5   Noise Gate

The noise gate simply removes any signal below a particular level by monitoring the input signal. If the input signal drops below a user-settable threshold, then the noise gate blocks the audio from appearing at the output (think of it as a "gate" closing that prevents audio from passing through). Once the signal rises above the threshold, the gate opens again.

The main use is to remove hiss in noisy devices. For example, suppose that the hiss hits a level of −50dB. By setting the noise gate to −49dB, it will reject any signal that consists solely of hiss. Signals above that level will pass through, but hopefully, they will be sufficiently loud to "mask" the underlying hiss.

9.3   Cubase's Dynamics Tools

Cubase has two dynamics processors, Dynamics and VSTDynamics.

9.3.1   Dynamics

This is the simpler of the two modules and therefore doesn't take as much processing power as the VSTDynamics processor. Dynamics consists of three modules: Compressor, Limiter, and AutoGate. The only functionality it has that VSTDynamics lacks is that you can determine the routing of the three processors.

Cubase's Dynamics processor does basic compression functions and doesn't draw too much processing power.

9.3.2 VSTDynamics

This includes the three modules that Dynamics has, and adds two more modules: Auto Level and Soft Clip. It also has higher latency than the Dynamics processor because of the extra modules.

The VSTDynamics processor adds Soft Clip and Auto Level to the Dynamics processor.

The Cubase Operation Manual explains the various module parameters from a technical standpoint and provides useful background information. We'll concentrate on the musical implications of these parameters and how they relate to the mixing process. After describing the modules, we'll then describe features unique to the individual processors.

9.4   AutoGate Parameters

The AutoGate is an advanced form of noise gate, with unique features. Enable it by clicking on the AutoGate label in the module.

The AutoGate module includes a means to restrict gating to specific frequencies.

9.4.1   Threshold

This sets the level above which the gate opens and below which it closes. For standard hiss removal applications, the threshold will be set fairly low. However, setting higher thresholds can do a variety of special effects, such as:

- Cut off the "ring" from sustaining drum sounds, like toms.
- Remove the room ambience "tail" from percussive instruments.
- Shorten reverb decay times.
- Reduce leakage—for example, if there's leakage from other drums on the snare track, it may be possible to reduce or elminate the leakage by setting the threshold below the snare but above the leakage.
- Make sounds more percussive by allowing only the peaks to play.

The Threshold parameter also has a calibrate option. This adjusts the threshold to stay above background noise. To use this feature:

1   Loop the track being gated around an area where background noise occurs.

2   Enable AutoGate.

3   Click on Calibrate. The button flashes for a few seconds to let you know it's busy thinking.

4   The threshold is now set just above the background noise. Note that this setting is not indicated above the threshold control, just take it on faith that Cubase has selected the proper threshold.

9.4.2   Attack

This sets how long it takes between the time AutoGate detects that a signal has risen above the threshold and when the gate actually opens. Normally, you want the attack to react as rapidly as possible, but there are some instances where an attack time is desirable:

■   If there's a click at the beginning of the audio when the gate cuts in. A short attack time (0.1 to 2ms) will usually be sufficient to reduce or eliminate any clicks.

■   Adding an attack time softens an instrument's attack so it's not quite so prominent. As this control is automatable, you can actually add dynamics to electronic drums by doing the equivalent of changing the "sample start point." When you want the drums to set a bit more in the background, increase the attack time. When you want them to move to the front, reduce the attack time to minimum.

■   Adding some attack time (usually around the 100ms range) allows a signal to "swell" to its maximum level. For instance, if you pause briefly between notes, when a new note exceeds the threshold it will fade in over the specified amount of attack time. This can alter the attack characteristics of percussive instruments like piano and guitar, or add "brass-like" attacks to sustained sounds. However, there must be a space before every note that needs an attack, to give the AutoGate a chance to reset itself. Also note that the Release and Hold parameters should be at minimum, with Auto and Predict turned off. Otherwise, the gate may remain open during the space between notes, which prevents triggering a new attack when a new note plays. Conversely, too short a decay can result in a "chattering" effect. So, use the shortest possible decay time, consistent with a smooth sound.

CD track 10 first plays a bass figure without envelope attack, then with envelope attack added by increasing the AutoGate's attack time.

■ Attack time is also useful with vocals, to reduce breath inhale noises. As the singer starts to breathe in, it triggers the gate. While the inhale fades in, so does the gate. This makes the breath sound less prominent, but doesn't cut it out completely (which can sound unnatural).

9.4.3 Attack Predict Function

The Predict mode allows a gate to open instantly in the presence of a signal, with no attack time. It does this by scanning ahead in the audio and noting where the gate should open. The main use for this is with very fast percussive transients that the gate might miss while it's opening, even at its fastest setting.

9.4.4 Release

This sets how long it takes for the noise gate to close completely after a signal goes below the threshold. With Auto selected, AutoGate chooses an optimum release time based on the program material. In general, it's a good idea to leave Auto on, unless you need to do some sort of special effect (e.g. attack delay) that require a specific release time setting.

9.4.5 Hold

After a signal goes below the threshold, Hold determines how long the gate remains open before the release time kicks in. It is particularly useful with signals that have long, slow decays (e.g. long reverb tails) where the signal crosses over the threshold several times as it fades. This can produce a "chattering" type of effect. Increasing the hold time allows the gate to stay open during those brief times when the signal drops below the threshold. Once the signal drops below the treshold for good, then after the hold time has elapsed, the release phase begins.

9.4.6 Trigger Frequency Range

This is an outstanding feature, because very often, you want to be able to gate on the basis of frequency range as well as level. For example, suppose a drummer and bassist are set up close to each other so they can have good eye contact, and "lock" into the rhythmic groove. But unfortunately, the bass amp sound leaks into the snare mic. If you restrict the gate's response to ignore the bass, then only the snare will trigger the gate, making it easier to reject the bass amp leakage.

Using this feature is quite simple:

1   Click on Listen. This bypasses the gate and lets you hear which frequencies are being filtered.

2   Adjust the left and right "handles" under Trigger Frequency Range to set the filter's low and high limits respectively.

3   Once you've isolated the sound you want to gate, click "On." The filter will now be active in the gating process.

4   To disable the filter, click on "Off."

9.5   AutoGate Applications

9.5.1   Grotesque Distortion

How about a fun, lo-fi effect? It's possible to get some pretty weird distortions, especially with low-frequency signals, by missetting the attack and decay controls. This causes the gate to trigger so fast it basically modulates the audio wave. Here's the procedure:

1 Turn off Predict and Auto.

2 Set Attack to 0.1ms.

3 Set Release to 10ms.

4 Set Hold to 0ms.

This technique works especially well with drums. In this context, the threshold now becomes an "ugly" control. At low thresholds, you'll hear an occasional buzz. Higher thresholds can give mean, spiky sounds. The effect isn't as dramatic as it would be if the Attack and Release times could be set shorter, but it's still pretty interesting.

9.5.2 Real-time Rhythm Track Tricks

Thanks to external control surfaces, you can play many of Cubase's modules like an instrument—and record your moves as automation. This technique can sound very cool with hip-hop, techno, and other types of music that rely on variations within drum loops.

With most loops, the snare and kick will reach the highest levels, with (typically) hi-hat below that and percussion (maracas, shakers, tambourine, etc.) mixed in the background. Tweaking the threshold in real time causes selected parts of the loop to drop out. For example, with the threshold at minimum, you hear the entire loop. Inch the threshold up, and the percussion disappears. Move it up further, and the hi-hat drops out. Raise it even higher, and the snare and kick lose their decays and become ultra-percussive.

> CD track 11 shows how changing the threshold control in real time changes the sound of a loop being processed by the AutoGate.

For this application, you want the fastest possible attack time and a fairly short decay (about 50ms). This can add really useful dynamics to a drum loop.

9.5.3 Selective Reverb

With a drum loop I'd already premixed to two tracks, in one particular application I wished just the snare had some reverb. However, being pre-mixed, it was impossible to extract the snare. Or was it?

I duplicated the drum loop. On one of the tracks, AutoGate was set to the range of only the snare (the low end was at about 800Hz). I raised the gate threshold so that only the snare peaks crept through and used a reverb (set for wet sound only) as an Insert Effect on the track. So, all you heard coming from this track was snare through reverb.

I then turned up the original track and set the right balance between the two. The end result: reverb on the snare only, with the rest of the drum track left unprocessed.

> CD track 12 plays the original drum loop without reverb, followed by the same loop with reverb added from the extracted snare.

9.5.4 Pseudo Peak Expander

Cubase doesn't have a dynamic range expander module, but sometimes this can be the ticket to making a drum part more dynamic (something that can really help with drum machines). However, there's a noise gate workaround: duplicate the track and adjust the gate so only the peaks come through. Adjust this track's level so that the peaks add to the original sound, thus providing a boost only on peaks. This also works with any kind of percussive transient—pick noise on guitar, for example, or percussive B3-type transients.

9.6 Compressor Parameters

Compress, the compressor section, has a comprehensive set of features, some of which are related to the gate parameters. Enable Compress by clicking on its label.

The compressor has a useful graph that shows the threshold (where the curve has a "knee" and bends). The slope to the right of the knee shows the ratio of output level to input level. This slope shows a 4:1 ratio of input level to output level—in other words, increasing the input by, for example, 4dB causes only a 1dB increase at the output. This is what compression is all about—the output level increases at a slower rate for higher input levels.

Note that compression is not always a transparent process. Overcompressing gives a pinched, unpleasant sound with "pumping" and "breathing." In fact, one of the more difficult decisions for beginning engineers is how much to compress, which is made even more difficult because the ear is not that sensitive to level changes. If you adjust the compressor so you hear it "working," it's probable you're overcompressing. My attitude is that you shouldn't really know a signal is compressed until you bypass it, at which point you should note a reduction in "punch" and overall level (if not, then you're probably undercompressing). Until you've trained your ears to recognize subtle amounts of compression, keep an eye on the gain reduction meters (described later) to avoid overcompressing.

Compression works mainly by lowering a signal's peaks. For example, suppose some peaks reach to 0, and compression manages to reduce those by −5dB, so the loudest peaks hit at −5dB. You can now turn up the signal's overall level by +5dB, at which point the peaks once again hit 0. In other words, you've been able to add +5dB of gain to the overall signal level simply by reducing the peaks.

9.6.1 Threshold

This sets the level at which compression begins. Above this level, the output increases at a lesser rate than a corresponding input change. With lower thresholds, more of the signal gets compressed, and the peaks become lower.

9.6.2 Ratio

This parameter defines how much the output signal changes for a given input signal change. For example, with 2:1 compression, a 2dB increase at the input yields a 1dB increase at the output. With 4:1 compression, a 16dB increase at the input gives a 4dB increase at the output. Higher ratios increase the effect of the compression and tend to sound more unnatural. Some compressors allow an "infinite" compression ratio, where the output will refuse to go past a certain point, no matter how much you pump up the input. This is the same function as a limiter. As the Dynamics module includes a limiter, the compressor is restricted to a maximum ratio of 8:1. If you require a greater ratio, use the limiter.

9.6.3 Attack

Similarly to the AutoGate, this sets how long it takes for the compression to start once it senses an input level change. Longer attack times let more of a signal's natural dynamics through, but remember, those signals are not being compressed, so make sure they do not overload the Master Channel.

9.6.4   Mode

The RMS setting causes the compressor to react to a signal's average level, whereas Peak causes it to react to peaks. RMS is used more to "beef up" sounds that don't have sharp attacks, including program material, vocals, pads, etc. However, this may still let peaks through. Peak is designed more for "transient control," making it appropriate for percussive sounds where you want to make sure transients don't exceed the available headroom.

Note that the VSTDynamics processor does not offer a choice of modes.

9.6.5   Release

Again recalling the AutoGate, this parameter determines the time required for the compressor to stop affecting the signal once the input passes below the threshold. Longer settings work well with program material, as the level changes are more gradual and produce a less noticeable effect. With Auto selected, Compress chooses an optimum release time based on the program material. Auto usually produces the best results with program material, but you may want to turn it off for special effects, like using a really short release time to give a more "squashed" drum sound.

CD Track 13 shows how a short release setting affects drums. This produces an effect often used for "psychedelic" 60s drum sounds, where hitting the cymbal modulates the entire kit with a pumping kind of sound (drum loop courtesy Discrete Drums, www.discretedrums.com).

9.6.6   MakeUp Gain and Gain Reduction Meter

Now that we've used Threshold and Ratio to squash the peaks, we need to turn the signal's overall level back up again—which is this control's function. To help in proper level setting, observe the Gain Reduction meter. The lit blue squares indicate how much "squashing" (gain reduction) is occurring at any given moment. You generally want to set the MakeUp

Gain control to a little less than the amount of reduction. (In the Compress screen shot, the gain reduction meter shows about 5dB of reduction, and the MakeUp Gain control is set to 4.0dB.)

9.7   Compression Setting Tips

Compression is difficult to set up correctly, so here are some tips.

■ Unless you're looking for a "compressed" sound, you usually don't want more than 6dB of reduction, and even that's stretching it. To reduce the amount of gain reduction, either raise the threshold or reduce the compression ratio.

■ Lower thresholds won't just tame the occasional peak, but also reduce the overall signal.

■ For a more natural sound, use lower compression ratios (1.5:1 to 3:1). Bass typically uses a ratio of around 3:1, voice 2:1 to 4:1—but these are approximations, not rules. To increase sustain of an instrument like guitar, try a ratio in the 4:1 to 8:1 range.

■ Attack times under 5ms may lead to clipping with high signal levels. But often, the clipping is short enough that it's not noticeable.

■ With minimum attack time, peaks are clamped almost instantly, producing the most drastic compression action. If it's crucial that the signal never hit 0 yet you want really high average levels, you're probably better off using a limiter. For most sounds, you'll have a more natural effect with an attack time of 3 to 10ms to let through some peaks, even if it means a somewhat lower average signal level.

■ Decay is not as critical as attack. Start in the 100 to 250ms range. Shorter times sound "livelier," longer times sound "smoother." But too short a time can give a choppy effect, while too long a release time homogenizes the sound.

■ Use the Release control's Auto function if you're new to compression.

- The bypass switch is your friend—check it frequently to compare the compressed and non-compressed sounds. You may find that even a little bit of compression gives the desired effect.

- When using compression as an insert effect, place it early in the chain so it doesn't bring up the noise from any effects that precede it.

- When increasing guitar sustain, remember that compressors/limiters are not miracle workers. They cannot make your guitar's strings vibrate any longer, but can only increase the apparent sustain. Don't think that a compressor can compensate for dead strings or guitars with poor sustain characteristics.

- Add compression before distortion for a smoother sound with more sustain.

- If it seems like there's been a sudden increase in compression but you didn't increase the compression amount, then the input signal going to the compressor may have increased.

9.8   Limiter Parameters

A limiter is a pretty uncomplicated module with just two parameters. As expected, you click on the label to enable it.

The Limiter isn't particularly difficult to either learn or use. Here, the "LED" is showing that the threshold of −1.0dB has been exceeded.

9.8.1   Threshold

This sets the absolute highest level a signal can attain (within reason—if you drive a limiter too hard, there will be distortion). There is no Make Up Gain control, so you'll probably keep the threshold pretty high in order to catch peaks. If you do want to lower the threshold for more of an effect (e.g., to add a more extreme effect to vocals), then you'll need to make up for any gain loss with the channel fader.

9.8.2   Release

This works the same as the Release control for the compressor and also has an auto function.

9.8.3   Indicator

The limiter has a single indicator: a light that shows when the threshold is being exceeded.

9.9   Routing Parameters

This module is unique to Dynamics—it's not included in VSTDynamics. It sets the order of the effects as follows:

- **1-2-3:** Compress > AutoGate > Limiter
- **2-1-3:** AutoGate > Compress > Limiter
- **1-3-2:** Compress > Limiter > AutoGate

Of these options, 2-1-3 is by far the most common: the AutoGate cleans up any noise before it hits the compressor and is amplified, while the limiter goes at the end to tame any peaks.

1-2-3 reverses the position of Compress and AutoGate. In a way this makes the AutoGate's job harder, because the difference between higher and lower signals is less obvious. However, this can be useful if the Auto-Gate has the filter engaged, and the input signal varies a lot. By compressing it, there's a more consistent signal presented to the filter.

1-3-2 seems, at least to me, as the least useful option of the bunch. It allows for some serious signal squashing, thanks to compression and limiting, prior to reaching the AutoGate. If you're using AutoGate as an effect to pass just the highest peaks of a signal, this routing option might be the best as the peaks will all be at a pretty consistent level when they hit the AutoGate input.

9.10 AutoLevel Parameters

This section is unique to the VSTDynamics module and works like the "sustainer" used by guitarists. Unlike a compressor or limiter, which is designed to work primarily on peaks, AutoLevel tries to keep a consistent output despite a widely varying input level.

AutoLevel turns up the gain during soft passages and turns it down during loud ones.

9.10.1 Threshold

This parameters sets the level above which AutoLevel does its thing. Generally, you'll keep this pretty low for the maximum amount of sustain.

9.10.2 Reaction Time

Here you have a choice of Fast, Mid, or Slow. The proper setting depends on the program material. Suppose a narrator goes off-axis with a microphone every time they look at the page they're reading, thus causing a drop in level. This represents a fairly slow change and would use the slow setting. On the other hand, if you're mixing in a recording of a city ambience and from time to time a sudden sound comes in (tire squeal, gunshot, car horn, etc.), then you want a fast setting to make sure the levels of these sounds are tamed as rapidly as possible.

9.11 SoftClip

SoftClip adds intentional distortion, which can actually be a good thing. Note that it has no controls, only an indicator meter.

This module is also unique to VSTDynamics; what's more, it has no adjustable parameters. In some ways, it works like analog tape: when an input signal increases past about −6dB, it is limited by being clipped, thus producing distortion. However, this is a fairly subtle, warm distortion that doesn't hit you in the face until the levels start reaching toward 0.

The indicator meter toward the top shows whether a signal is in the "distortion zone" or not. In the green area, no distortion occurs. Distortion starts to kick in with the orange band, and increasing signal levels become increasingly distorted from that point on.

My favorite SoftClip application (and it will probably be yours, too!) is with drums. In the section on compression, I mentioned that with drums, setting a small attack time allows some of the drum's natural percussive transients to come through, thus giving a more dynamic sound. In the old days of analog tape, people didn't worry about this too much when using attack time with compression, because the tape would "absorb" the transients. The only penalty was a slight amount of added distortion, however, some would say that the distortion was actually a good thing. This is because it added harmonics to the clipped transient, making it seem stronger and making up for the fact that it didn't have as strong a peak.

SoftClip can do exactly the same type of thing. Because it follows the compressor (VSTDynamics has a fixed signal routing: AutoGate, AutoLevel, Compressor, SoftClip, and Limiter, as shown by the handy graphic in VSTDynamics' lower right), you can set a bit of attack to let the initial drum attacks through, then clip them in SoftClip.

Note that you can increase the input level until you run out of gain, and SoftClip will stubbornly refuse to let the signal exceed 0. However, past some point it's likely the amount of distortion will get on your nerves ... or maybe not, depending on the type of music you do!

9.12 Cubase's Other Noise Gate

The AutoGate is quite sophisticated and part of a plug-in that draws CPU power. However, if all you need is a simple noise gating function, or if you want to apply noise gating only to a selected portion of audio, a noise gate is available by going AUDIO > PROCESS > NOISE GATE.

The parameters are very similar to what we encountered for AutoGate: Threshold, Attack Time, Hold (called "Minimum Opening Time" in this processor), and Release. However, there are a few options not present in AutoGate.

9.12.1 Link Channels

With stereo signals, when Link is checked, the noise gate opens if the signal in either channel exceeds the threshold. With Link unchecked, the noise gate works independently for the two channels (think of this as a "dual mono" noise gate).

9.12.2 Dry/Wet Mix

Access this parameter by clicking on the "More" button. This allows some of the dry signal to go through, so that the gate attenuates the signal rather than mutes it when the gate is closed. Conceptually, you can think of this as a "leakage" control.

9.12.3   Pre-crossfade and Post-crossfade

These are also accessed by clicking on the "More" button. You specify a time over which the effect fades in (pre-crossfade) and/or fades out (post-crossfade).

> To hide the extra parameters that appear when you hit the More button, click on the Less button.

9.12.4   Preview

Click on this to hear the results of the noise gating on the selected audio.

9.12.5   Process

If everything sounded okay when previewed, click on Process to "make it so." Note that this is not a permanent or destructive change; you can always go to EDIT > HISTORY and undo the operation.

Chapter 10

About Reverberation

For thousands of years, music was heard exclusively in an acoustical environment. Recording direct (i.e. plugging an instrument directly into the mixer console) forfeits this sense of acoustical space. A reverb unit helps put this space back in again by simulating the sound of playing in a large room.

A room's acoustical characteristics create a characteristic "ambience." The audience hears not only the sound that comes directly from an instrument or amplifier, but myriad sound waves reflecting and re-reflecting off the room's walls, ceiling, and floor. As a result, what hits the ears of listeners is a composite of the original audio signal, the first reflections from various surfaces, and the delayed reflections. Eventually these sound waves lose their energy and become inaudible.

What's in the room also affects the sound. A thickly carpeted room will easily absorb reflected waves, while a room with extremely hard surfaces will tend to keep the sounds bouncing around. Also, high frequencies are more prone to absorption than lower frequencies.

The best reverb is a large, acoustically-treated room, but few of us can borrow the local cathedral or auditorium as our own personal reverb units. Reverb plug-ins provide a convenient, inexpensive way to add these types of effects.

> Most plug-in reverbs, including Reverb A and Reverb B in Cubase, do not have true stereo inputs but mix the two inputs to mono, then create a stereo field from that signal.

•

Digital reverb can also create spaces that don't exist in nature, such as "gated reverb." This does the equivalent of adding a noise gate to the end of the reverb, allowing for an abrupt cutoff of the reverb tail. This effect is most often used with drums.

10.1   Reverb A and B Parameters

As reverbs go, Reverb A and Reverb B are fairly limited. However, they're bundled with Cubase, and toward the end of this section, we'll give some tips on how to maximize their sonic potential.

Reverb A and B have similar parameters, although Reverb A has more sophisticated filtering and they both have rather different sound qualities because they use different reverb algorithms.

10.1.1   Room Size

The Room Size parameter determines the apparent volume of the room, from a small space like a room to a large space like a hall. The larger the room size, the more complex the reflected sound. This is the most fundamental reverb parameter as it influences the other parameters as well; generally, small sizes sound best with shorter delay times and larger sizes work best with longer delay times. However, you can of course experiment with these to obtain less natural, but nonetheless interesting, effects.

10.1.2 Predelay

Predelay sets the amount of time before the first group of reverberant reflections begins, and is usually less than 100ms (20 to 50ms are typical values). A longer predelay setting gives the feeling of a larger acoustical space, but can also produce an overly "echoed" effect with percussive sound.

10.1.3 Reverb Time

Reverb Time sets how long it takes for the reverb tail to decay to the point of inaudibility. In more costly reverbs, there are usually separate decay times for higher and lower frequencies (and possibly midrange as well), so you can more precisely tailor the room characteristics.

10.1.4 Filter and Damp

Filter (Reverb A) and Damp (Reverb B) both affect the frequency response of the decay. Increased damping causes the high frequencies to roll off more rapidly than the low frequencies. To do this with Reverb B, rotate the Damp control counterclockwise—more negative values increase the damping. Conversely, the closer the Damp number is to 0, the greater the high frequency response during the decay.

Reverb A offers two filter controls, "High Cut" and "Low Cut." Frankly, I think they're labeled backwards—setting High Cut to 0.00 dB gives the most low-frequency response, while more negative numbers decrease low-frequency response. With Low Cut, 0.00 gives the most high-frequency response, while more negative numbers decrease high-frequency response. Well ... whatever. The main point is that you can use these controls to determine how "bright" or "boomy" the reverb is.

10.1.5 Mix

This determines the mix between the reverberated (wet) and unprocessed (dry) signals. This is sometimes referred to as the "wet/dry" mix. With Reverb A, a setting of 100% means all reverb and 0% means all dry signal. With Reverb B, there's a continuously variable readout that shows the percentage of dry and reverberated signal.

10.2 Building a Better Reverb

Good reverbs take a lot of processing power, because the reflections that occur in a natural space are extremely complex. Calculating a sound that takes all the complexities into account is a daunting task even for dedicated DSP, let alone a microprocessor that's busy attending to other chores.

Of the two Cubase reverbs, Reverb B is somewhat grainier and has a lower, bassier timbre. Reverb A is smoother and brighter. Neither is particularly satisfying by itself, but fortunately they complement each other well; adding them as Send Effects creates a far more rich, authentic tone.

Using two different reverbs as send effects gives a much deeper, more realistic reverb effect than either one by itself.

CD Track 14 plays three sections: five hits through Reverb A then one second of silence, five hits through Reverb B then one second of silence, and finally, five hits through both reverbs as described in this section. Note how the reverb sound is far better in the last example.

Generally, it seems you want the two reverbs to be set similarly with respect to decay time. I prefer setting a relatively large room size, even with not too long a delay, because that seems to produce a less periodic sound (especially when the two are combined). Also, it seems both reverbs have a hard time handling sharp transients without "splattering" a bit. However, setting different predelays in the 8 to 25ms range often helps diffuse the sound.

As to setting up the sends, I found the effect was a little richer if Reverb A received a bit more send level than Reverb B, but that's a matter of personal taste. The point is, you need to experiment to find that combination where one reverb fills in the other's "holes." But once you find it, the reward is a far richer reverb sound than what comes stock with Cubase.

10.3 Other Reverb Parameters

At some point, you will likely feel the need to add a more powerful reverb to your recording environment. However, be aware that reverbs do require a lot of CPU power. As a result, using DSP cards and running reverbs on them (e.g., TC Works PowerCore, Universal Audio UAD-1, CreamWare Pulsar XTC) is a common technique. This relieves the host processor of having to spend too many CPU cycles on creating a room environment. However, there are native plug-ins that produce good reverb effects without compromising too much on CPU power.

In any event, many will have additional parameters compared to Reverb A and B. Different manufacturers sometimes use different names to describe the same parameters, but usually they aren't so different you won't be able to figure them out.

For example, let's look at the parameters you'll find in the WaveArts MasterVerb, which strikes a good balance of sound quality and CPU loading. However, one difference compared to higher-end reverbs is that the parameters affect the reverb "tail" only. More sophisticated reverbs, which we'll look at shortly, usually offer another set of parameters for the early reflections (the echoes that first happen when a sound wave starts bouncing off of surfaces) as well as for the reverb tail.

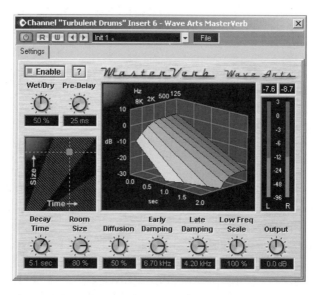

The WaveArts MasterVerb is a good example of a reverb plug-in with more flexibility than the ones included with Cubase SX/SL.

"Decay Time" is the same as Reverb Time in the Cubase Reverbs. Room Size and Pre-Delay are the same as the identically-named parameters in Reverbs A and B.

"Diffusion" sets the "spacing" between reflections. Lower diffusion settings space the echoes further apart, which sounds good with sustained sounds, like vocals, because the spaces don't "crowd" the vocals. With drums, though, lower settings can add so many discrete echoes that percussive sounds take on the quality of marbles bouncing on a steel plate. For percussive sounds, higher diffusions are generally preferable.

"Early damping" is a high-cut filter that sets the range of frequencies permitted into the reverb. Lower values create a bassier, more muffled effect, whereas higher values produce a brighter sound.

"Late damping" sets the frequency response characteristics of the reverb tail itself. Lower settings cause the high frequencies to decay faster, as would happen in a room with absorptive surfaces (heavy carpeting, lots of people, etc.). Higher settings create the effect of a room with harder surfaces, where the high frequencies bounce around for longer before finally decaying.

"Low frequency scale" determines the decay time ratio for low frequencies compared to the midrange frequencies. For example, with a setting of 100%, the decay time occurs equally at all frequencies. Higher percentages cause the low frequency decay to be longer (e.g. a setting of 200% means that the low frequency decay time will be twice that of the midrange), whereas lower percentages set a shorter low frequency decay time. This helps if, for example, you're adding reverb to a drum set and don't want the kick to reverberate as long as the other drums ... or you want it to reverberate longer.

10.4 High-end Reverb Plug-ins

Let's close out our discussion of reverbs by looking at a high-end plug-in, the RealVerb Pro from Mackie/Universal Audio. This runs on the UAD-1 "powered plug-ins" card, so using it takes nothing away from the host CPU.

The "Shape" section provides two different algorithms which are not just limited to rooms, but can also include spring and plate reverberation. You can then set a blend of the two shapes, which has a major impact on the character of the reverb's early reflections. The size of each is also variable.

Furthermore, a "Material" module lets you choose from a wide variety of materials, including wood, glass, air, etc. Similarly to Shape, you can select two different materials and blend between them, so you can have a surface that's half-marble and half-hardwood, one-third glass and two-thirds cork, etc. Each of these also has a thickness control; think of this section as a super-sophisticated set of damping controls.

Universal Audio's RealVerb Pro offers a wide variety of control over multiple reverb parameters.

The "Resonance" section is configurable as a parametric or high-shelf EQ, or a hybrid between the two. This allows simulating the natural kinds of resonances that occur in rooms.

"Timing" has two views: an upper one that's dedicated to early reflections, and a lower one for the reverb's tail. Both have "handles" for setting amplitude and amount of predelay, while the strip along the right-hand side of the lower view controls diffusion. This graphic approach, with a numeric readout strip along the bottom to show parameter values, provides useful visual feedback on the reverb settings.

Other plug-ins take a less graphical approach and correlate these parameters to specific names. Here are some of the parameters you'll find:

- "Early reflections diffusion" is similar to the main reverb diffusion parameter but affects only the early reflections. This can be thought of as a "smoothness/thickness" parameter; increasing diffusion packs the early reflections closer together, giving a thicker sound. Decreasing diffusion spreads the early reflections further apart.

- "Early reflections level:" Early reflections are closely spaced discrete echoes, as opposed to the later "wash" of sound that constitutes the tail of the reverb. This parameter determines the level of these discrete echoes.

- "Early reflections shape" is a less-commonly found parameter that imparts an envelope to the early reflections. The envelope may attack instantly then decay slowly, build up over time then decay, take a long time to attack then decay abruptly, etc.

- "Reverb density" or "spread" determines the space between the first reflection and subsequent reflections. With lower density settings, the first reflection is audible as a separate event, followed by the remaining reflections. Higher density settings move the remaining reflections closer to the first reflection, so that the first reflection joins the overall "wash" of reverb.

There is some disagreement among manufacturers as to the exact definition of "diffusion" and "density," so your reverb may function somewhat differently than described here. Hey, it's not my fault!

- "Crossover frequency" applies only to plug-ins with separate decay times for high and low frequencies. This parameter determines the "dividing line" between the highs and lows. For example, setting the crossover frequency to 1kHz means that frequencies below 1kHz will be subject to the low frequency decay time, while frequencies above 1kHz will be subject to the high frequency decay time. Really fancy reverbs may have separate high, mid, and low frequency crossover frequencies. Each of these may have a level control too.

■ Some reverbs include "gated reverb" parameters within the reverb itself, while others treat it as a separate effect or expect you to follow up a traditional reverb with a noise gate. Typical parameters are gate "threshold" (how much of the reverb tail is cut off), gate "shape" (even "reverse" or "backwards" reverbs are possible, where the tail increases to a certain level instead of fading out), and others. It's best to consult the manual for more information on these types of effects since they vary so much among different units.

Getting back to the RealVerb Pro, it has one other very interesting set of parameters: positioning controls. This section provides separate panning options for the direct, early reflections, and reverb tail components, as well as a "Distance" parameter that sets the perceived distance from the sound source. This allows not just creating an acoustic space, but determining where the listener is in that acoustic space.

Yes, we've sure come a long way from sticking a speaker and mic in a concrete room ... although let's not forget that even though real reverb doesn't have presets and options, it gives the most realistic sound.

Part 4

Using Effects in Cubase

Chapter 11

The Three Types of Effects Slots

Effects are a key to good mixes, as they allow tweaking sounds so that they blend in better, stand out more, add interest to parts that are somewhat lacking in terms of sound, or whatever is needed to create the ultimate mix.

As with traditional physical mixers, Cubase offers three places where you can insert effects. It is important to choose the right location to maximize the effect's impact, as well as conserve processor power.

11.1   Insert Effects

Insert effects are named after the "insert" jacks found in hardware mixers, which are found within individual mixer channels. (By using the insert jacks, you're inserting the effect into the channel's signal path. Insert jacks are often wired as 1/4" tip-ring-sleeve jacks with the send on one connector and the return on the other connector.)

In hardware mixers, channel inserts are located between the input preamp and the fader/panpot circuitry. This allows for proper gain-staging, as few effects are designed for mic level signals. The preamp can bring the incoming signal up to a consistent level for feeding the effect. Also, if the effect generates any noise, pulling down the fader reduces both the signal and any generated noise.

Cubase follows the same concept:

- Inserted effects appear within a specific channel and affect only the channel into which they are inserted.

Popular insert effects include dynamics control, distortion, delay, chorusing, and flanging, although almost any effect can be used as an insert effect.

Stereo channels need to use effects with stereo inputs; a mono effect will process only the left track. Mono channels can use stereo or mono effects, but if used with a stereo effect, only the left channel output will be present.

Technically, an EQ is also an insert effect. In fact, in some hard disk recorders, the EQ needs to be inserted into a channel. However, because of the EQ's importance, Cubase "hard-wires" it into each channel so you don't have to insert it—just like almost all hardware mixers.

11.1.1   Using Insert Effects with Cubase SX

One of the main differences between Cubase SX and SL is that SX offers an expanded mixer view, where a section opens up above the faders to show inserts, EQ settings, and effects sends. This offers a very flexible way to deal with EQ and effects. Cubase SL users can skip ahead to the section "Using Insert Effects with Cubase SL (or SX)" on page 253.

Narrow versus Wide Mixer Channels

Cubase SX's mixer has both wide and narrow channel modes, as selected by clicking on the small arrow above each fader that points down at the fader.

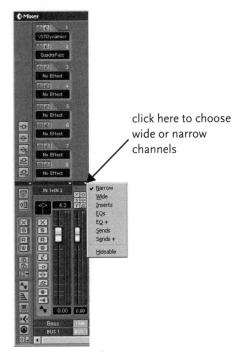

click here to choose wide or narrow channels

Clicking the small arrow above the fader allows selecting a narrow or wide channel strip. The extended section above the fader, in this case showing insert effects, is available only with Cubase SX.

Because of the expanded mixer option, with Cubase SX I usually work in wide view, as narrow view does not display the expanded section. However, if you're mixing in Cubase SX and using the narrow view in expanded mode, it is still possible to access effects for a particular channel.

■ Click on the arrow above the fader, as if you were going to choose between the wide and narrow versions. If you select Inserts, the channel will automatically go to wide mode so you can see the Inserts (this is also true if you choose any of the other options—EQs, EQ+, Sends, or Sends+).

■ Another option is to click on the channel strip's Edit icon (the "e" symbol), as described later. This brings up the channel VST strip where you can see Insert effects, Send effects, and EQ simultaneously.

Getting Ready to Insert Effects

Let's look at the mixer to see how to select, enable, and edit effects. Cubase SX allows many ways to do the same function, so you can use whatever is comfortable for you.

In Cubase SX's expanded mixer mode, the global strip toward the left of the mixer is one way to call up effects.

The Cubase SX mixer needs to be in expanded mode so you can see the inserts. Click on "1" to toggle between normal and expanded view.

Another method is to click on "2" and a menu appears. Select Expanded, as indicated by a check mark. If you select Normal, the top area above the faders that shows the inserts, EQs, and send controls goes away.

Now that the mixer is expanded, click on the Insert icon ("3"). The area above the faders will show the 8 available insert slots. Insert effects are always routed in series, which means that one effect follows another (i.e., the output of the effect in the top slot feeds the input of the effect in the next slot down, whose output feeds the next slot down, and so on).

Note that effects need not be inserted consecutively; a "No Effect" slot is effectively acting like a bypass that feeds the output of the slot above it to the input of the slot below it. This is important because you might have a particular way of working, like always placing dynamics in the top slot, distortion in the second slot down, delay at the end, or whatever. Thus, if you want to see which channels use a particular type of effect, you can scan that particular slot across all the channels to see if the effect is present.

Enabling and Editing Insert Effects

Now that we can see the inserts, let's make them work for us. Insert effects slots default to saying "No Effect."

You can insert any VST or DirectX effect into an empty slot or replace an existing effect. Here the QuadraFuzz is being selected.

To select an effect:

1   Click and hold on the insert effect slot. It can be either empty or hold an existing effect.

2   A list of available effects appears.

3   Drag down to the desired effect and select it.

4   Release the mouse button.

Working with Insert Effects

Now that we can see the insert effects and have inserted effects, here's how to enable and use them.

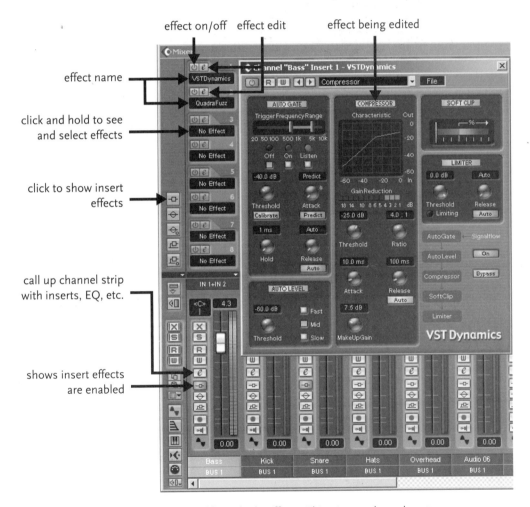

Cubase SX offers several ways to enable and edit effects. This picture shows how to do so directly from the mixer and summarizes what we have covered so far.

The two small icons above each slot control effect On/Off (Active/Bypass) and Effect Edit. These are toggles; blue means the function is active. When you click on the Edit icon, the effect screen appears in front of the mixer. In the picture above, the VSTDynamics effect (which was inserted in the top slot) has been selected for editing.

To the left of each fader, an icon that's a smaller version of the Global Strip insert icon glows blue if any channel insert effects are enabled. This is handy if the mixer is in the Normal rather than Expanded mode, as you can still see if effects are being used for a particular channel. You can also click on this icon to enable (glows blue) or bypass (glows yellow) the insert effects as a group. If you click on the icon when it's gray (bypassed) and it doesn't turn blue, that means there are no insert effects for that channel.

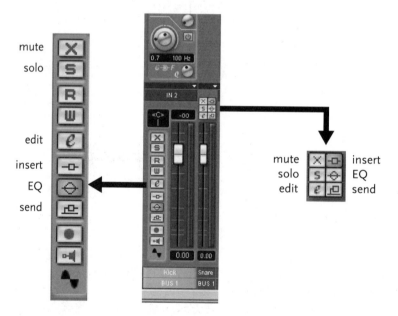

Note that even if you are using the narrow channel view, there are still six icons available above the fader, including the familiar square Insert active/byass button in the upper right.

With either view, the Edit icon "e"calls up the VST channel settings and presents yet another way to deal with Insert effects. This is described in the next section.

11.1.2 Using Insert Effects with Cubase SL (or SX)

With Cubase SL or SX, you can access the VST Channel Settings window (which allows you to edit Inserts, EQ, Send Effects, and more) by clicking on the Edit ("e") button. This is accessible from either the wide or narrow channel view.

clicking on the the "e" icon in either wide or narrow mode calls up the VST Channel Settings

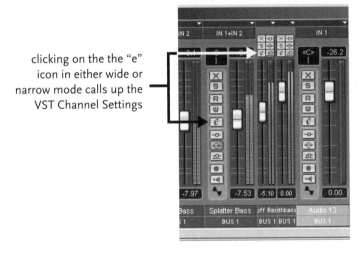

The "e" icon is located to the left of the fader in wide view and on top of it in narrow view.

The VST Channel Settings window shows insert effects similarly to the expanded view in Cubase SX; the Insert icon to the left of the fader (just below the "e") acts as a master active/bypass switch for the Inserts.

fader   insert effects   4-stage EQ   send effects

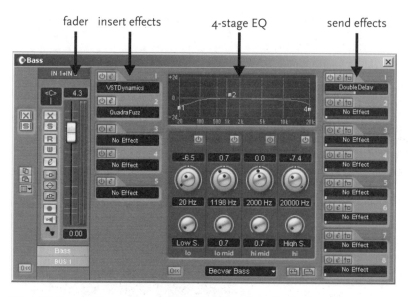

The VST Channel Settings include the fader, insert effects, EQ, and send effects. Note that you can save and load EQ presets. This shows the window from Cubase SL, which has five insert effects slots instead of the eight found in Cubase SX.

As with SX, insert effects are routed in series so one effect follows another (i.e. the output of the effect in the top slot feeds the input of the effect in the next slot down). A "No Effect" slot effectively acts like a bypass, so it is not necessary to insert effects consecutively. Even though SL is limited to five insert effects, this should be enough for almost all applications.

Enabling and Editing Insert Effects

Insert effects slots default to saying "No Effect." Selecting an effect is done as with Cubase SX:

1   Click and hold on the insert effect slot. It can be either empty or hold an existing effect.

2   A list of available effects appears.

3 Drag down to the desired effect and select it.

4 Release the mouse button.

DaTube distortion is about to be added to the third effects slot. Clicking and holding on an effects slot brings up the effect selection menu.

Working with Insert Effects

Above each effects slot, there are two small icons. The left one controls effect On/Off (Active/Bypass), while the one on the right brings up the effect's "front panel" for editing. These are toggles: when blue, the function is active.

In wide mixer view (or in the VST Channel Settings window), there's an icon to the left of the fader, just below the "e" icon. This glows blue if any channel insert effects are enabled and can also be clicked on to enable or bypass the insert effects as a group (when insert effects are bypassed, the icon turns yellow). If you click on the icon when it's gray (bypassed) and it doesn't turn blue, then there are no insert effects in that channel.

these icons glow blue if insert effects are
enabled in the corresponding channels

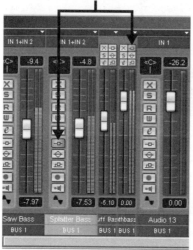

The insert effect indicator icons let you know if effects are inserted and if so, whether they're enabled or bypassed as a group.

11.1.3   Placing Effects in the Right Order

Cubase's 4-stage channel EQ always follows the inserts, but otherwise, you can place any effect in any order, including additional EQ from other plug-ins. Where effects are placed in the chain have a major influence on the overall sound, so here are some observations on particular pairs of effects.

EQ before or after Compression

There is no universal answer for this situation, because compression can serve different purposes.

Consider this scenario: you've recorded a fantastic synth bass line with a highly resonant filter sweep. On some notes, the level goes crazy when a note's frequency coincides with the filter frequency. Otherwise, the signal is well behaved. But, you also want to boost the lower midrange a bit to give a beefier sound.

In this case, I'd put the compressor first to trap those rogue transients, then apply EQ to the more dynamically consistent sound. Because the EQ change is minor, it probably won't change the signal's overall amplitude too much.

Now suppose you don't have any problems with overly-resonant filters, but you do need a *massive* lower midrange boost. This much boost could greatly increase the amplitude at some frequencies, so putting compression after the EQ will help even these out a bit.

But there's a complication. Because significant boosts in a certain frequency range increase level in that range, the compressor will scale those levels back down a bit. So, this reduces the effect of what the EQ is trying to do—it tries to boost, but the compressor won't let it go much further. However, signals below the threshold remain boosted, and this just might give the sound you want.

Another reason to place EQ before compression is to make the compression more "frequency-sensitive." Suppose you have a great guitar part and want to emphasize the melody. By boosting EQ slightly for the range to be emphasized and then compressing, the boosted frequencies will go into compression sooner than the other frequency ranges.

Or, suppose you have a "buzzy" digital synth. Cut the highs a bit prior to compression, and the compressor will bring up everything else more readily than the highs. This type of technique isn't quite the same as multi-band compression, but gives some of the same results as there's more "punch" to the boosted frequencies.

Loudness Maximizers/Boosters

This is a specialized form of compressor that is more like a limiter, as it establishes a strict dynamic range ceiling. However, today's maximizers that are designed to put as much level as possible on CDs operate somewhat differently than standard limiters, as they are designed to give extreme amounts of limiting while still sounding relatively natural.

On individual instruments, maximizers work very well to bring out a solo: select the region containing the solo, then apply a couple dB of maximization (don't add too much). This will lift it out of the mix compared to other sections of the part. For individual instruments, maximization generally goes last in the signal chain. One exception is that I prefer putting maximization before echo or reverb; processing the tails of these effects can result sound unnatural.

Also, maximizers can help out with the compressor/EQ order dilemma. I often place a compressor first to trap excessively high peaks, then add EQ to provide the desired timbre, and finally use a maximizer to give a "hot" sound.

Distortion

Distortion has worked well for the Hammond B3 and for guitarists, and now others are starting to discover the joys of messing up your signal.

I invariably place distortion before anything else, with one exception described later. Although you might think distortion should be, well, distorted, any guitarist will tell you there's clean, pleasing distortion and ugly, dirty distortion (which one they prefer is another issue entirely!).

If the distortion is followed by a number of "clean" effects, they make the distortion sound smoother as well. The classic example is reverb. Add some really gorgeous room ambience to a distorted signal, and it takes out some of the edge, creating a "sweeter" distortion sound. But placing distortion *after* reverb will distort all the reverb tails, which sounds unrealistic as well as dirty.

The same is true for discrete echoes (delay): you want to echo a distorted sound, not distort an echoed sound. If there's a lot of feedback, the distorted echoes will eventually degenerate into intermodulation distortion. If the echo is after the distortion, then the echoes will remain clean and distinct.

The one possible exception is with EQ. Most of the time, you want EQ after distortion, so it can alter the distorted sound's timbre. But just as we used EQ before compression to give a more "frequency-sensitive" effect, EQ before distortion allows certain frequency ranges to distort more easily than other ranges. For example, you might boost a synth's midrange to distort more easily than the bass, so that the melody gets chunky but the bass doesn't intermodulate too much. This is an ideal situation for placing EQ before distortion. I often add EQ both before and after distortion—the first to alter what gets distorted, and the second to alter the distorted sound itself.

Flangers and Phasers

The situation here is complicated because proper placement depends on the effects settings you chose, so you're better off experimenting and choosing whatever sounds best. Following are some general tips:

- Placing these effects in front of distortion may be ineffective, as heavy distortion can pretty much cancel out the effect. Or you might like the way the sounds "cuts" through the distortion.

- Flangers can generate massive frequency response peaks and deep valleys. Therefore, you probably want to follow the flanger with a compressor to restrict the dynamic range somewhat. Caution, though: if you add too much compression, the flanging sound will be less intense.

- EQ placement requires experimentation. I'd usually put it before the flanger, because you can then optimize the sound to work well with the flanging effect.

Generally, flangers, phasers, delays, reverb, and other time-based effects go toward the end of the chain, just prior to any loudness maximization (except as noted earlier, with individual tracks you might want reverb after the maximization).

The Virtues of Parallel Plug-ins

Most software requires a series connection of plug-ins. However, some really great effects can occur by placing effects in parallel. As of this writing there are two plug-ins that let you plug in combinations of parallel effects: TC Works FX Machine and BIAS Vbox. Essentially, these are plug-in effects matrices where you plug in VST or DirectX effects, depending on the host. (TC Works' Spark, a digital audio editing program, also includes a matrix into which you can insert effects in series or parallel.) You can also use Cubase's Send Effects capability, or simply copy a track several times and use different plug-ins for different parallel effects. As these tracks can also have plug-ins, then you can also do parallel chains of series effects to create what's called a series-parallel effects chain.

Setting up effects in parallel can be essential to producing very vivid, vintage-style flanging. This is because flanging is the result of mixing a modulated, delayed signal in equal proportion to a "dry" signal; as the time difference between the signals varies between oms to around 5 to 10ms, you'll hear that characteristic "whoosing," jet plane-like effect. However, the modulated/delayed signal can generally not hit oms of delay and will have a minimum delay time (typically 1ms). This limits the range of the flanging effect. If you put the modulated signal in parallel with a dry signal delayed by 1ms, when the modulated/delayed signal hits its minimum delay of 1ms, there will be a oms difference between the two paralleled signals. This effect is called "through-zero flanging" and is more dramatic than if the flanging can't reach a oms time difference.

Parallel effects are also good for creating stereo signals from older, vintage gear that had only a mono output. I often use parallel EQs to do this, notching in one channel while boosting in the other. Short delays in the

10 to 20ms range (just make sure they're long enough to avoid comb filtering problems if you re-combine the signals back into mono) also help expand the sound.

11.1.4 Insert Effects Tips

Richer Vocals

A proven technique for creating richer vocals is to have the vocalist double a line by singing along with the original take. The doubled take is usually mixed behind the main line at anywhere from –3 to –10dB.

However, sometimes it isn't always possible to cut a doubled line—like when you're mixing, and the vocalist is on tour somewhere. For those occasions, here's a quick workaround.

1   Duplicate the vocal track you want to thicken so you now have two tracks of the same vocal.

2   Select the copy and go AUDIO > PROCESS > PITCH SHIFT.

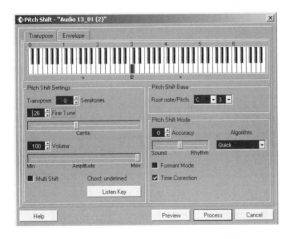

The Pitch Shift DSP sounds quite good and can create useful timbre changes for instruments.

3 Set the Fine Tune around −20 to −30 cents.

4 Make sure Time Correction is enabled, then click on Preview to make sure everything sounds okay.

5 Click on Process.

6 You will likely get a warning that other clips also use this audio and any processing will apply to them as well. Click on New Version so that the processing affects only the selected clip.

7 Bring the doubled track down a bit so it doesn't compete with, but instead complements, the lead vocal.

For the thickest sound, pan the two vocal tracks to center. If you pan one vocal full right and one full left, you'll hear two individual vocals instead of a composite effect (which may be what you want), and the stereo image will be weighted toward the slightly louder vocal.

Also try panning lead vocals slightly left and right (e.g. left channel at 10 o'clock, right channel at 2 o'clock). This gives a little stereo imaging and makes the vocals sound bigger.

11.2   Master Effects

The chapter on Mastering with Cubase SX/SL delves into the master channel, and master effects, in great detail. This section is designed to present an overview of how the master section relates to effects.

Master effects patch in series like insert effects, but they insert in the mixer's master output section, so they're applied after the separate channels have been mixed to a stereo signal. As a result, master effects process the entire mix, not individual tracks. (There are also effects designed for processing the multiple channels involved in surround productions, and Cubase SX—but not SL—can do surround sound. However, mixing in surround is an entirely different topic that deserves a book of its own.)

Master effects must have stereo ins and outs. A mono effect will not load into a master effects slot.

The Global strip's second button down from the top shows or hides the master faders, which appear toward the right of the mixer. The module's upper right corner has an Edit ("e") button; clicking on this calls up the Master Effects window, which is sort of like an abstract equipment rack. Each "rack panel" accepts a VST or DirectX plug-in.

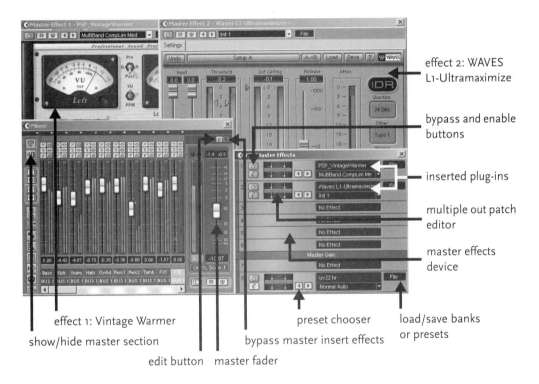

effect 2: WAVES L1-Ultramaximize

bypass and enable buttons

inserted plug-ins

multiple out patch editor

master effects device

effect 1: Vintage Warmer

show/hide master section

edit button   master fader

bypass master insert effects

preset chooser

load/save banks or presets

The mixer is on the lower left, the Master Effects section on the lower right. The two plug-ins being used in the first and second effects slots are in the background. The last slot has Cubase's built-in dithering patched in.

Note how there are six effects slots prior to the master gain and two effects slots after the master gain control. The reason for having two effects slots after the master is so that if you want an effect that continues even after the main level has been turned down (for example, a long, repeating echo or long reverb "tail" that fades into silence), that effect would go here. Typically, the very last slot is where Dithering gets added to the signal chain. We'll explain much more about dithering in Part 6, "Mastering with Cubase SX/SL."

The most commonly used mastering effects are for Equalization and Dynamics (particularly multi-band compressors, loudness maximizers, limiters, and sometimes stereo compressors). Equalizers applied to program material tend to be broader, like the TLAudio EQ-1 plug-in. This produces very gentle, natural-sounding EQ curves.

Steinberg's TLAudio EQ-1 plug-in was designed with mastering applications in mind.

If you use any master effects, be careful not to overload the master channel output. If this happens, one or both of the small red "LEDs" above the master fader will light. Again, we'll talk more about this under mastering.

11.3 Send Effects

The Cubase mixer has multiple "busses." Each acts as a "terminal" for signals flowing through the mixer channels. In most applications, the most important of these busses is the stereo master output bus, which is controlled by the Master Channel. All the channel outputs dump into this bus for a stereo mixdown. Buses are discussed in more detail in Chapter 26, "Interfacing with the Physical World."

However in addition to output busses, Cubase includes eight mono send (also called "auxiliary") busses. Any channel can send some signal to one or more of these aux busses; this signal can come either pre-channel fader (therefore, the level going to the bus doesn't change when the channel volume changes) or post-channel fader (where bringing down the fader also brings down the amount going to the aux bus).

> If you have selected pre-fader send, be aware that if you mute the channel, the pre-fader signal will not be muted. As muting is the same as pulling a fader all the way down, muting a track mutes the send effect signal only if the send effect is post-fader.

There's a good reason why you would rather use Send Effects under some circumstances than Insert Effects. Every plug-in requires some amount of computing power, so the fewer plug-ins you use, the more processing "headroom" is available. Therefore, if you want to process several channels with the same effect, you're better off loading a single Send Effect instead of inserting the same effect multiple times as a channel insert effect. For instance, when adding reverb, it makes more sense to use it as a send effect, synthesize the desired acoustic space, and mix in varying amounts of signal from the send bus, as determined by each channel's send effect level control.

> Send effects need to be mono in/stereo out. This is not as much of a limitation as it may seem, as many effects sum stereo inputs anyway and create a stereo output. For example, the DoubleDelay works in the this manner.

The output of each send bus can go to the output bus of your choice. For a conventional stereo mixdown, they would go to Bus 1, which terminates in the Master Channel.

The lower arrow represents the master bus, which mixes together the signal from each channel and sends the combined output to the Master Channel. The other arrows represent send busses. The send controls for each channel (whether accessed here via SX's expanded mixer view or from the VST Channel Settings window in Cubase SX or SL) determine how much of the channel signal gets sent to a particular bus.

In the VST Channel Settings window, you can see all the various send bus parameters. The blue line below the send effect name controls the send level. Above the name, the icons (from left to right) include Effect On/Off, edit effect parameters, and send pre/post fader.

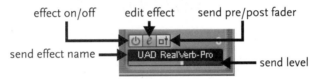

The VST Channel Settings window provides full control over each channel's send parameters for all eight send channels.

In Cubase SX's expanded mixer view, looking at the send effects in linear view provides access to the Effect On/Off, Pre/Post, and effect edit buttons. In knob view, only the Effect On/Off button is visible.

With hardware mixers, send effects are generally outboard gear. A mixer's send bus output feeds the effect input; the effect output returns to the mixer either via dedicated send return jacks or to an ordinary mixer channel.

Of course, in the Cubase Virtual Studio, send effects are inside the computer. You choose the send effects by going DEVICES > VST SEND EFFECTS. You choose effects as you do for insert effects (click and hold on the slot, then select the effect). The Send Effects device also provides other useful editable parameters:

■ Master send level: This is very handy when setting send levels. Suppose you start turning up more and more sends on the mixer, to the point where the input of the send effect is overloaded. Simply turn down the master send to obtain the correct level. Another example would be if you decide that the overall reverb amount needs to be louder or softer, but you don't want to re-adjust every single send control because the balance of the sends is already perfect. Simply use the send effects master to change the overall amount of the send signal.

- Effect on/off: You can quickly take an effect out of the send bus with this button.

- Effect edit: This accesses the send effect parameters for editing.

- Preset select arrows: Go quickly to a previous preset (left arrow) or the next preset (right arrow) in the send effect's list of presets.

- Preset select drop down menu: This shows a list of all available presets.

- File select: Click on this to save or load individual effects or banks of effects.

- Bus select: This determines where the effects bus output terminates. For a normal stereo mix, this would be the master bus. Why you might want to use this with other busses is covered in the chapter "Interfacing with the Physical World" on page 399.

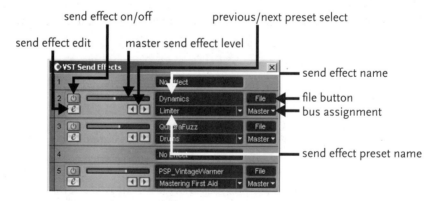

The Send Effects device serves as a "control center" for send effects, presets, effect on/off, master send effects level, etc.

Note that send effects are generally set for processed (wet) sound only. This is because the channel fader provides the unprocessed signal to the master bus, while the send effects contributes only the effect sound, adding it to the unprocessed signal. In fact, it is recommended that you not include any straight sound in a send effect because of possible latency issues within the effect. Combining the straight signal from the channel along with a straight signal contributed by the send effect could lead to phase cancellation problems.

11.4 Gain-staging

When working with send effects, there are three places to alter levels:

- the channel's send effect control,
- the main channel fader, if the send effect control is set to post-fader,
- the master send control in the Send Effects device, which regulates the overall level going to the send effect.

Furthermore, any signal processor the send effects bus feeds may have input and/or output level controls, and their sound may depend on the incoming level (e.g., distortion—more input signal generally increases the amount of distortion). If these controls aren't set correctly, overly hot levels may cause distortion, while too low a level can lead to an unfavorable signal-to-noise ratio. Here's the general procedure for proper level-setting:

1 If the send effect has an input level control, set it to unity gain (i.e. the signal is neither amplified nor attenuated).

2 Set the master level control in the VST Send Effects device (this is the unity gain position for the master level).

3 Adjust the individual send controls for the desired amount of effect. Channel send controls are at unity gain when turned all the way up. The higher you turn the individual send controls, the more that channel will contribute to the effected sound.

4 As the sends from the individual channels start to add up, they may overload the processor's input. Leave the processor input at unity gain and use the master send control to reduce the level going to the effect.

If the signal going to the processor is too low, then use the master send control to bring it up. If turning it up leads to distortion at the mixer and there still isn't enough level, increase the processor's input level as needed.

11.5 Putting Two Send Effects in Series

At first, it seems Cubase will not allow you to put two send effects in series. However, what happens if you want to, for example, add stereo delay before reverb on a track?

There is a workaround; we'll use adding DoubleDelay before Reverb A as an example:

1 Duplicate each track that should go through the combination of effects.

2 Set up Reverb A as a send effect.

3 In the duplicate channel(s), make sure the send signal going to the reverb is pre-fader.

4 Pull the duplicate channel's main fader down all the way.

5 Insert the DoubleDelay effect as an insert effect in the duplicate channel.

6 Set the DoubleDelay parameters as desired.

7 The duplicate channel now goes through the DoubleDelay before going into the Reverb A send effect.

Note that if you want to send several channels through the combination of effects, then you would first need to duplicate each channel you wanted to have go through the combination of send effects. Then, on each duplicate, set up the send effects bus as described above (pre-fader to Reverb A, master fader all the way down). You would then need to use DoubleDelay as an insert effect in each of the duplicate channels. If you want the DoubleDelay effect to be identical for each channel:

1   Adjust the DoubleDelay parameters as desired in one of the tracks.

2   Save this setting as a preset using the File button (located in the VST Send Effects device).

3   Load this preset into the instances of DoubleDelay that are in the other duplicate channels.

11.6   Multiple Send Effects in Series: the "Virtual Send Effects Bus"

The method mentioned above is workable, but designed mostly for the occasional situation where you want a couple of send effects in series, on a limited number of tracks. If you have a project where there are, for example, four drum tracks and you want them processed through several series send effects (and want them all processed similarly), there's a more elegant way to do this using Group tracks. What's more, the send effects can even be in true stereo, not just mono in/stereo out.

You create a Group track as you do any other track: right-click in the Track List. Then, select Add Group Channel Track. This creates a track that shows up in the Track List and has a corresponding channel strip in the mixer. When using Group tracks, I prefer using the Mixer view as it shows everything needed for this application with Cubase SX and can access everything you need in Cubase SL.

This Group track contains two insert effects; its fader serves as a master send effects level control. Also note that the Group track has a reverb inserted as a traditional send effect, which is in parallel with the "virtual send effects." For the four tracks assigned to the Group track, their master faders serve as effects send controls to the Group track, while their normal effects sends are now assigned to the master output bus, so the associated controls determine the track's level in the mix.

The Group track will become our "virtual send effects bus." Here's how it works; we'll use four audio drum tracks as an example:

1   Assign the Group track output to Bus 1 (or whatever you're using for a main output bus). This assignment can be done toward the bottom of the mixer, just below the channel fader's name.

2   Click on the Group track's "e" button (visible only from the mixer, not from the track in the Track List) to open the track for editing.

3   In the Group track, insert the effects you want to use as "virtual send effects" in the Insert Effects slots—*not* the Send Effects slots! Set the individual effects to processed sound only (no dry signal).

4   Assign each channel to be processed by the virtual send effects (in this case, the four drum tracks) to the Group track. As with the Group track, this assignment can be made just below the channel fader's name.

5 For each drum track, click on a send effect field and select Bus 1 (or whatever you're using as your main output bus). Again for each drum track, enable the effects send and select pre-fader send. We are *not* using any send effects here—just routing the track to Bus 1 though the send section.

6 With the Group track fader down, for each drum track adjust the send to Bus 1 for the desired level. Essentially, the effect send to Bus 1 now becomes each track's main fader.

7 Turn up the Group track fader, which is essentially the virtual send effect's bus master control. Now each drum track's channel fader becomes a virtual effects send, because it's determining the amount of signal going to the Group track effects; the output of the final effect in the chain returns back into the master bus.

As the signal flow can get a little confusing, the following flow chart diagram summarizes what's going on.

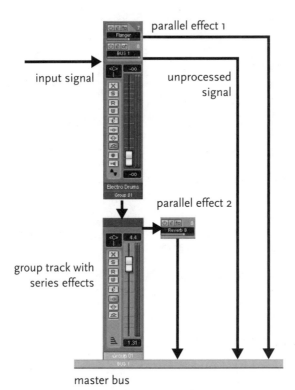

parallel effect 1

input signal

unprocessed signal

parallel effect 2

group track with series effects

master bus

The input signal goes through the channel's main fader, then into the Group track, which contains some series effects. The output of these effects terminates in the master bus. The channel fader serves as an effects send to the Group track, while the Group track fader is a master for the send effects. Meanwhile, the unprocessed input signal also splits off to the master bus via a channel send effect. This doesn't have an effect inserted, but instead is assigned directly to the master bus. The send level here determines how much dry signal goes to the master bus.

There are also two options for additional parallel effects: parallel effect 1 taps off the original signal at the channel fader, while parallel effect 2 taps off the processed signal from the Group track. The mind boggles! Note that the series effects in the Group track and the parallel effects should be set for processed sound only.

Here are a few more notes regarding this technique:

- The Group fader controls the output of the virtual send effects, not the signal going to the input of the effects chain. Therefore, make sure the channel faders feeding the Group track are set low enough so that they don't overload the Group track's insert effects.

- You can add send effects to the Group channel as well, which allows you to put send effects in parallel with the virtual send effects. Pretty cool, eh?

- The above recommends using the pre-fader setting for the straight level so that this level is maintained independently of the level going to the send effects. However, you can of course select the post-fader setting, in which case the send level and straight level will track each other.

- You can add an effect that parallels the Group track effects—just insert it into a track's send effect. Make sure it's set for wet sound only.

11.7   Send Effects Applications

The classic Send Effects application is reverb. This is because the reverb is generally used to simulate an acoustic space, and the send controls for individual channels determine how much of the signal gets reverberated in the "room." But send effects are good for a lot more than just reverb.

However, there is an important caution: the latency that's added by going through a send effect means that the effect sound not only has to be set for processed sound only, but must be different from the source channel. Otherwise, when the send effect signal is combined with the channel signal, there will be comb filtering and signal cancellation effects (on rare occasions this can be cool, but most of the time it's a problem).

> In case you're thinking "Well, I'll just use a delay for an insert effect and set it so the delay time is equal to the amount of effect send latency," that won't work because the effect send signal, regardless of whether it's pre- or post-fader, will come after the delay anyway.

As a result, this leaves out using processors like harmonic exciters, compressors, limiters, or anything else that doesn't change the signal very much. However, distortion, reverb, ring modulation, etc. are all excellent candidates for send effects.

11.7.1 Distortion

Judicial amounts of distortion can add some "grit" and "bite" to the signals that pass through it and help "lift" them out of the mix.

When using distortion as a send effect, the trick is to pick a couple of instruments to be emphasized and bring up a little distortion behind them in the mix. Favorite candidates for this include vocals, drums, and particularly, bass. I believe this also helps bring back some of the distortion-related aspects of saturating analog magnetic tape, which we associate with "pushing" the sound.

Using distortion for obvious effects à la Nine Inch Nails is one thing; getting a subtle, warming effect takes some work with EQ. Not surprisingly, I favor using the QuadraFuzz because the multiband operation minimizes intermodulation distortion, which doesn't sound as pure in the context of a mix. Also, you can pull back on the QuadraFuzz high frequency band, which gives a smoother, rounder tone, thereby letting you bring up the distortion higher before it becomes noticeably ugly.

Cutting bass is another matter altogether. This produces a brittle, bright high end that is effective if mixed *way* in the background—treat it like an exciter with an attitude problem, and the levels should be just about right.

Another plug-in that I find very useful for a distortion-based send effect is PSP Audioware's Vintage Warmer. This provides a smooth type of overdrive sound, but also lets you reduce high frequencies if needed.

11.7.2 Vocoder

Using a Vocoder as a send effect is remarkably cool for dance music. For those who haven't yet played with Cubase's vocoder effect (found under "Other" in the effects pop-up menu), it makes "talking instrument" sounds—sort of like the talkbox effect that was so popular in the 70s (Peter Frampton, Stevie Wonder, Joe Walsh).

The Vocoder is really not intended to be used as a send effect, but there is one application where it works just fine: using the internal vocoder carrier signal (basically, a synthesizer) and modulating it with an external audio track, such as drums or some other percussive sound.

If the drums are all on one audio track, then you can use the Vocoder as an insert effect for that track. This would also allow you to modulate a second audio signal with the drums (this is all explained in the Cubase Operation Manual help file). However, what happens if the kick is on one track, snare on another, toms on a third track, the hi-hats on a fourth, etc.? You will probably want to include some sounds, like the kick and snare, but exclude the hi-hats.

By inserting the vocoder as a Send Effect, you can send it signal from only the kick and snare track, in whatever proportion you want. Meanwhile, set up a MIDI track to drive the carrier (set the MIDI track out to Vocoder). Record your playing on the MIDI keyboard or other MIDI controller, and you'll have some cool, rhythmically-modulated synth sounds.

11.7.3 Short Delays

Short delays are a useful supplement to conventional reverb. Using a combination of room reverb and short delays can build a bigger ambience than just adding more or less "standard" reverb, as the tracks with more short delays generate the equivalent of more early reflections.

Another technique is to use only short delays to create ambience effects, as described later in the section "The New Ambience."

11.7.4   Ring Modulator

Ring modulation adds a "klangorous," metallic sound and is generally used as an insert effect. However, adding it as a Send Effect and sending multiple channels into it, can make the sound even ruder and nastier.

11.7.5   Using "Outside World" Analog Send Effects

If you have a favorite analog effect that you want to use with Cubase (like a high-end hardware reverb), no problem. A send effect can be assigned to any of the available busses (see the chapter "Interfacing with the Physical World" on page 399 for more info about busses), and there's no reason this bus couldn't feed an external analog effect, whose output patches back into Cubase. However, as soon as a signal leaves Cubase's controlled digital environment and ventures out into the analog work, latency becomes an issue—more so than latency within Cubase's virtual environment itself. At the very least, there will be a 1 to 2ms delay caused by going through a D/A converter to the analog device, followed by returning through an A/D converter.

In some cases, this won't matter—an extra millisecond of pre-delay going to a reverb, or a 1ms delay in the reverb output is pretty much inconsequential. But if you're using something like a compressor, the sound is similar enough to the dry sound that you might hear problems, such as comb filtering, caused by the compressed signal being slightly delayed.

One workaround is to bounce to a Cubase track through the analog processor. Once the track is recorded, you can simply advance it to compensate for any delay. If it's essential that you monitor the effect in real time rather than bounce it to disk (for example, if you want to play the controls as part of the mix), here's a second option: bounce the track you want to process, then advance that before sending it out a bus to the signal processor. After the advanced track gets delayed by the signal processor, it should all line up okay.

Part 5

Specific Techniques

Chapter 12

Re-Amping and Live Monitoring

Wouldn't it be great if you could choose a guitar's amp tone while mixing down instead of being locked in to the tone you used while recording? Well it *is* great, and thanks to plug-in technology, it's possible as well.

12.1 About Re-Amping

For years, engineers and guitarists have used a technique called "re-amping." With this, a guitarist splits the guitar signal in two: one feed goes direct to an amp, and the other goes straight into the recorder via a direct box. As the guitarist plays, the amp signal is recorded—but so is the straight signal, on a separate track.

During mixdown, if the amp track sounds fine, that's great. But if not, the engineer can mute the amp track, feed the straight track's output into a different amp, then record the output of the other amp. Or, another option is to keep the original amp track, but add a new amp track to get stereo or layered effects.

This raises a question: as the sound can be changed later, why not just record the straight signal and not even worry about the amp? The reason is that most guitar players need the aural satisfaction of a good amp sound while playing. Also, if the guitarist uses feedback to create sustain, then that sustain influences the straight sound, and the sustained straight signal gets recorded as well.

12.2 Monitoring through Cubase

Cubase makes traditional re-amping unnecessary, thanks to the use of plug-ins and low-latency audio interfaces. With older, slower audio interfaces, monitoring through plug-ins was impractical due to latency. There would be the delay of converting analog to digital, then the delay caused by going through the plug-in and program, then additional delay while converting from digital back to analog.

Unfortunately, there will always be delay due to the analog-to-digital and digital-to-analog conversion process. Fortunately, this is typically under 1.5ms—no big deal. However, with today's fast computers, the latency added by going through a plug-in running in Cubase, even when added to the conversion latency, can still be well under 3 to 4ms. To put things in perspective, 3ms of latency is about the same as the delay that would occur from a sound wave travelling 1 meter (3 feet). In other words, the amount of delay is about the same as if you moved your head 1 meter further away from your amp—not serious at all, and not really enough to affect the "feel" of your playing.

In my experience, if the overall latency is less than 5ms, playing through a plug-in will not be a problem. In the range of 5 to 10ms, you might find the amount of delay a little bit disconcerting. Above 10ms, this technique doesn't really work because you hear more of an echo. In this case, I suggest using traditional re-amping techniques where the guitarist plays through an amp, and you record both the amp and straight signals simultaneously to Cubase.

12.3 A Practical Example: Recording Guitar

Let's suppose you're recording a guitar part in Cubase. Here's how you would record while monitoring through a plug-in (e.g., Steinberg Warp VST guitar amp, IK Multimedia AmpliTube guitar amp, QuadraFuzz, etc.).

1 Create a track and assign its input to the input being fed by the guitar.

2 Click on the track's Record and Monitor (Speaker icon) buttons so that the track is record-ready and in monitor mode.

You have a choice of several monitoring modes; go FILE > PREFER-ENCES > VST and click on the arrow in the Auto Monitoring field. I generally choose Tapemachine Style, as this automatically enables input monitoring while stopped and recording, but monitors the recorded track on playback.

3 Play your guitar and check the track's meter to verify that it's receiving the guitar signal.

4 Open up the track's VST Channel Settings window by clicking on the "e" button.

5 Add the desired Insert Effect plug-in. Now when you play, you should hear the guitar being processed by the plug-in.

6 Start recording.

The key to what makes "virtual re-amping" possible is that Cubase records the straight guitar signal to the track. So, any processing that occurs depends entirely on the plug-in(s) you've selected; you can process the guitar in any way you'd like during the mixdown process, including changing "virtual amps."

Also note that you can use the VST Channel Settings EQ as well as set level and pan in the mixer to get a better idea of how the instrument will integrate with the final mix.

12.4 Other Applications

Although we've presented everything in a guitar re-amping context, monitoring through plug-ins has other uses:

■ Vocalists often like to hear themselves with compression, reverb, EQ, etc. while singing. By monitoring through Cubase, they can hear what their voice will sound like through particular plug-ins. And of course, these can be changed on mixdown.

- Session musicians don't have to bring their effects racks or other processors if they don't want to; they can use the plug-ins within Cubase.

- Bassists are used to recording direct, but with this technique, they can monitor through more of an amp sound.

- If you want to use an effect like tempo-synched delay on a drummer, that will influence the part that gets played. By monitoring through Cubase, the drummer can hear the effect the delay will have on the drum part and play accordingly.

12.5 ASIO Direct Monitoring

Another way to monitor, ASIO Direct Monitoring, requires an ASIO2-compatible audio interface. However, this does not allow for virtual re-amping, as the signal appearing at the audio interface input is simply directed to the audio interface output (however, enabling or disabling can be controlled from within Cubase). The advantage of this approach is that it allows for near instantaneous input signal monitoring, and computer latency is not an issue. However, I'm willing to put up with a few milliseconds of delay to take advantage of the benefits of doing virtual re-amping.

Chapter 13

Pseudo-Multiband Compression

Multiband compressors are powerful tools; they allow focusing on a specific frequency band and compressing just that band. In extreme examples, you can do something like zero in on one tom, compress it, and pull it forcefully into the mix.

Cubase does not include a true multiband compressor, but this application shows how to use parallel compression or limiting to emphasize a specific range of frequencies. For example, older samplers that lack high frequency "sparkle" or drum machines that need a solid low-end whomp, can benefit greatly.

The basic idea is to duplicate the track, tailor the duplicate's frequency response with EQ to isolate the range you want to compress, then send this track to a dynamics-oriented Send Effect. (This is necessary because in Cubase it is not possible to switch the EQ pre-insert effect. If this was possible, you could simply use a dynamics processor as an insert effect.) This sounds simple enough, but there are several subtleties that can influence the sound even further.

13.1   Setting Up

Here's how to set up the pseudo-multiband compression.

1   Duplicate the track you want to process by right-clicking on the track in the Track List and selecting Duplicate Track.

2 Solo the duplicate track so you can hear the results of the EQ tweaks you are about to do.

3 Call up the VST Channel Settings.

4 Adjust the EQ to emphasize the range of frequencies you want to compress or limit.

5 Call up the VST Send Effects window and insert the dynamics processor of your choice (e.g. Dynamics, which has lower latency than VST-Dynamics).

6 On the VST Channel Settings window, make sure the effect send is post-fader and up all the way. Pull the channel fader all the way down.

7 Now loop the section you want to process so you can easily adjust the dynamics settings.

8 Adjust the Effects Master slider to taste for the desired amount of compressed/limited signal.

9 If you're using the Compressor, adjust the parameters as desired. If you're using the Limiter, there may not be enough input level to initiate limiting as much as you might like. To fix this, enable the Compress button, set Threshold to 0.00 and ratio to 1.0:1, and use the compressor's MakeUp Gain control to boost the level going to the limiter. You can also use the Compressor and Limiter, as shown in the following screen shot.

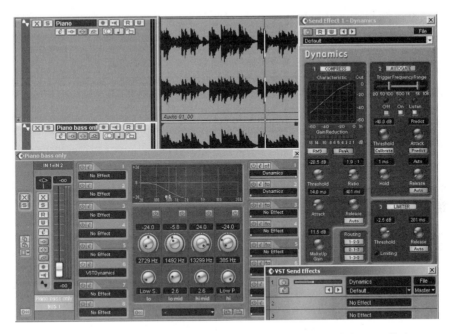

The lower track contains the duplicated audio. Its main channel fader is pulled down, and the pre-fader signal goes through low-pass EQ prior to going to the dynamics send effect.

CD track 15 first plays a sampled piano by itself, which is definitely lacking bass. Next you'll hear the same part in a duplicated track, set to compress only the bass range. Finally, the two tracks play together. Note how the final piano example sounds much fuller than the original one.

13.2 Which Filter Type?

For general high or low frequency processing, I prefer using the high pass or low pass filter option respectively (available by setting the bandwidth control for the highest and lowest EQ stages fully clockwise or counterclockwise), because this restricts the frequency response to just the range to be processed. Shelving also works well if you don't want the range to be quite so isolated. Of course, if you're looking to compress a fairly specific range of frequencies, a parametric stage will do the job.

Typical settings are hard to give, because "your mileage may vary" depending on the material. However, here are some guidelines.

For a high frequency lift, start off with a high pass corner frequency of around 1 to 2kHz. For low frequency emphasis, I generally use this technique to add a sort of "pseudo-subwoofer effect," so the corner frequency ends up being quite low—around 100Hz or so. Anything higher can make the sound overly "tubby." (The low frequency boost is particularly useful when using a loop that originated on vinyl; low frequencies were often rolled off to keep the vinyl cutter from freaking out.)

As to the compressor settings, because the compressor is post-EQ, it's not seeing a lot of signal, particularly if you're working on the high frequencies. Start with a ratio of around 3:1 to 5:1, and the threshold will be quite low (sometimes under −40dB or so). As with any type of dynamics control, check the gain reduction meter: you want a maximum of around 3 to 6dB of gain reduction.

Midrange band compression is much trickier. Here you need one parametric stage to select the band to be processed and use whatever you have available to cut the frequencies higher and lower than the selected band. In general, this "pseudo-multiband compression" technique works best with high and low frequency processing, but I mention the midrange option for the experimentally-minded.

13.3   Final Tweaks

As you tweak, start off by soloing just the additional channel(s). With high frequency emphasis, the sound will be very tinny. Set the compression to avoid an overly squeezed sound; it's particularly important to include around 5 to 10ms of attack time so the compression doesn't nuke all the transients. The same general advice goes for low end processing, but remember to select only the very lowest frequencies. If you can hear too much of the music, the overall result will be muddy.

Now turn down the duplicated channel and bring up the main channel. Listen to the unprocessed material for a while as a "reality check." Slowly bring up the duplicate channel until there's just the right amount of processing, then bring the faders back a dB or two just to make sure you're not going overboard—done.

By the way, although I've emphasized using the compressor post-EQ, also try using the compressor or limiter as an insert effect and go for a pre-EQ setting. Personally I've found this to be the less satisfying than post-EQ, but it does create its own sound that might work for some applications.

Finally, if latency is an issue, you may need to nudge the original track back in time just a tiny bit.

Chapter 14

Creating "Virtual Mics"

I often record acoustic rhythm guitars with one mic for three reasons: faster setup time, no issues with phase cancellation s among multiple mics, and besides, these parts tend to sit more in the background anyway. I then add some ambience with electronic delay and reverb to obtain a somewhat bigger sound. However, on an album project with classical guitarist Linda Cohen, the guitar was definitely the "up front" instrument in many tunes and required a somewhat different approach.

Due to a very tight schedule, rather than experiment with multiple mics and deal with phase and ambience issues, we decided to go for the most accurate sound we could extract from one high-quality, condenser mic. This was successful, in the sense that moving from the control room to the studio sounded virtually identical.

Upon starting the mix, though, the sound was—well, *too* accurate. It sounded like an expensive mic picking up a guitar in a studio with good acoustics, not a friend sitting in front of you in her living room.

I fooled around with various techniques to make the guitar sound somewhat more intimate, including adding ambience. Nothing clicked until I thought about what you actually hear when sitting in front of a guitar, which provided some valuable clues on getting the desired sound.

14.1 A Question of Image

A classical guitar doesn't have a wide stereo image if you hear it from more than a 2 to 3 meters away, but up close, it's a different story. If you're facing a guitarist, your right ear picks up on some of the finger squeaks and string noise from the guitarist's fretting hand. Meanwhile, your left ear picks up some of the body's "bass boom." Although not as directional as the high-frequency finger noise, it still shifts the lower spectra somewhat to the left. Meanwhile, the main guitar sound fills the room, providing the acoustic equivalent of a "center channel."

Simulating these effects started with copying the original guitar track to two more tracks. The first copy had a drastic treble cut and was panned somewhat left. The second copy had an equally drastic bass cut and went a bit toward the right.

Adding these two tracks had two immediate effects. First, it pulled out some of the "finger squeaks" and "boom" components that were in the original sound and positioned them in a more realistic stereo location. Second, it stretched out the stereo image somewhat. Because these were signals extracted from one mic, there were none of the phasing problems associated with multiple mic setups.

14.2   Real World Settings

The original guitar track had a −6dB cut at 225Hz, where the guitar exhibited a strong resonant peak. It was also necessary to add a −3dB cut at around 100Hz after pulling the bass-heavy channel into the mix.

The track with the "squeak" component used a highpass filter that cut off the low end starting around 3kHz, with 11dB of total cut. A parametric stage, set to −24dB at 220Hz, took out some additional low end. The end result was a bright, articulated, low-level sound, panned somewhat to the right.

The main EQ for the "boom" channel was a lowpass filter that started a sharp cutoff from 350Hz on up. An additional shelf added a mild 3dB of boost, kicking in at 125Hz. This comes in a little closer to center than the squeak channel.

These three EQ curves, when panned as described and mixed for the proper balance, create a much larger guitar image that belies the fact it was recorded with a single mic.

Regarding the mix of these three elements, the drastic amounts of high-pass and lowpass filtering on the duplicated channels brings their overall levels way down, even without touching the channel fader. In isolation, it sounds as if their impact would be non-existent due to the low level and restricted frequency range. But if you mix them in with the main channel, the entire sound comes to life.

CD track 16 plays the first figure in mono; after the short pause, the same material repeats but using the channel EQ/splitting technique described in this section. The difference isn't huge, but the second figure definitely has a more ambient, bigger sound. This difference is particularly obvious when listening with headphones.

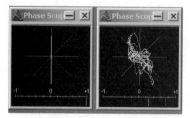

The left picture shows the phase relationship of the mono section. As expected, there's no difference between the two channels, as represented by the straight vertical line. The right picture shows that there are indeed significant differences between the left and right channels, which is why the sound is more spacious and has better stereo imaging.

14.3   Adding Subtle Delay

To further differentiate the added channels, I nudged the squeaks about 5ms late compared to the main track and the boom about 5ms early. Granted, this is enough to reach into the "phase cancellation" zone—5ms is the period of a 200Hz wave, and a guitar's lowest frequency is just under 100Hz—but both of the extra channels were sitting far back enough in the mix that the delay added a slight bit of "room realism," without causing other problems. Careful monitoring in mono as well as stereo confirmed that the phase shift issue wasn't a problem.

You might wonder why I didn't just use three mics and good miking technique in the first place. Well, that certainly is an option, and possibly the most desirable one. But it's not the only option. Three mics is three times the noise, three times the preamps, and three times the variations in frequency response. Also, if you depend on mic placement for this specific a sound, you're pretty much locked into it, and it's harder to change after the fact if the nature of the finished song demands something else.

The technique described above is almost like adding "virtual mics," but mics that are designed to pick up only one specific element of an instrument. Adding the 5ms delay is equivalent to putting the mic 5 feet away from the instrument, which also helps add some of the intimate feel. So in a way, we're adding ambience, but it's a frequency-dependent ambience.

I've started to use this technique in other ways, such as adding a high-frequency "virtual mic" to some percussion parts to help spread their stereo image a bit, which allows them to be placed a little lower overall in the mix. You can also obtain mammoth tom sounds by splitting off a little of the bass component, delaying it very slightly, and panning it a little off from the main tom sound.

However, the key to all this seems to be not so much to boost the part of the spectrum you want to emphasize, but to cut the parts you *don't* want to emphasize. Boosting adds an unnatural element, whereas cutting gives a more natural sound. This is why the highpass and lowpass filters responses were used as the main filtering elements.

No matter how you use this technique, though, check it out when working with acoustic instruments. It can add an intimacy and spaciousness that is difficult, if not impossible, to achieve using only reverb or other delays.

Chapter 15

Modeling Acoustic Spaces with Short Delays

The reverb-drenched sound of the 60s and 70s is well behind us, as is the chorused gauziness of the 80s. The current tendency is toward high-definition, "in your face" sounds; you hear less and less reverb on records.

But although reverb isn't as common as it once was, we're still used to instruments having some "air," both from resonances within the instruments themselves and from the room in which they are played. Listen to a drum machine that was recorded direct into Cubase or a drum plug-in with no processing: yes, the sound is clean—but there's also a certain deadness. The stereo is *too* wide, and drums become individual points of sound instead of being part of a cohesive, unified kit. With more and more sounds being recorded direct or being generated during mixdown from plug-ins, this is becoming an increasingly important issue.

Fortunately, there's an easy and predictable way to give your electronic sounds some air—model a room.

15.1 The New Ambience

While "modeling" is sort of a buzzword, the concept has been around for a while. Any electronic reverb is essentially modeling what happens when sound waves run around loose in a room.

Recording in a very tight, sparse, hard "box" of a room is one way to get that in-your-face sound. Back in the very early days of digital delay, one technique to simulate this kind of ambience was to put several delays (with delay times of 1 to 10ms or so) in parallel. Mixing these delays well in the background creates the "comb filtering" effects associated with typical small rooms.

Although most of today's reverbs, including the ones in Cubase SX/SL, tend to optimize the room, plate, spring, and hall reverb simulations for fairly long decays with lots of reflections, there are workarounds if you want to experiment with short delays.

Cubase includes two delays suitable for this application: ModDelay and DoubleDelay. The basic idea is to use several delays as Send Effects (set to processed sound only—no dry sound), model your room with them, and then feed in some drum signal.

Two DoubleDelays set up as Send Effects. These can add "room ambience" to sounds that were recorded direct, or to plug-ins that include no processing.

15.2   Typical DoubleDelay Parameter Values

Our first example requires two DoubleDelays used as send effects. Try these values as a point of departure:

	Fedbck	Pan1	Pan2	DlyTim1	DlyTim2	Mix
DoubleDelay 1	50%	−40%	−100%	5ms	7ms	100%
DoubleDelay 2	50%	+40%	+100%	3ms	9ms	100%

This option seems to work best with the short delays panned closer to center, and longer delays panned left and right. However, feel free to experiment—even small changes in pan and delay settings can make a big difference in the sound.

The effect this produces is called "comb filtering," and most of the time, we try to get that effect out of our recordings. However, this effect is so tied in with the sound of miking an instrument in a small room with hard surfaces, that psycho-acoustically a little comb filtering makes our brain says "Aha! This was recorded in a small room with hard surfaces!"

Of course, you need not limit yourself to two DoubleDelays—you can add even more to create a more complex "room" with additional reflections.

15.3 Typical ModDelay Parameter Values

This next example is based on ModDelay settings. The main difference here is that the ModDelay, because of the modulation, gives a less "hard" and more diffused sound. It sounds like the room is a little bigger and softer. Also, comb filtering is less of an issue (although you should still check the master output in mono). Here are some suggested values:

	Fedbck	DlyMod	DlyTim	Mix
ModDelay 1	50%	6%	8ms	100%
ModDelay 2	50%	7%	5ms	100%

Like the example with the DoubleDelays, the ModDelays are also installed as Send Effects.

The slow modulation effect adds a bit of animation that dynamically colors the sound. To change the room characteristics, try other delay times between 1 and 15ms.

> CD track 17 first plays a drum part with no delays. After a one-second pause, the next section uses fixed short delays, followed by a one-second pause, then mod delay with 5+8ms of delay, another pause, and finally, mod delay with 10+12ms of delay.

15.4 Additional Short Delay Tips

- If you turn up the aux returns to obtain lots of processed signal, beware of phase cancellations. Although the whole point of this exercise is to add the phase cancellation/addition effects found in the average room, high levels of processed signal can cause excessive cancellation. At some point, solo the drums and check the master output in the mono position. Confirm that the sound is still acceptable. The likelihood of any thinness occurring will be most likely in the bass range, so you may want to use the VST EQ to add a slight bass "bump."

- A little bit of delay is all you need. Just a subtle feeling of ambience is enough to persuade the listener that the sound is more "real."

- With mostly mono source material, this technique will tend to give better stereo imaging. With stereo source material, using short delays may "monoize" the signal and make the stereo spread less obvious. In some situations, this a benefit as it provides an overall sonic ambience for the drums.

- These types of delays can sound good on vocals, but there's still nothing like a nice, warm chamber for wrapping around a voice. I always have at least two reverb devices available—one to create these short, ambient delays, and the other a more traditional plate sound for vocals. This gives the best of both worlds. Sometimes I'll use both sounds on an instrument.

15.5   Gourmet Short Delay

Before leaving the subject of delay, note that technology has transformed the delay lines of old into entirely new identities. For example, Native Instruments' Spektral Delay plug-in splits the signal into hundreds of bands, each of which can have its own delay time and feedback. These are relatively short delays, and therefore can impart a variety of tonal and arpeggiated effects that are quite stunning. The examples on the CD will give you an idea of how delay can be used for far more than just echoes.

CD track 18 shows off what the Native Instruments Spektral Delay plug-in can do. The first part is a straight piano sound, followed by the same part played three more times through different effects.

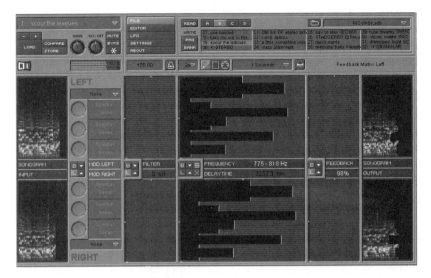

The Spektral Delay combines filtering and delay into a very versatile and novel plug-in. Each channel can have radically different parameters if desired.

Chapter 16

Automation in Cubase

Back in the days of analog consoles, automation was extremely expensive. For the few who could afford it, though, automation simplified the mixing process to a previously unimaginable extent. No longer did you have to worry about blowing a mix because you forgot to mute a bad note toward the end: you just programmed a mute to do the job for you.

Cubase VST's automation was useful, but quite primitive; mix automation data was stored in a single, difficult-to-edit track. On the other hand, Cubase SX and SL's automation is modern, intuitive, and efficient. For audio and group tracks, you can automate level, pan, mute, EQ, FX send (on/off, level, pre-post), insert effect program selection and parameter values, and more. MIDI tracks implement automation similarly, but of course have a different repertoire of parameters they can control (including volume, pan, mute, transpose, etc.).

There's also master automation for master gain, left and right levels for all master busses, and send effects master input levels. Furthermore, soft synth plug-in parameters can be automated (which show up on a dedicated automation track), as can signal processing plug-in parameters (these appear as automation sub-tracks of the tracks they're processing). All automation tracks are editable in several ways.

Each of these types of automation (audio/group, master, and instrument) has a corresponding automation track.

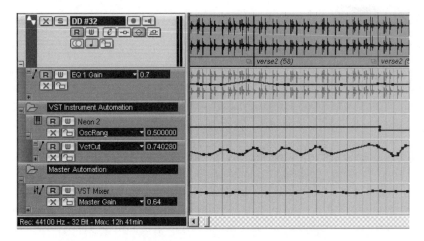

The audio track at the top has an automation subtrack for EQ gain. As VST instruments don't have an associated audio track, automation sub-tracks are dumped into a folder track called VST Instrument Automation. Each instrument within the folder has its own sub-tracks for automation. Finally, the track at the bottom is the Master Automation track.

What makes automation so wonderful while mixing is that it allows adding nuanced expressions to electronically-oriented music. Of course, automation has been used for levels and mutings for decades, and when MIDI came along, automation of outboard MIDI gear parameters became possible. But now with automatable signal processing plug-ins, we can impart greater expressiveness within a sequencing environment like Cubase. And don't forget that you can overdub (and edit) automation data so you can tweak one parameter to perfection, then another, and so on.

We'll start with an overview of automation options, then segue into some typical applications. I highly recommend reading the section on Automation in the Operation Manual, as it's very clear. This allows us to get more into applications rather than simply re-state the manual.

16.1 Cubase Automation Methods

Cubase has three main automation methods: recording on-screen control motion in real-time, drawing envelopes (offline editing), and recording/editing MIDI controller messages (can be in real time or offline). VST instrument automation was covered briefly earlier in the book, but we'll expand on the subject here.

16.1.1 Method 1: Record On-screen Control Motion

Steinberg calls this Write/Read automation. This type of automation accommodates the human touch; you can push changes to the beat and work intuitively—as well as go back and edit your moves if touch-ups are needed.

But this requires a low-latency system, or there will be a disconcerting lag between moving the control and hearing the parameter change. Also, you're limited to moving one parameter at a time when using a mouse (another reason why you might want to invest in a control surface—see the chapter "Using Hardware Control Surfaces" on page 383).

You'll find "R" (read) and "W" (write) icons on the VST Channel, next to mixer faders, and along the top of plug-ins and soft synths. Click on "W" when you want to write automation data by moving controls; click on "R" to have Cubase read that automation data.

The VST Dynamics and QuadraFuzz are patched into the Audio 01 channel. If you click on "R" or "W" in anything that's part of a channel, automation data is recorded for anything within that channel. The VST instrument automation is independent of any particular channel. In this case, Neon's "R" is lit, indicating that it can read automation.

There are three automation recording modes; let's describe them, as well as how you'd use them.

A pop-up menu lets you choose among the three automation modes.

- With "Touch Fader," automation begins when you click on a parameter and continues for as long as the mouse button is held down. This is the "standard" automation method because it's easy to avoid overwriting previous automation information—just release the mouse button. In particular, when writing automation over a section that loops, if you release the mouse button at the end of the loop you don't have to worry about overwriting automation data at the beginning.

- "Autolatch" is the same, except that automation isn't turned off until you click on the "W" icon to de-select write mode or stop playback. You have to be careful with this mode, because if you move another control accidentally, it will continue to overwrite any existing automation data until stopped (if this happens, remember to undo immediately). This isn't so much an issue when automating with Cubase, but rather if you use an external fader box or controller, where it can be easy to brush against a control accidentally. Speaking of remote control, this is the preferred mode to use because the mouse button is not a part of the process.

- "X-Over" is the same as Autolatch, except that automation turns off if the new automation curve crosses over an older automation curve. This is useful in situations where you want to preserve some parts of the existing automation while overwriting others.

  For example, suppose you're automating level for a rhythm guitar part. You bring the level down a bit behind the vocal, then fade up again just before the solo hits. You then decide that you really need the level a bit higher behind the vocal, but you want to retain the automation data for the part that fades up into the solo. So you go into X-Over mode and record the new data; when the fade-in part of the curve crosses over the value of the data you're writing, and if the mouse button is released while this happens, Write mode is automatically disabled. If you keep holding the mouse button down, new data will be written regardless of whether there are crossovers or not.

In any event, note that the "R" and "W" buttons can be on simultaneously so the program can read existing automation while you write new automation. Whether and how old information will be overwritten depends on the automation mode you've chosen, as described previously.

Here's the specific procedure to record control moves:

1   Select the desired automation mode, as described above. In most cases you'll use Touch Fader.

2   Click on the "W" (write) icon in the plug-in. This enables automation writing. Cubase does not need to be in record mode; recording automation is a separate process that's determined by the status of the "W" button.

3   As Cubase plays, manipulate the controls as desired.

4   End automation as required for the method of automation you've chosen (e.g. release mouse button, turn off "W" icon, stop playback, or have it occur automatically if in X-Over mode).

5   Prior to playback, click on the "R" (read) icon in the plug-in. The automation moves you recorded will play back.

Some parameters produce small clicks or other glitches as they're changed. This is a technical limitation for which there is no workaround.

16.1.2 Method 2: Envelope Control

Moving an on-screen control while recording automation creates a corresponding automation envelope. You can see this by clicking on the small "+" symbol in a track's lower right corner. This "unfolds" the automation track, and then turns into a "–" symbol, indicated that if you click on it, the track folds up again.

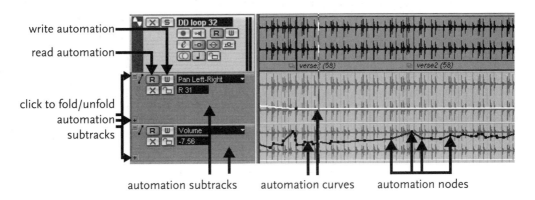

This shows an audio track, with two of its automation sub-tracks "unfolded." You can unfold as many sub-tracks as you like, as well as select any automation parameter within a single sub-track.

Once unfolded, you can edit an automation sub-track's parameters (or draw a new curve from scratch), as well as choose which parameter to edit. Cubase has a particularly rich selection of ways to view or hide automation:

■ You can select any of the available automation parameters for editing within a single subtrack—just click on the parameter name, and a pop-up list lets you select the parameter for editing. Selecting a parameter does not erase or eliminate other parameters, which remain "in the background."

- Within the pop-up menu, parameters with automation data are marked with an asterisk (*). From this menu you can also choose to remove automation sub-tracks with unused parameters.

- You can view as many automation sub-tracks as you want by unfolding more sub-tracks.

- Note that a "ghosted" graphic of the audio track is behind the automation, making it easy to correlate automation to audio events.

- By right-clicking on the blank space within a track in the Track List, you can choose to Show Used Automation for All Tracks, or Hide All Automation.

Drawing and editing envelopes is simple:

- Click anywhere on the curve with the standard arrow cursor to add a "breakpoint" (node).

- Click on the node and drag to move.

- To draw an envelope, click on the Pencil tool. Note that if you click on the little arrow in the Pencil icon, you can choose various drawing tools—draw repeating waveforms (sine, triangle, square), straight lines, or parabolic changes.

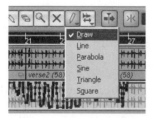

The Pencil tool offers numerous drawing options. The periodic waveforms can sync to the current snap value, assuming snap is enabled.

- Nodes can snap to grid, or turn off the grid to move them around freely.

- To delete a single node, click on it and hit the keyboard's ⌦ or ← key.
- To delete multiple nodes, draw a selection marquee around them, or shift-click on the nodes to be deleted. Then hit the ⌦ or ←.

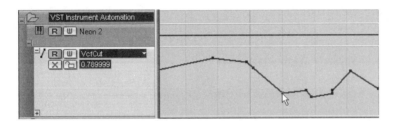

This envelope affects the VCF cutoff for the Neon synthesizer. Virtual instrument automation shows up within its own folder track; plug-in signal processor automation becomes a sub-track for the track being processed.

Note that as moving controls creates envelopes and drawing envelopes moves the on-screen controls they affect, these methods are somewhat interchangeable. The method to use depends on the application. If I wanted to add a wa-wa effect, I'd go for recording control motion; but the envelope approach works better to add automation changes that need to be synched precisely to the beat (like having a volume swell that ends right on the beat).

16.1.3 Method 3: Recording MIDI Data from an External Control Box

Most Cubase parameters accept MIDI data sent from an external hardware controller (see also the chapter "Using Hardware Control Surfaces" on page 383). Using an external controller for automation follows the same basic procedure as recording a control's on-screen motion, because the on-screen control is mirroring the external controller. Therefore, after setting up a parameter to respond to an external control signal, simply place the associated track in Write mode, and the data will appear as an automation sub-track—just as if you'd moved an onscreen fader.

A related method also works with soft synths. For example, suppose a soft synth's filter cutoff responds to controller #74. Set your hardware controller to generate controller #74, then record the controller into the MIDI track that drives the soft synth. On playback, the MIDI controller messages will drive the synthesizer and also appear as standard controller data within the MIDI track.

16.2   Applying Automation

Okay, now that you know how to automate, here are some of my favorite plug-in automation tricks.

16.2.1   Better Chorusing and Flanging

I'm not a fan of the whoosh-whoosh-whoosh of LFO-driven choruses. Even when tempo-synched, the repetition can get more boring than AM radio.

There are two simple workarounds. One is to vary the LFO rate control so that it's constantly in motion rather than locked into one tempo. The other is to set the LFO to a very slow rate, or turn off LFO modulation entirely, and automate the Initial Delay parameter. Play with the delay so the effect rises and falls in a musically appropriate way. Sometimes it's worth overdubbing a second control track with automated feedback (regeneration).

16.2.2   Creative Distortion Crunch

With distortion plug-ins, usually the input level control sets the degree of "crunchiness." For those times when you want to kick up the intensity without causing a massive increase in volume, turn up the plug-in's "drive" control or equivalent to add crunch. Assuming the signal is already clipping, turning it up more will create a more crunched sound but without an excessive level increase. With the DaTube and Overdrive plug-ins, use the "Drive" control. With the QuadraFuzz, use the "Gain" control, which affect all stages simultaneously.

If the distortion plug-in's drive parameter cannot be automated for some reason, use the distortion effect as a Send Effect rather than as an Insert Effect. As Cubase can automate the effects send going to the bus, this can vary the input level to the distortion plug-in, thereby altering the "crunch factor." Of course you need to give up an aux bus, but it's worth it.

16.2.3   Delay Feedback

This was the application that sold me on the concept of effects automation, and it remains one of my favorites. I often use synchronized echo effects on solos, and heighten the intensity at the solo's peaks by increasing the amount of delay feedback. This creates a sort of "sea of echoes" effect. Sometimes, I also bump up the delay mix a bit so there's more delay and less straight signal.

Actually, any feedback control can benefit from automation. For example, the Predatohm plug-in (by Ohm Force) is one of my favorite plug-ins. Its combination of multiband compression and hardcore distortion with feedback is just the thing for some really powerful, industrially-slanted effects. But its controls, particularly the Feedback Amount parameter, can be touchy. Using automation to bring this up and create the feedback effect, then reduce the feedback before it becomes overbearing, works really well. I also like to automate the Feedback Frequency, especially making it rise or fall slowly over the length of a loop.

16.2.4   The Parametric Wah-Wah

On one of my earliest sessions, the producer decided I should have recorded my guitar with a wah-wah effect. I was ready to re-record the part, but the engineer said not to worry, he'd create the wah-wah effect in the mix. He inserted a parametric EQ, turned up the resonance, and swept the frequency control during the mixdown.

It sounded pretty good, but I must say it didn't sound like a real wah-wah. That's because a parametric EQ has a flat response, with the peak poking above it. A real wah-wah *rejects* frequencies around the resonant peak so you don't hear anything except the peak.

But it is possible to create a very realistic wah-wah effect with Cubase. Here's how:

1   Duplicate the track to which you want to add the effect.

2   Select all events in the copied track.

3   Go AUDIO > PROCESS > PHASE REVERSE.

4   You will be warned that the audio duplicates existing audio. Click on "New Version" so that he processing applies only to the selected events.

5   Click on Play—you won't hear anything because the two tracks cancel each other out. You can verify this by changing the level slightly on one of the tracks, at which point you'll hear audio.

6   Call up the VST Channel for one of the tracks by clicking on the Edit ("e") button.

7   Enable one of the middle parametric stages, and as a starting point, set the controls as follows:
   ■ Bandwidth = 10 to 12
   ■ Boost = 14dB
   ■ Frequency = vary between around 200Hz to 1kHz

As you vary the frequency, you'll hear a pretty decent wah-wah effect. Write the automation as you vary the control.

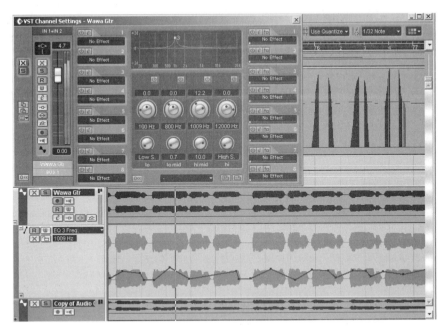

There are two guitar tracks, each identical but out of phase with each other. One channel has a parametric stage applied that boosts the midrange. As the equalized range is the only part that's not out of phase, that's the only part of the waveform you hear.

CD track 19 plays a straight guitar part (from a "Technoid Guitars" sample CD guitar preset, played via HALion), then through a shifting parametric frequency without cancellation effects, then through the "canceled" wah-wah effect described here.

Just for kicks, mute the track that doesn't have the parametric EQ enabled and play the part again. The effect is still cool, but it doesn't thin the sound out the way a real wah-wah does.

Because of the high gain and narrow bandwidth, watch out for distortion! You'll probably need to trim the controls very carefully. But at least you don't have to spray the wah-wah pedal potentiometer with contact cleaner.

16.2.5 Sample-and-hold Effects

While we're in vintage-land, you can use the same concept to create synth-like sample-and-hold effects right out of the 1970s.

A sample-and-hold synth module would sample (at a sub audio rate) a waveform and create a control voltage equal to the value of the sample. It would then apply this to a resonant filter's center frequency and hold it for a particular duration (e.g. an eighth note). An eighth note later, it would take another sample and hold the filter at that new frequency.

The effect was a series of stepped filter changes—sort of like a quantized wah-wah pedal. Using the "imitation wah-wah" setup described previously produces a classic sort of resonant filter effect.

Creating a sample-and-hold "stairstep"-type automation control signal pretty much requires drawing an envelope, as you can't move a control fast enough to create instant filter frequency changes. Fortunately, Cubase has a great tool—a pencil that can draw in particular waveform shapes, synced to a particular rhythmic value. To do this:

1 Click on the arrow in the toolbar's Pencil icon.

2 There's a choice of several waveforms, including the one we want—square.

3 To choose the rhythmic value, enable Snap and select Snap to Grid. For the Grid, select Use Quantize then specify the quantize value.

4 Start drawing! If you get diagonal lines instead of squared-off edges, just draw over the diagonals. Pretty soon you'll get the hang of it.

5 To add variety of emphasize certain parts, change the quantize value as desired.

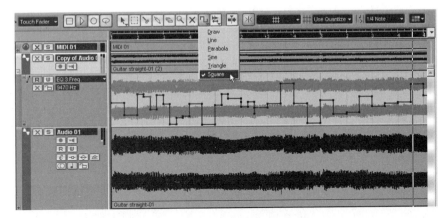

The concept is similar to the wah-wah, but the control signal is entirely different. Here, the pencil draws a square shape. Repeatedly drawing at different quantized resolutions produced the distinctive sample-and-hold pattern you see here.

CD track 20 first plays a power chord from the Technoid Guitars sample CD, then processes it with the sample-and-hold technique.

16.2.6 Envelope-based Tremolo

Amplitude changes are fun, but a tremolo is pretty limited. Instead, automate amplitude changes in time with the music by using the triangle pencil tool.

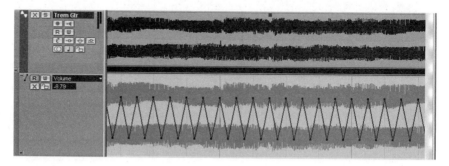

Having a track pulse rhythmically is easy to do—just draw in a tremolo waveform with the Pencil tool.

> CD Track 21 plays some power chords (again, from a Technoid Guitars sample CD preset) without processing, then with the rhythmic tremolo effect.

Of course, just because tremolo circuits in old guitar amps used sine or triangle waves doesn't mean you have to feel bound by tradition; you can use square waves here too. And when you have nothing better to do someday, write an email to Steinberg and say you want to see sawtooth and random waves added to the Pencil options as well.

Let's recap this section with a step-by-step example of adding processing to a guitar sound. We'll take a fairly non-descript guitar sound and make it bigger; check out the audio example.

> CD Track 22 plays the same rhythm guitar power chord six times as it traces the evolution of its sound through signal processing. The first chord is as the guitar was recorded. The second chord goes through

Sonic Foundry's Smooth/Enhance plug-in, which takes off some of the highs. The third chord goes through the VST parametric EQ to give a bit of an upper midrange lift. The fourth chord is processed by the compressor in Steinberg's Mastering Edition to give some more sustain, while the fifth chord goes through Steinberg's WunderVerb. Finally, the sixth chord goes through Steinberg's Stereo Expander plug-in; the seventh chord merely repeats the original first chord for comparison. The difference isn't huge, but the processed version has a wider stereo image, sounds more defined, and sits in a track better.

16.3 Applying Automation with Soft Synths

Cubase comes with an outstanding software synthesizer, Waldorf's A1 Analog Synth Unit. (Okay, it's not really analog, but it can sound that way.) It's very representative of what soft synths can do these days, and one of the key aspects is the ability to automate parameters for greater expressiveness. There's no need to have the sound always be static when, with a little automation, you can make it far more animated and lively.

The main reason why electronic sounds often aren't as interesting as acoustic sounds is that the latter evolve over time in a very complex way. Synthesizers tend to produce somewhat static sounds that fail to hold our interest after the initial attack transient; sampled sounds generally aren't much better since despite an interesting attack, they often settle down into a repetitive loop. Once you introduce variations in a sample to increase the degree of evolution over time, you'll be well on the way to producing more interesting sounds that can greatly increase the effectiveness of any mix.

As is standard with Cubase, you can automate the A1 with the Write/Read buttons and move onscreen faders, as well as draw envelopes, use MIDI control, or some combination of the three. Following are some tips on how to tweak synth parts on mixdown so they contribute to a greater overall feeling of motion and expressiveness.

- I love the sound of a guitar going into feedback, when it kicks up an octave or an octave+fifth higher. With the A1, set up your basic patch around Oscillator 1, tune Oscillator 2 an octave, octave+fifth, or two octaves higher, then automate its level. For example:

1 Call up the "Muhg WMF" lead patch on the A1.

2 Turn up Oscillator 2 two octaves.

3 Turn down the Oscillator 2 level control in the mixer.

4 As you play the keyboard, fade up the Osc 2 level toward the end of notes, like the way a guitar generates a sympathetic tone when it starts to feed back.

5 Add a little mod wheel vibrato to make the sound even more animated.

This is a typical chorus setting for fattening up an instrument sound: Frequency around 1Hz, delay around 2 to 5ms, and two stages of chorusing. Automating the Frequency and Delay parameters adds even more interest, especially when the A1's internal chorus is active.

- With some synths, a patch will use its second oscillator mostly to provide a fatter sound, so using it only to add emphasis as recommended above might make the sound too "thin" when the oscillator's level is down. One way to fatten up the sound is to add a chorus in the synth's mixer channel. The A1 already knows this trick, and includes an onboard chorus/flanger to fatten the sound—but you can take things even further by throwing in another chorus as well.

- A similar track works for bass sounds, but tune Osc 2 an octave lower, so turning up its level brings in a nice, fat suboctave. In this application, try using a sawtooth or pulse wave for the sub-harmonic. This increases its "presence" in the signal, increasing the sub-bass effect. I've also done the reverse in breaks—when the bass keeps going and the drums drop out, pull back on the sub-octave. Then, when the bass comes back in again, push the sub-octave and it will sound really big.

- You'll often find the chorus is engaged on the A1 for pads and other "large" patches. It can be very effective to automate the chorus Speed and Feedback controls slowly so that the pad is constantly changing and evolving. However, it's not a good idea to automate Depth, as it can introduce little spikey glitches when swept.

- For rhythmic synth tracks, like arpeggios or ostinato, three of my favorite parameters for automation are filter cutoff, filter envelope decay, and amplitude envelope decay. Changing these in real time can make what might be an overly-repetitive part far more interesting. When mixing, also try tweaking the control that ties velocity to filter cutoff if it wasn't used in the original recording. This too can add variety.

Chapter 17

The Wide World of Panning

Part of listening in the "real world" involves locating sounds in space. Although 5.1 surround sound excels at providing spatial cues, most of the world still runs on stereo, which has been with us for decades. While stereo's spatial options are limited to left, right, or somewhere in between, it remains an important part of recording and we need to make the most of it.

Consider what happens when you sit down and play the piano. There's a definite sense of lower notes emanating from the left and higher notes coming from the right. Try recording a piano in mono, then again in stereo. If properly miked, the stereo version will be far more realistic.

17.1 How Cubase Panning Differs for Stereo and Mono Tracks

The pan control works differently for stereo and mono audio tracks, as well as for MIDI. If you enable Write automation while moving the pan control, it creates an automation sub-track that contains the panning envelope.

> For fine pan adjustments, hold down ⌷shift⌷ when moving the fader.

- With mono tracks, pan places the track at a specific point within the stereo field—anywhere from full left to full right.
- With stereo tracks, moving the pan control off center to the right turns down the left channel until when all the way to the right you hear the right channel only and nothing from the left channel. Moving the pan

control toward the left works in the opposite manner—the right channel becomes progressively softer.

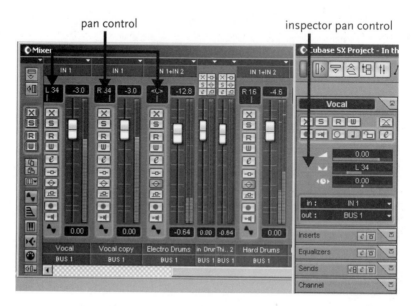

You can access the pan controls from the mixer, or for a particular channel via the Inspector. Note that if a mixer channel is in narrow mode, no pan control is visible.

There are situations where you may want to hear both stereo channels equally, but not spread them across the full stereo range. For example, suppose you have two rhythm guitar parts recorded in stereo. You might want one to span the range from left to center, while the other covers the range of center to right. This still gives a bit of a spread, but keeps the guitars spatially separate from each other.

The only way I've figured out to do this in Cubase is to save a stereo file as two separate mono files and bring each file into its own channel.

Wavelab, Steinberg's digital audio editor, makes it easy to save a stereo file as separate left and right channels. Go FILE > SAVE SPECIAL

(WAVE) > SAVE LEFT CHANNEL AS, name the channel, then click on "Save." Similarly, go FILE > SAVE SPECIAL (WAVE) > SAVE RIGHT CHANNEL AS, name the channel, and again click on "Save."

You will probably want to use the same effects, EQ settings, and effects send levels on both channels. So you don't have to do these settings from the ground up for each channel, Cubase has a useful shortcut to copy one channel's complete set of parameters to another channel.

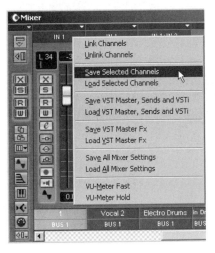

You can save all of a channel's parameter values as a file, then load those values into a different channel. This is also handy if you have a particular combination of EQ, effects, etc. that sound good with an instrument you record a lot.

1   Set up one of the channels exactly as desired and select only that channel.

2   Right-click on this channel in the mixer and select Save Selected Channels.

3   Save it under a distinctive name.

4 Select the other channel of the pair (the one that should have the same settings).

5 Right-click on it and select Load Selected Channels.

6 Navigate to the file you just saved, select it, then click on "Open."

7 Both channels will now have the same settings. Set the pan controls to create the desired stereo spread.

17.2 Panning and MIDI

With MIDI tracks, the mixer's pan control creates an automation sub-track and sends MIDI pan messages (standardized as controller #10). The plug-in being fed by the track should recognize these. Sub-track automation can also go to a MIDI port for controlling outboard gear. However, if you attempt to export this data as a Standard MIDI File, note data will be included but sub-track data will not.

With MIDI mixer channels, the pan controls are located in the same place as with audio channels—toward the upper left of the fader. As with audio panning, you can *ctrl*-click on the pan control to reset it to zero and hold *shift* while moving the control to fine-tune the value.

You can also do panning by drawing controller #10 data in the Key Editor window's controller strip, as you would any other MIDI data. This will control any plug-in that responds to panning data as well as go to a MIDI output port if so directed. With pan data entered this way, it will be saved as part of a Standard MIDI File.

> You can convert sub-track automation data to a standard controller signal by simply feeding Cubase's MIDI out back to the MIDI in, recording the controller information on a different channel (to avoid a MIDI feedback loop), then re-assigning the controller data to the desired channel.

17.3   Panning Tips and Techniques

Stereo placement (panning) isn't just about realism, though. It's also used to keep instruments from interfering with each other as well as to add special effects. Here are some tips designed to help further your skills in the art of stereo.

17.3.1   Audience Perspective or Performer Perspective

As you set up stereo placement for instruments, think about your listener's position. For example, for a drummer the hi-hat is on the left, and the toms on the right. For the audience, it's the reverse. I generally go for the performer's perspective, unless the object is to emulate a concert experience.

17.3.2   Frequency Response and Panning

Low frequencies are fairly non-directional, whereas highs are very directional. As a result, low frequency sounds (kick, bass) generally appear in the center of a mix, whereas higher frequency instruments (shaker, tambourine) go further out to the left and right.

With synthesizers that have assignable, multiple outputs, split functions can be very useful for spatial placement. One option (especially if you're handling the bass line with your left hand) is to send the lowest split to the center, a middle split to left of center, and the top split to right of center. This is not necessarily the most realistic option with respect to imitating the real world, but hey, it's a synth. If there's also a bass part to contend with, then kick the bass to center and spread the keyboard from left to right (or right to left), going from lower keys to higher keys. This keeps your low frequencies spatially separated from the bass player.

The easiest way to spread a keyboard is if a key range can tie panning to note numbers. This creates a wide spread when you feed the keyboard's stereo outs to two mixer channels. However, unless the keyboard is the major focus of the music, you'll probably want to narrow the final range down a little bit. For example, if guitar is another major melodic instrument in the piece, try spreading the guitar from left of center to center, and the keyboard from center to right of center.

17.3.3 Panning and Delay

Placing a delayed sound in the same spatial location as the main sound may cause the end result to become somewhat indistinct, especially if the echoes are the same note as what's currently playing.

There are two ways around this problem: if your instrument is weighted to one side of the stereo spread, weight the delayed sound (set to delayed only/no dry signal) to the other side of the spread. If you're using stereo delay on a lead instrument that's panned to center, you can get some lovely results by panning one channel of echo toward the left and one toward the right. If the echoes are polyrhythmic, this can also give some lively ping-pong type effects. Of course, this may sound gimmicky (not always a bad thing, mind you!) but if the echoes are mixed relatively low and there's some stereo reverb going on, the sense of spaciousness can be huge.

CD track 23 illustrates how panning and delay can change the sound. In the first part of the file, the sixteenth note ostinato figure is generated by a string of sixteenth notes feeding Steinberg's Neon, and the LM4-Mark II tom part has no echo. After the pause, in the second part, the Neon is being fed with quarter notes (everything else about the part is the same), and the sixteenth notes are being generated by delay and panned off to the side via the DoubleDelay effect. The tom part has delay that pans across the stereo field (also courtesy of DoubleDelay). The second part sounds much more animated than the first part.

Other notes about the mix: the kick drum is going through the Quadrafuzz, the snare drum is being bitcrushed down to 6 bits, and the Waves L1-Ultramaximizer+ is inserted as a master effect to provide about 3dB of loudness maximization.

17.3.4 Plan Ahead

One way to pan is just to arbitrarily move pan controls around until things sound good. But I prefer to plan ahead by drawing a diagram of the intended "soundstage," much like the way theater people draw "marks" for where characters are supposed to stand. The further back the sound, the lower in level and sometimes, the more reverb. Closer sounds are louder and drier. When it's time to mix, this diagram can be a helpful "map" to stay on track.

17.3.5 Bigger Guitars and Pianos

Here's a tip from Spencer Brewer on an effect that Alex de Grassi uses a lot on his guitars to create a wider stereo image with two mics, but it also works well with piano.

1   Pan the right mic track full right.

2   Pan the left mic track full left.

3   Duplicate the right mic track and left mic track.

4   Pan the duplicated tracks to center.

5   Bring the duplicated tracks down about 5 to 6dB (or to taste).

This "fills in" the center hole that normally occurs by panning the two main signals to the extreme left and right. While you're at it, experiment with adding reverb in different ways—only the main channels, only the middle channels, weighted toward the left or weighted toward the right, etc.

17.3.6 Creating Wider-than-life Sounds with Delay

Many signal sources are still essentially mono (voice, vintage synths, electric guitar, etc.), but there are ways to "stereoize" sounds. With a Cubase audio track, the easiest option (although not necessarily the best) is to copy a track and "slip" it ahead or behind the original track to create a slight delay between the two, then pan the two tracks oppositely. In some cases, it's most effective to slip the original track ahead of the beat a bit and the copy a little late, so that the two end up "averaging out" and hit in the pocket. But you can also use slipping to alter the feel somewhat. To drag the part a bit, keep the original on the beat and slip the copy a little later. For a more insistent, on-top-of-the-beat feel, slip the copy ahead.

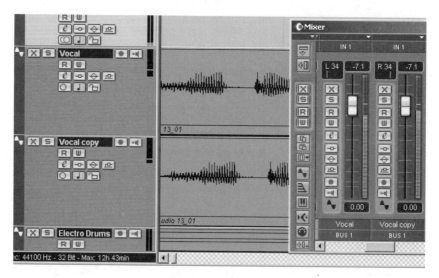

Note how the two vocal tracks are offset just a bit; also note the pan controls on the mixer channels, which place the two tracks somewhat spread out from the center.

How much slip to add depends on the instrument's frequency range. If the delay is too short, the two signals may cancel somewhat and create comb filtering effects. This results in a thin sound, much like a flanger stuck on a few milliseconds of delay. Lowering the copied signal's level can reduce these negative effects, but then the stereo image will be correspondingly less dramatic.

If the delay is too long, then you'll hear an echo effect. This can also be useful in creating a wider stereo image, but then you have to deal with the rhythmic implications—do you really want an audible delay? And if the delay is long enough, the sound will be more like two mono signals than a wide stereo signal.

Thankfully, it's easy to slide parts around in Cubase and experiment. Just be sure to check the final result in mono. If the sound ends up being thin or resonant, increase the delay time a tiny bit until both the stereo and mono sounds are satisfactory.

Chapter 18

Linking and Grouping Tracks

We met Group tracks briefly when using them to set up chains of send effects, but they certainly have other uses. When mixing, it's often convenient to be able to apply one set of edits and have it affect multiple tracks, or raise and lower the level of a group of tracks in one motion, rather than having to raise or lower each track in the group individually. Cubase has two ways to streamline the mixing process: Group tracks and Linked tracks. Both accomplish quite different tasks.

18.1 Group Tracks

Group tracks are a powerful way to manage multiple tracks when mixing. There are often times when several tracks are related, such as when multiple mics are used to record a drum set, individual background singers are recorded to separate tracks, brass sections, multiple outputs from a drum machine or synthesizer, etc. You want to be able to vary the relationship of the levels among all these tracks and process them independently, but ideally, you'd also want to be able to vary the overall volume of all the tracks as a Group, with one fader. That's what Group tracks are all about.

You can think of a Group track as a mini-mixer with a master volume control. To assign tracks to a Group track:

1   Create a Group track. The easiest way is to right-click on the Track List and select "Add Group Channel Track."

2 For each track you want to assign to the Group, click in the field just below the track name, and a pop-up menu will show possible assignments: whatever output busses, Group tracks, or master setup options (left or right channels with stereo, or any of the surround channels with surround projects).

3 Choose the desired Group track.

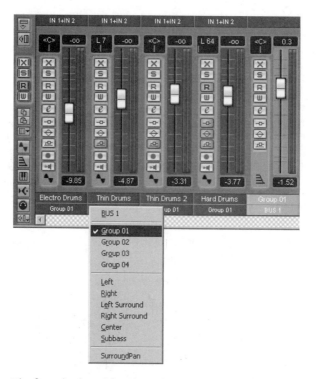

The first, third, and fourth tracks have already been assigned to the Group track toward the right; the second track is in the process of being assigned to Group track 01 (the same as the others).

18.1.1 Group Track Characteristics

■ Group tracks are always stereo. Any panning in the tracks that belong to a Group track is preserved.

■ Group tracks are like other tracks with respect to effects: There are Insert Effects slots (8 for Cubase SX, 5 for SL), Send Effects slots, and EQ. This is very handy if you are combining several drum tracks into a group track and want to have a common reverb setting for all of them.

■ Group tracks can be automated and have automation sub-tracks.

18.2 Linking Tracks

Linking tracks allows an edit made on any one track to be made on any Linked tracks. Note that linking tracks does not automatically cause one track to assume the characteristics of another; the track parameters remain as they were before they were linked. Only when a parameter is edited does it change the other track.

Linking can save a lot of time during mixing. Here's an example:

Suppose you've cut a vocal part, then doubled it. You've panned the tracks, set their levels, added some effects, and all seems well ... but then you decide that the vocals really need some EQ. Rather than set the EQ for one channel and copy it over to the other, you can temporarily (or permanently) link the two, so that as you make EQ changes to one vocal, they are also applied to the other vocal. This is also handy when setting send effects levels or other characteristics you want two or more channels to share.

> You can temporarily "unlink" a parameter by holding down ⟨alt⟩ as you change the value. When you stop holding down ⟨alt⟩, the parameter rejoins its linked companions.

Not all parameters mirror each other when linked. Automation sub-tracks are independent, as are insert effect settings, pan, and input and output routing.

To link channels:

1 *shift*-click on the names (just below the faders) of the tracks you want to link. The background of the name for selected tracks will turn brown.

2 Right-click on any empty space in the mixer, or on the fader of a linked channel.

3 Select Link Channels.

4 To unlink channels, click on one of the linked channel's name. Other channels linked to that channel will show they are selected by having the background of the name for the selected tracks turn brown.

The two "Thin Drums" channels have been linked prior to applying EQ to them. Note that one is panned left and the other right; this relationship is preserved, even when linked. Also, note that the levels are offset. When moving either fader, Cubase will try to maintain a constant relationship between them.

The ratiometric relationship between faders cannot be maintained if one fader reaches the limit of its maximum or minimum travel before the other one does. However, once the fader is pulled back from that limit, the linked faders return to their prior relationship.

Note that any number of channels can be linked. However, a fader cannot be linked to more than one fader. If a fader that has an existing link is linked to a different fader, the original link will be broken.

Chapter 19

Mixing—More Than Level Changes

When mixing, you don't always have to use level to make one instrument stand out compared to another. There are several ways to make an instrument leap out at you or settle demurely into the background, that don't involve level in the usual sense.

Much of mixing without level changes relies on the fact that the ear is most interested in the first few hundred milliseconds of a sound, then moves on to the next sound. (This is likely due to years of evolution, when we wondered whether that sound in the bushes was the wind or a sabretooth tiger.) What happens during that first few hundred milliseconds greatly affects the perception of how "loud" that signal is, as well as the relationship to other sounds happening at the same time.

Here some ways to change the prominence of a sound without using traditional level changes.

19.1   Adjusting Start Time

If two sounds of approximately equal level play at almost the same time, the one that started first will appear to be more prominent. For example, suppose kick drum and bass hit at the same time. If you want the bass (and therefore the melodic component) to be a little more prominent than the rhythmic component represented by the kick drum, move it ahead of the kick. To make the kick more prominent, slide the bass a bit late compared to the kick.

This is a handy technique when you want to shift the emphasis from, for example, a chorus to an instrumental break. You might want the chorus to accent the melody, while the break has a more rhythmic feel. Remember to move sounds in relation to the kick, as that anchors the tempo.

There are two easy ways to shift a track:

■ Click on the audio segment and drag it. As the amount of shift needs to be quite small, you'll probably want to zoom in a fair amount. It's a good idea to use the Scissors tool to cut the audio into a specific region you want to shift; otherwise, you might end shifting portions that you don't really want to change.

■ With the Infoline showing, click on a segment, and adjust its Start time. There are two ways to show the Infoline: click on the toolbar icon or right-click on the audio segment and select Show Info.

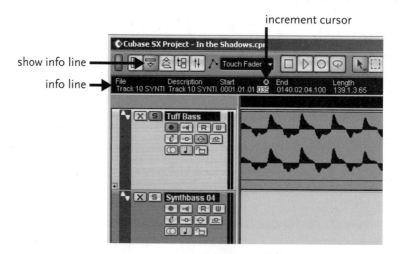

The Infoline shows information about a particular audio segment: its name, start time, end time, length, and so on. You can shift the start of the segment precisely by altering the start time parameter using one of the ways mentioned in the text.

The Infoline shows the time in whatever units you have selected for the time ruler (bars and beats, seconds, SMPTE, samples, etc.). There are three ways to adjust the start time:

- Hold the cursor just above one of the start time fields; it will turn into a little "+" sign. Click to increment the value by one, or click and hold to increment the value continuously until you release the mouse button.

- Hold the cursor just below one of the start time fields. The cursor turns into a little "-" sign. Click to decrement the value by one, or click and hold to decrement the value continuously until you release the mouse button.

- Click on a field, type in the desired number, and hit [return].

19.2 Using Exciters

Try inserting an "exciter" plug-in to "lift" an instrument out of the mix, with no significant increase in level. These add a boost in the very highest frequencies (e.g. the top or two octave of hearing), where instruments normally don't have a lot of acoustical energy. When an instrument does have energy in this region, it tends to stand out quite a bit.

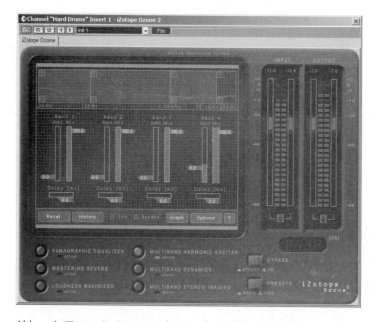

Although iZotope's Ozone is designed more for mastering, you can use its multiband harmonic exciter as an insert effect if desired. Here, a tiny bit of excitation has been added between 3 and 10kHz, and a slight amount more between 10 and 20kHz. As the example on the CD demonstrates, even this little bit of added boost can affect the sound.

You can also insert an exciter as a Send Effect and mix in a little bit from several instruments you want to emphasize.

CD track 24 demonstrates the drums and bass, playing together. The first two measures have the exciter enabled, the second two measures do not. Note how the drums in the first two measures are much more prominent compared to the bass.

19.3 Pitch Changes in Soft Synth Envelopes

This involves doing a little programming at your synth or sampler, but the effect can be worth it if you want a sound to really cut through. It is essential that you be able to add envelope modulation to the oscillator pitch.

The basic idea is to add a very short (around 10 to 20ms), very steep (from maximum modulation to zero) decay so to give an extra "punch" at the attack of a note. If two sounds are layered together, try adding a similar but inverted envelope to the second layer (in other words, the envelope goes from flat to standard pitch over the same 10 to 20ms interval).

Envelope 1 has been set for a very fast decay (0.014ms). On the Mod/Tune page, this is applied to the oscillator pitch, thus "snapping" the pitch down to normal over a very short time and adding a percussive "blip" to the sound.

The proper amount of pitch bend depends on what you're trying to do. With a pad sound like a choir or other sustaining sound, even a small amount of pitch bend might create the desired effect. With a sound that already has a fairly percussive attack, you might need as much greater amount of pitch bend.

CD track 25 plays a patch from my Technoid Guitars sample CD through Steinberg's HALion sampler. The first part does not have the pitch envelope added; the second part has an added downward pitch bend, which makes the attack more prominent in a subtle way.

19.4 Mini Fade-ins

If you need to make an attack less prominent so a part "slides" in behind another one rather than come on too strong, you can add a fade in. However, if you do a fade starting from the beginning of a sound, you'll lose the attack altogether, which will probably sound too mushy. Instead, extend the start of the fade to before the sound begins. When the audio starts, it does so partway into the attack rather than coming up from zero, thus creating the desired effect.

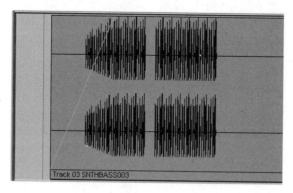

Track 03 SNTHBASS003

By starting the fade in before the sound starts, you reduce the attack but don't eliminate it. This makes the part's entry into the music more subtle.

19.5   Diffusing a Sound with Chorusing

If you want to diffuse a sound and have it sit back more in the mix, a chorus/flanger can help. Set it for a short delay (under 10ms or so) with no modulation (important!). If available, use an out of phase output mix (e. g. the output control that blends straight and delayed sounds says −50 instead of +50). Alter the mix by starting with the straight sound, then slowly adding in the delayed sound. As the delayed sound's level approaches the straight sound's level, a comb-filtering effect comes into play that essentially knocks a bunch of holes in the signal's frequency spectrum. If you're trying to make a background piano or guitar take up less space in a track, this technique works well.

19.6   Mixing via EQ

EQ is a very underutilized resource for mixing. Turning the treble down instead of the volume can bring a track more into the background without having it get "smaller," just less "present." Some engineers go for really bright sounds with instruments like acoustic guitars, then trim the volume when the vocals come in (or some other solo happens). Try turning the brightness down a bit instead. Don't forget about using automation to control these kinds of changes.

Chapter 20

Cleaning Vocals

Part of the mixing process involves cleaning up small problems and glitches that occurred during the recording process. As mentioned earlier, to prepare for mixing it's a good idea to listen to every track by itself through headphones in order to identify problems that need fixing. Vocals in particular are likely to need some editing as part of the mix preparation process, so let's look at ways to create cleaner vocals.

In the early days of digital audio, this type of fixing usually required transferring the track into a two-track editor like Steinberg's Wavelab. However, Cubase's sample editor has almost all the flexibility of stand-alone editors and can take care of almost all vocal cleaning problems you may encounter.

20.1 Specific Tips

Following is a collection of tips, but several of them relate to other tracks as well, not just vocals.

20.1.1 Silence the Spaces between Verses, Choruses, etc.

If you isolate vocal tracks, you'll often hear a lot of tiny little glitches—a pop due to a switch being closed, mic handling noise, throat-clearing, etc. To edit these:

1   Double-click on the audio you want to edit, which opens the Sample Editor.

2   Use the Vertical Zoom slider so that low-level signals are easy to see.

3 Click and drag across the region you want to silence.

4 Go AUDIO > PROCESS > SILENCE—the noise is gone.

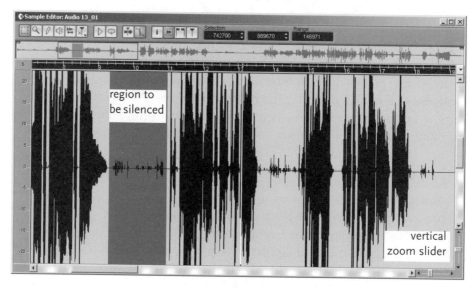

The region to be silenced contains mic handling noise, which we do not want to hear.

Sometimes there will be enough noise on the vocals that descending abruptly into silence, or returning to the vocals after silence, sounds choppy. There are two possible solutions:

- Make sure the region starts right where the vocals end and continues to right where the vocals begin. If there's no space between the vocals and the silence, the effect is like a noise gate and you won't notice any transition.

- Silence most of the noise, but leave about 100 to 200ms just before and after the vocals. Use the AUDIO > PROCESS > FADE IN and AUDIO > PROCESS > FADE OUT commands to "fade" from silence to noise or noise to silence.

If you need to add a fade out or fade in, do it while the region is still defined. That way you can just "pull" the region's left edge past the right edge to create a fade in, or pull the region's right edge past the left edge to create a fade out.

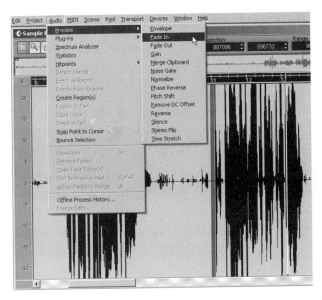

Here a fade in has been added to the previous example. The fade starts where the silent part ends and fades back into just before the vocal begins.

20.1.2 Dealing with Compression

Like most engineers, I use a lot of compression on my vocals. Although this makes the vocals smoother, compression also emphasizes the inhales at the beginning of phrases. Don't silence these, as that creates an unnatural effect (subconsciously, we use the inhale to lead us into the vocal). However, sometimes it's a good idea to at least reduce their levels somewhat. To do this:

1 Use the vertical zoom and horizontal zoom sliders to zoom in and make it easy to see where the inhale begins and ends.

2 Click and drag across the region with the inhale

3 Go AUDIO > PROCESS > GAIN and select a suitable amount of gain reduction (somewhere between -3.00 and -6.00 is a good starting point). Use the Preview button to determine the correct amount.

4 An alternate approach is to add a fade in (AUDIO > PROCESS > FADE IN). Sometimes this gives a better-sounding result. Use the Preview button to verify that the effect works.

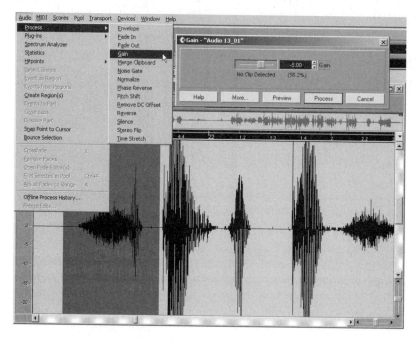

Reduce the gain on vocal inhales, or add a fade-in, to make them less prominent.

20.1.3 P-Popping

A "p-pop" is the sound that occurs when a plosive sound (such as "p" or "b") hits the mic full force. Although wind screens, pop filters, and the low frequency cut switch on a microphone are supposed to get of these, sometimes a pop will get through anyway. It's frustrating when a vocal is perfect except for one p-pop, but there is a solution.

As pops are mostly low frequency energy, there are two choices for the desired fix.

1   Use the horizontal zoom slider to zoom in on the area with the p-pop. You do not necessarily want to zoom in vertically, because the pop should be obvious. It will be lower in frequency than the rest of the signal, so the waveforms will be fairly broad.

2   Click and drag across the region with the p-pop.

3   Go AUDIO > PROCESS > GAIN and reduce the gain by a significant amount—for example, -12dB. Use the Preview button to make sure it's the right amount (and don't forget, you can always undo if it isn't).

4   If reducing volume doesn't solve the problem, try adding some low-cut filtering. Go AUDIO > PLUG-INS and choose the filter plug-in of your choice. Set it to low-shelf and begin as steep a rolloff as possible around 50 to 100Hz.

5   If necessary, use a combination of volume reduction and low cut filtering.

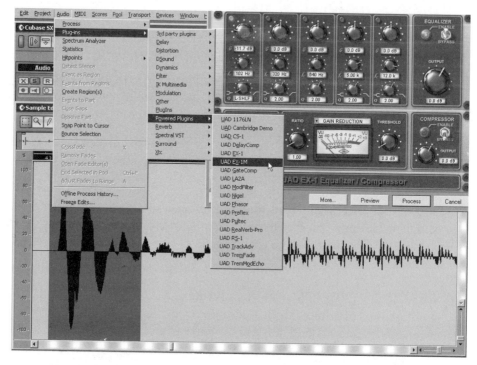

Note the highlighted p-pop, which is much lower in frequency, and louder, than the subsequent vocal signal. In this situation, the UAD EX-1 equalizer plug-in is being selected to provide a low frequency shelf (the stage on the left, which rolls off starting at 100Hz).

20.1.4 Phrase Shifting

One popular vocal technique is to double a vocal to create a richer, thicker sound. However, it can be extremely difficult for a vocalist to duplicate a part. There are two common workarounds: have less inflections in the main vocal so it's easier to copy, or use a digital delay (which sounds stiffer than doing two "real" overdubs).

In Cubase SX, there's a far more elegant solution: just "borrow" good phrases from one channel and paste it into the other. For example, suppose a vocal doubling works fabulously except that the last phrase of the overdub was off. No problem; just take the last phrase from the first vocal and drag it over ([alt]-click and drag) to the track with the bogus phrase. Offsetting the start time a bit gives a more realistic effect.

Chapter 21

Mixing and MIDI

Thanks to soft synths, MIDI has enjoyed a resurgence in recent years. More and more "tracks" in Cubase are not traditional digital audio tracks, but virtual instruments playing in real time and triggered by MIDI data.

As a result, tweaking MIDI tracks is just as important as tweaking audio tracks. The biggest difference is that MIDI tracks are almost infinitely variable—you can tweak individual parts of individual notes if you so desire, and those tweaks can have a huge impact on your mix.

21.1   Soft Synth CPU Issues

The biggest problem with soft synths is they tend to need a fair amount of CPU power. As a result, after getting a track right, it's common practice to export the audio prior to mixdown so it can be brought back into the project as a hard disk track (which requires less CPU power). You can then disable the soft synth to reclaim CPU power for other things, like high-quality reverb plug-ins.

The procedure for exporting soft synth audio is as follows:

1   In the VST Mixer, solo both the VST instrument track and the MIDI track that drives it. Set all effects, enables, sends, etc. exactly as desired.

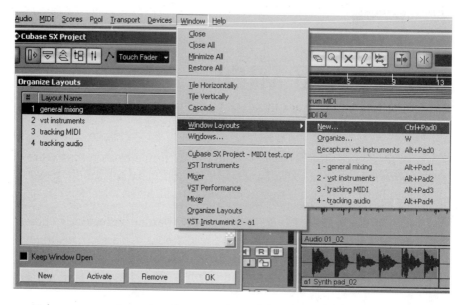

Make sure you solo not just the mixer channel that carries the audio, but the MIDI channel that drives it as well.

2   Use the Locators to set up the right and left boundaries of the area you want to mix to a hard disk track.

3   Play the area to be mixed and check that neither the instrument nor master meters hit overload. If so, trim levels at the MIDI track or instrument track (or the master out) as needed to get the level as close as possible to 0.

4   Once the levels are correct, go FILE > EXPORT > AUDIO MIXDOWN.

5   A dialog box appears where you can enter the file name, file type, destination, attributes, whether to include automation and effects, etc. Enter the desired values then click on "Save."

6   Cubase renders the track to hard disk.

7   Select the track where you want the audio to appear and place the cursor where you want the audio to begin.

8 Go FILE > IMPORT > AUDIO FILE, navigate to the file, select it, and click on "Open." Check the desired parameters in the "Import Options" dialog box (usually the defaults are fine), then click on OK. The file will appear starting at the designated location.

Note that you can also automatically import the mixed file to the Audio Pool or to an audio track by checking the corresponding boxes in the Export dialog, thus eliminating the need for step 8.

The MIDI file that drives a soft synth requires almost no CPU power. I strongly recommend keeping the MIDI file (I usually create a Folder track to hold "old" soft synth MIDI tracks) so that if you decide the part needs tweaking, you can simply re-load the desired soft synth, assign the appropriate MIDI track to it, and re-render the part after it's perfected.

21.2 Enhancing MIDI Drum Parts in the Mix

With so much rhythmic emphasis in today's music, it's no surprise that virtual drum boxes and drum modules have become very popular. Products like Native Instruments' Battery, Steinberg/Waldorf's Attack and LM4 Mk II, Fxpansion DR-008, and several others are becoming increasingly responsible for providing the rhythms that drive today's music.

To get the most out of these programs during mixdown—or, for that matter, soft samplers playing drum sounds or software suites with percussion instruments (such as Reason, Storm, Fruity Loops, etc.)—you'll want to take advantage of the many editing possibilities they offer. This includes modifying the MIDI data feeding them and/or tweaking how their parameters respond to MIDI data. Here are some common, useful drum tweaks.

21.2.1 Pitch Shifting

A drum synth's pitch control parameters are surprisingly useful. You can:

- Tune drums to the song's key. This is particularly applicable to toms and resonant kick drums (such as the famously overused TR-808 "hum drum"). If out of tune, the kick can fight with the bass to make mud or just confuse the song's sense of key. If fine tuning is not available as a control (sometimes you can change tuning only in semitones), you may be able to feed in a constant amount of pitch bend as a workaround.

- Create multiple drum sounds from one. Want to play a two-hand shaker part, but you have only one shaker sample? If you can copy sounds from one pad to another, copy the sound, then detune the copy by a semitone or so to provide a slight sonic variation. Detuning can also create a family of cymbals or toms out of one cymbal or tom sample.

- Accommodate different musical genres. A lot of house music pitches drum sounds lower, whereas drum 'n' bass often pitches sounds up. You may not need a new set of samples; try retuning the ones you have.

- Use radical transpositions to create new sounds. Most drum boxes don't have a gong sound, but don't let that stop you. Take your longest cymbal sound and detune it by −12 to −20 semitones. Create another version of the cymbal and detune it by about −3 semitones. Layer the two together; the slightly detuned cymbal gives a convincing attack, while the highly detuned one provides the necessary sustain.

- If your drum sound source lets you assign velocity to pitch modulation, you can increase dynamics by programming high velocity levels to add a very slight upward pitch shift. This works best if you apply velocity to the amount of pitch envelope and then modulate the drum's pitch from the envelope, so that after attacking at a higher pitch, the drum will fall back to the normal pitch. Of course, the increase doesn't have to be slight if you want to create a disco-type falling tom sound. A small increase emulates a drum's skin being stretched, hence pitched higher, when it's first hit.

21.2.2 Changing the Sample Start Point

Altering a sample's start point under velocity control (most synths and samplers, and many virtual drum instruments, offer this feature) can add convincing dynamics that make a mix come more "alive." Generally, you set the initial sample start point several tens, or even hundreds, of milliseconds "late" into the sample so it's past where the attack occurs. Now assign *negative* velocity to modulate the sample start point. At low velocities, you don't hear the signal's initial attack; higher velocities kick the sample point further toward the beginning, until at maximum velocity you hear the entire attack.

The highlighted section of Battery's virtual front panel shows the controls for modulating, setting, and monitoring the sample start point. (Note: the front panel graphic has been modified to focus attention on the sample start point elements.) On the envelope, observe the line about a fifth of the way into the waveform: this indicates the initial sample start point, as set by the Start control. In the Modulation section, velocity is modulating Sample Start by −92.

If you already have a good MIDI drum part but it lacks dynamics, you can add sample start modulation after recording. Simply overdub a controller track using a mod wheel or MIDI fader and assign the controller to sample start time.

21.2.3   Filter Modulation

For dynamic control beyond tying velocity to level and/or sample start point, assign velocity to filter so that hitting the drum harder produces a slightly brighter sound. This gives extra emphasis to the hardest hits. Soft taps will sound a bit muted.

21.2.4   Hi-hat Amplitude Envelope Decay Modulation

One of the most annoying "features" of electronic drums is the hi-hat. A real drummer is constantly working the hi-hat, open and closing it with the pedal, but the electronic version is an unchanging snapshot. Sure, you can program a combination of open, half-closed, and closed hi-hat notes and assign them to a mute group (see below) so each will cut off the others, but programming a rhythm with three hat sounds is tedious and doesn't always sound that realistic.

A more expressive option is to use a MIDI controller, such as mod wheel, to vary an open hi-hat sound's envelope decay time. Close the decay for a closed hi-hat; as you extend the decay, the hi-hat opens gradually. I usually play the hi-hat note with my right hand and move the mod wheel with my left, but this is also an operation that lends itself well to "post-processing"—record the part, then overdub the controller changes necessary to create a more expressive track.

21.2.5   Overdrive

This is a signal processing tip more than a MIDI or drum programming one, but it's still a good one.

Most drums have a quick initial attack, followed by an abrupt decay. Adding a little bit of overdrive distortion will "crunch" the first few milliseconds of the attack, while leaving the decay untouched. This affects the sound in three important ways:

- You can raise the overall average level of the drum for a louder perceived sound, because the overdrive effect will limit the percussive attack.

- This creates a short period of time where the sound is at its maximum level, thus contributing a feeling of "punch."

- Distortion increases the attack's harmonic content, producing a brighter attack.

21.2.6 Mute Groups

When drums are assigned to a mute group, hitting a drum that's part of the group will cut off any other drum from the group that's still sounding. This is mostly intended for hi-hats, so that playing a closed hi-hat sound will shut off an open hi-hat.

This LM4-Mark II "DrumnBass" preset has the hi-hats assigned to the same group (in this case, Group 1), as set up on the instrument's Edit page.

There are other uses for mute groups:

- Assign toms with long decays to the same mute group. Too many simultaneous tom decays can muddy up a track. When you assign them to the same mute group, not only do tom rolls sound cleaner, but you conserve polyphony, which can be a problem with older samplers. Also, toms sampled with a lot of reverb can acquire gated reverb effects when multiple drums are playing.

- If you have some rhythmic loops loaded into a soft sampler along with individual drum sounds, make the loops part of a mute group (assuming, of course, you don't plan to layer them). This is particularly important if you're playing the loops in real time. Suppose you have a bunch of four-measure loops, but you're hitting a build and you want to switch quickly between the first measure, or first two measures, of various loops. Assigning loops to the same mute group means you can start them with impunity, knowing that the other ones will shut up when you do.

21.2.7   Click Layering

Sometimes modulation of an existing sample just isn't enough to create serious dynamics. This is where a click sample or sound can come in handy.

For virtual instruments that can load samples, create a click sample. I made mine by simply drawing some spikes in a digital audio editor for about 35ms and saved that as a file. With synthesized drums, you can make a good click by applying maximum, extremely short pitch modulation to a white noise source or buzzy oscillator, then impose a very quick amplitude decay.

The goal is to layer the click with another sound, such as kick. But the key is to choose a velocity curve where the click is very quiet at lower velocity levels. The click's entire dynamic range should be given to the upper dynamic range of the sound with which it is layered. As you play harder, the click will become more audible, adding punch to the drum sound. A little lowpass filtering on the click will help you blend the two sounds to taste.

21.3 Enhancing Synth Parts in the Mix

Layering two bass sounds with different velocity responses during mix-down can turn a so-so bass part into one with absolutely thrilling dynamic effects. For example, one synth can have no velocity response and be the main bass sound, while a second synth, with a harder or more percussive sound, can have full velocity response so that it comes in only with higher-velocity notes. Of course, you could also automate the level of the second bass, or automate specific controls (e.g., filter) to produce more intense effects. Here's how to do this sort of layering:

1 Insert the second instruments that will layer with the first one in the VST Instruments device.

2 Duplicate the MIDI track that plays the existing bass part.

3 Assign the duplicate MIDI track to the layered synth.

4 For the "main" synth sound, turn the velocity control all the way down.

5 For the "accent" synth sound, turn the velocity control all the way up.

Now when the sequence plays back, the layered sound will produce a more dynamic part. You may need to tweak the MIDI data a bit to obtain the desired results. Of course, it would be easier to just record the layered part in the first place, but it's nice to know this is something that can also be done on mixdown.

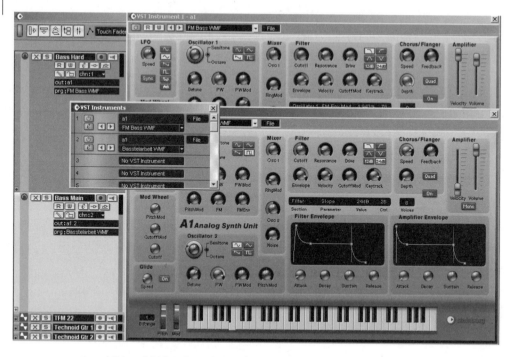

An additional A1 has been layered to complement an existing bass part. The second one is set so that higher velocities bring in the sound, thus producing more of an "attack" to create a more dynamic feel.

A similar technique works with leads, but use the same synth patch for both layers, and detune one slightly compared to the other. Use maximum velocity response on the detuned one so that hitting harder creates chorusing. Normally chorusing tends to diffuse the sound a bit, but in this case, because the level is simultaneously increasing from the other layered instrument, the end result is simply a bigger, fatter sound.

21.4 "Humanizing" Sequences

Timing is everything, and that's especially true with music. Yet mathematically *perfect* timing is most certainly not everything, otherwise drum machines would have replaced drummers a long time ago. Good drummers enhance music by playing with the time—subtly speeding up or slowing down to change a tune's "feel," and leading or lagging specific beats to push a tune or make it lay back a bit more in the groove.

Often, these time changes ahead of or behind the beat are very small; even a few milliseconds can make a difference. This may be surprising, as sound itself moves at about 1 foot per second, so a 6ms change theoretically affects a track about as much as moving a guitar amp 6 feet (2 meters) further behind the drummer. Yet once you start experimenting with timing shifts, it becomes obvious that even very small timing differences can change a tune's groove when you hear these changes in comparison to a relatively steady beat.

When working with MIDI, musicians and engineers often forget about the importance of timing changes and quantize everything, which is the quickest way to suck the life out of a piece of music. Fortunately, we can use some of Cubase's MIDI editing features to put the "feel" back in to sequenced music.

Before proceeding, I'd like to acknowledge Michael Stewart, who first made me aware of the importance of small timing shifts to music, and whose research on the topic has influenced the entire industry.

21.4.1 How Timing Shifts Produce "Feel"

Feel is not based on randomizing note start times (but randomization is useful if you want to simulate the effect of a drummer who's had too many beers). Human drummers add variations in a mostly non-random way—often subconsciously, so these changes tap directly into the source of the drummer's "feel."

You may want to apply randomization in some situations, such as a chord so that all the notes don't hit at exactly the same time. We discuss how to do this under "Quantization Options."

Drummers frequently hit some drums slightly ahead of, or behind, the beat to give certain effects. For example, jazz drummers tend to hit a ride cymbal's bell a bit ahead of the beat to "push" a song. Rock drummers frequently hit the snare behind the beat (listen to any Led Zeppelin album) to give a "big" sound. Of course, the sound isn't really bigger; but our brain interprets slight delays as indicating a big space, since we know that in a big space, sound travels a while through the air before it reaches us.

The easiest way to shift timing in Cubase is with the Logical Editor. Don't be scared of it, the Logical Editor is your friend! Just set it up as follows:

- Top Line:
  Filter Target = Type Is
  Condition = Equal
  Parameter 1 = Note

- Lower Line:
  Action Target = Position
  Operation = Add (moves notes "behind" the beat), or Subtract (moves notes "ahead" of the beat)
  Parameter 1 = The amount to move the notes, in Ticks (1 tick = 1/480th of a quarter note)

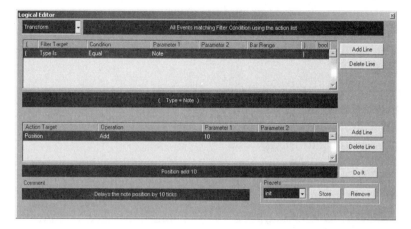

The Logical Editor makes it easy to move events ahead or behind the beat. In this example, a track's notes are being shifted 10 ticks behind the beat to delay them somewhat compared to the kick.

Keep the kick drum on the beat as a reference, and use track shifting to change the timing of the snare, toms, and percussion by a few milliseconds. Here are some specific track timing tricks:

■ For techno, dance, and acid jazz tunes try moving any double-time percussion parts (shaker, tambourine, etc.) a little bit ahead of the beat to give a "faster" feel.

■ Sometimes it pays to shift individual notes rather than an entire track. With tom fills, delay each subsequent note of the fill a bit more (e.g., the first note of the fill is on the beat, the second note approximately 2ms after the beat, the third note 4 to 5ms after the beat, the fourth note 6 to 8ms after the beat, and so on until the last note ends up about 20ms behind the beat). This can make a tom fill sound gigantic.

■ If two percussion sounds often hit on the same beat in a rhythm pattern, try sliding one part ahead or behind the beat by a small amount (a few milliseconds) to keep the parts from interfering with each other.

■ Track shifting does not apply only to drum parts. Suppose there are two fairly staccato harmony lines in a tune. If you advance one by 5ms and delay the other by 5ms, the two parts will become more separate and distinct instead of sounding like one combined part. If the parts are panned oppositely in the stereo field, the field will appear even wider.

■ Hitting a crash cymbal a bit ahead of the beat makes it really stand out. Moving it behind the beat (later) meshes it more with the track.

21.4.2   Quantization Options

Strict quantization is favored for some types of music, but it's an artificial process because no human plays with crystal-controlled precision.

Fortunately, Cubase has some wonderful options that make quantization far less dictatorial. To adjust these, go MIDI > QUANTIZE SETUP (or select Setup from the Quantize field in the MIDI Key Editor).

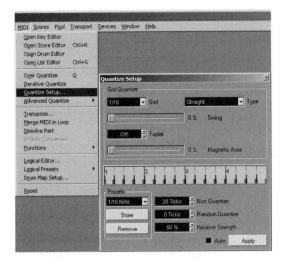

Quantize Setup is where you can create more subtle variations on standard quantization.

Non Quantize

Notes that are closer to the quantize value than the number specified here in ticks will not be moved. In other words, if you set Non Quantize to 50 and a note is 45 ticks away from the nearest rhythmic value (e.g., the nearest 16th note if quantize is set to 16th notes), it will not be quantized. But if it's 55 ticks away, it will be. Thus, if your playing is mostly okay but there are a few out of control notes, they'll be pulled in and the rest will remain untouched.

Random Quantize

This moves quantized (or unquantized) notes around randomly within the "window" specified in this parameter. For example, if you've entered 25 ticks and apply quantization to a group of notes, they will all be placed at some random amount within 25 ticks of the nearest rhythmic value.

Iterative Quantize

This is my favorite quantize option, because it moves notes a certain percentage closer to the beat. Thus, if your playing is basically all right but isn't quite as tight as you'd like, this option tightens it up without strangling it. The Iterative Strength parameter in the Quantize Setup dialog sets how much closer the notes move each time you apply quantization (I usually set this to 50%). When quantizing, I usually just invoke iterative quantize as many times as necessary (but as few times as possible) for the part to sound right; the result is a track that sounds rhythmically correct, but retains most of a performance's "feel."

You can invoke quantization in several ways:

- From Quantization Setup, click on "Apply."
- In Quantization Setup, click on "Auto." Any changes you make to Quantize Setup will be applied immediately.

- To apply the Quantization parameters in the Quantization Setup dialog (except for Iterative Quantize), go MIDI > OVER QUANTIZE or type ⓠ.

- To apply Iterative Quantize, go MIDI > ITERATIVE QUANTIZE.

Incidentally, I suggest avoiding the Auto Quantize feature (enabled by clicking on the "AQ" button in the transport). This quantizes your playing while recording; I think it's preferable to just record any notes the way they come in and tweak the data afterward.

21.5   Groove Quantizing

There are times when you're mixing that two parts just don't seem to work well together, but tend to "fight." For example, suppose you have an ostinato eighth-note synthesizer pattern and a drum loop played by a live drummer. Unless the drummer is a machine, the odds are quite good that the timing between the synth and drums will be a bit off, because the synth's rhythm will be perfect, while the drummer will have a few "human errors." In this case, you want to be able to quantize not to some absolute standard, but to another instrument.

Cubase includes a function that lets you quantize a MIDI track to a rhythmic reference provided by an audio track. It does this by analyzing the audio track, detecting where the drum hits occur, then using those detected "Hitpoints" as a quantization template instead of the usual rhythmic value.

To illustrate how this works, we'll use the example above of quantizing the eighth-note synth pattern to drums.

1   Double-click on the drum loop; the sample editor appears.

2   Click on the Hitpoint mode icon (the right-most icon that looks like a golf tee).

3   Cubase performs an analysis and places Hitpoints at each drum transient.

4 You can vary the sensitivity of the detection process with the Hitpoint Sensitivity slider. Moving it further to the right places more Hitpoints as Cubase lowers the threshold for deciding what constitutes a percussive transient.

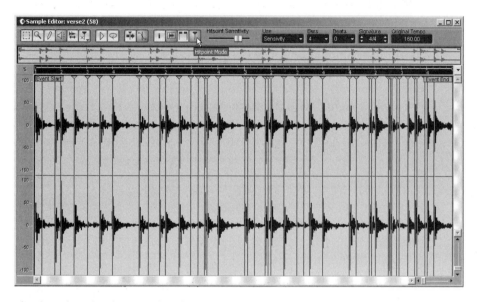

The drum loop has been analyzed, and a Hitpoint placed at percussive transients. Now it's almost ready to become a quantization template.

5 You can zoom in and add Hitpoints with the pencil icon, move them with the standard arrow cursor, or delete them by selecting Disable from the Hitpoint Edit icon (the one that looks like a golf tee with an "X"). You don't have to go too crazy here; remember our goal is to indicate where the eighth-note hits fall so the synth pattern can lock to that groove.

6 After adjusting the hitpoints to your satisfaction, go AUDIO > HITPOINTS > CREATE GROOVE QUANTIZE.

7   Now when you open up the quantize value pop-up in the MIDI Key Editor or Quantize Setup dialog, the name of the file to which you added Hitpoints will be included as one of the quantization options. Apply it using any of the previously-mentioned techniques (e. g., click on "Apply" in the Quantize Setup window, go MIDI > OVER QUAN-TIZE, etc.).

21.6   Tempo Track Timing Tweaks

People generally set the tempo in a sequencer to the desired beat, then just let it sit there. But that's not the way real music works. In a fascinating study, Ernest Cholakis and Ray Williams compared the tempo tracks of two classical pianists playing Moonlight Sonata, and plotted out the tempo changes. The results were anything but a constant tempo—the changes looked like a relief map of the alps.

Even though pop music doesn't change tempo as much as classical pieces, real drummers insert subtle tempo changes, inserted over several measures or just in selected parts of individual measures, to build anticipation and change moods.

To edit the tempo track, first click on the Master button in the Transport so the song knows to follow the Master Tempo Track and not just the tempo in bpm entered into the Transport's tempo indicator. Then go PROJECT > TEMPO TRACK. Use the pencil tool to draw in a new tempo by clicking where you want the tempo to change, and the tempo to which it should change.

Unfortunately, digital audio tracks cannot easily follow tempo changes, because that requires stretching the audio on-the-fly so that it speeds up and slows down in tandem with the tempo changes. However, tracks that use hitpoints, MIDI, and REX files have no problem following tempo changes.

Because tempo track changes can have a powerful effect on a song, I sometimes set up a rhythm track using MIDI and tweak the tempo as desired. I can then record digital audio parts, like vocal and guitar, over that because the tempo changes are already in place, so the audio tracks go on top of those tempo changes—just like recording vocals over a drummer who speeds up and slows down.

The only caution is that once you've created a varying tempo track and recorded audio to it, you can't really make any more tempo changes. The only exception is if the tempo changes move in "steps" (e.g. the tempo is 125bpm over the first 16 measure, then jumps to 126bpm over the next 16 measures). You can cut the audio into pieces and use time-stretching to match each piece to the existing tempo, but that gets pretty tedious.

Here are some examples of tempo track tweaks:

■ To boost a song's energy level, increase the tempo slightly (by 0.5 to 1 bpm). This is the timing equivalent of modulating pitch upward by a semitone; both increase excitement. Decreasing tempo has the reverse effect. Tempo shifts are useful when transitioning between song sections (verse to chorus, chorus to instrumental, etc.) as well as within a particular section (such as upping the tempo for the last two measures of a solo).

■ Change tempo a little bit before the first beat of the measure you want to change. For example, if you're going from verse to chorus, increase the tempo halfway through the measure prior to the chorus. This creates a smoother lead-in than having the tempo change coincide with a measure change.

■ For really dramatic effects, ritard the tempo over the course of a measure (e.g., 1bpm or less lower on each beat) then return to the original tempo. Having a drum roll during the ritard creates a particularly effective transition.

21.7 "Proofing" Your Sequences

Do you sometimes get the feeling your sequence isn't all it could be? As you mix you try different arrangements, different instruments, different signal processing ... and still, something is not quite right. Possibly the problem lies deep within the MIDI data stream—small glitches and problems that may not be obvious individually, but when added together during the mixdown process, detract from the tune's ability to sound rhythmically tight and sonically "clean."

Typical glitches are double triggers caused by quantizing two notes so that they land on the same beat, excessive or unwanted controller data that messes up timing, and voice-stealing that abruptly cuts off notes. Although a group of instruments playing together will often mask these problems, they nonetheless detract from the overall quality of a piece by robbing clarity and/or creating timing errors.

Fortunately, the same technology that created these problems can also help remove them as you can "tweak" a sequenced track while mixing, long after the actual recording took place. Before exporting your final mix, consider "proofing" any MIDI data, much like you would use spelling or grammar checkers to check a word processing document before printing it out. Cubase has several functions to help "clean up" MIDI tracks. Let's investigate:

■ If your keyboard generates aftertouch (pressure) but a patch isn't programmed to use it, it's easy to record a track with pressure data that serves no purpose other than to take up memory and clog the MIDI data stream. A more subtle problem is that sometimes pitch bend and mod wheels are mounted on the same support bar, so moving one wheel energetically can cause the other to move slightly, thus generating low level but fairly constant data. Although you can disable aftertouch by going FILE > PREFERENCES > MIDI > FILTER and checking the Aftertouch box for recording, in the heat of creative passion this is easy to overlook. To check for excessive aftertouch, call up a MIDI track's Key Editor, set the controller strip to Aftertouch, and erase unwanted data.

■ If you know you didn't record any controller data in a track, go MIDI > FUNCTIONS > DELETE CONTROLLERS and all controllers will be removed from the selected track.

■ Doubled notes can eat up polyphony and cause strange flanging on occasional notes. It's easy to deal with this: Go MIDI > FUNCTIONS > DELETE DOUBLES. This removes any note that doubles an existing note with the same pitch and placement.

■ Cubase's Delete Notes function lets you specify notes that are below a certain velocity or shorter than a certain duration. Go MIDI > FUNCTIONS > DELETE NOTES, and you'll be presented with a dialog where you can enter the criteria by which notes should be deleted. This is an incredibly valuable tool when cleaning up MIDI guitar tracks, which are often loaded with low-velocity "ghost" notes.

■ When listening to parts in isolation, you might note excessive variations in dynamics, such as a kick drum occasionally dropping too low, some "rogue notes" being too loud, or too wide a dynamic range for velocities. The Velocity function can fix all of these problems. Go MIDI > FUNCTIONS > VELOCITY, where you can add or subtract a certain amount of velocity to the MIDI part, compress or expand the dynamics, or limit the upper or lower velocity range for all notes. This is a tremendously helpful tool for cleaning up tracks; for example, it's very convenient to be able to compress the velocity values of notes for a bass track.

■ Cubase offers a Legato edit (go MIDI > FUNCTIONS > LEGATO) that lets you set a minimum amount of space between notes by lengthening short notes and shortening long ones so that the end of one note occurs the specified amount of time before the beginning of the next note. This is again a very useful function for MIDI guitar, as it guarantees that note re-triggering will occur.

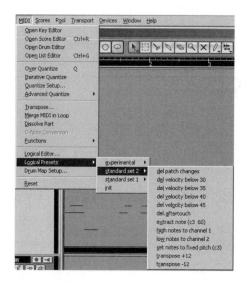

The Logical Editor has several presets that clean up MIDI tracks and can be accessed very quickly. For example, if you go MIDI > LOGICAL PRESETS > STANDARD SET 2, you will find functions to delete aftertouch data, delete all notes with velocities under specific values, etc.

Chapter 22

Mixing with Noise

Different people approach mixing differently, but I don't think anyone has described something as truly strange as the concept we're about to discuss. Some people will read this and just shake their heads, but others will actually try the suggested technique, and craft tighter, punchier mixes. I have several friends who swear that this really does work ... see what you think.

22.1 The Mixing Problem

What makes mixing so difficult is, unfortunately, a limitation of the human ear/brain combination. Our hearing can discern very small changes in pitch, but not level. You'll easily hear a 3% pitch change as being distinctly out of tune, but a 3% level change is nowhere near as dramatic. Also, our ears have an incredibly wide dynamic range of greater than 200dB—much more than a CD, for example. So when we mix and use only the top 20 to 40dB of average available dynamic range, even extreme musical dynamics don't represent that much of a change for the ear's total dynamic range.

Another problem with mixing is that the ear's frequency response changes at different levels. This is why small changes in volume are often perceived as tonal differences, and why it is so important to balance levels *exactly* when doing A-B comparisons. Because our ears hear low and high end signals better at higher levels, just a slight volume boost might produce a subjective feeling of greater "warmth" (from the additional low end) and "sparkle" (from the increased perception of treble).

The reason why top mixing engineers are in such demand is because through years of practice, they've trained their ears to discriminate among tiny level and frequency response differences (and hopefully, taken care of their ears so they don't suffer from their own frequency response problems). They are basically "juggling" the levels of multiple tracks, making sure that each one occupies its proper level with respect to the other tracks.

Remember, a mix does not compare levels to an absolute standard; all the tracks are interrelated. As an obvious example, the lead instruments usually have higher levels than the rhythm instruments. But there are much smaller hierarchies. Suppose you have a string pad part and the same part delayed a bit to produce chorusing. To avoid having excessive peaking when the signals reach maximum amplitude at the same time, as well as better preserve any rhythmic "groove," you'll probably mix the delayed track around 6dB behind the non-delayed track.

The more tracks, the more intricate this juggling act becomes. However, there are certain essential elements of any mix—some instruments that just have to be there and mixed fairly close in level to one another because of their importance. Ensuring that these elements are clearly audible and perfectly balanced is, I believe, one of the most important qualities in creating a "transportable" mix (i.e., one that sounds good over a variety of systems). Perhaps the lovely high end of some bell won't translate on a $29.95 boombox, but for the average listener, if you can make out the vocals, the leads, the beat, and the bass, you have the high points covered.

Ironically, though, our ears are less sensitive to changes in relatively loud levels than to relatively soft ones. This is why most veteran mixers initially work on a mix at low levels, because it makes it easier to tell if the important instruments are out of balance with respect to each other. At higher levels, differences in balance are harder to detect.

22.2 The Origin of "Mixing with Noise"

The following mixing technique is a way to check whether a song's crucial elements are mixed with equal emphasis. Like many other techniques that ultimately turn out to be useful, this one was discovered by accident.

I currently live in Florida, where it gets very hot in the summer—and my air conditioning makes a fair amount of background noise. One day, I noticed that the mixes I did when the air conditioner was on often sounded better than the ones I did when it was off. This seemed odd at first, until I made the connection with how many musicians use the "play the music in the car" test as the final judge of whether a mix is going to work or not. In both cases the background noise masks low-level signals, making it easier to tell which signals make it above the noise.

Curious whether this phenomenon could be defined more precisely, I started injecting pink noise into the console while mixing. This just about forces you to listen at relatively low levels, because the noise is really obnoxious! But more importantly, the noise adds a sort of "cloud cover" over the music, and as mountain peaks poke out of a cloud cover, so do sonic peaks poke out of the noise.

22.3 Applying the Technique

You'll want to add in the pink noise very sporadically during a mix, because the noise covers up high frequency sounds like hi-hat. You cannot get an accurate idea of the complete mix while you're mixing with noise injected into the mixer, but what you can do is make sure that all the important instruments are being heard properly.

CD track 26 consists of 60 seconds of pink noise that you can use to try mixing with noise. The file is crossfade-looped if you want to load it into a sampler, otherwise you can just drag in enough instances to last the duration of the song you're mixing.

Typically, I'll take the mix to the point where I'm fairly satisified with the sound. Then I'll add in lots of pink noise—no less than 10dB below 0 with dance mixes, for example, which typically have restricted dynamics anyway—and start analyzing.

While listening through the song, I pay special attention to vocals, snare, kick, bass, and leads. (With this much noise, you're not going to hear much else in the song anyway.) It's very easy to adjust their relative levels, because there's a limited range between overload on the high end and dropping below the noise on the low end. If all the crucial sounds make it into that "window" and can be heard clearly above the noise without distorting, you have a head start toward an equal balance.

Also note that the "noise test" can uncover problems. If you can hear a hi-hat or other minor part fairly high above the noise, it's probably too loud.

I'll generally run through the song a few more times, carefully tweaking each track for the right relative balance. Then it's time to take out the noise. First, it's an incredible relief not to hear that annoying hiss. Second, you can now get to work balancing the supporting instruments so that they work well with the lead sounds you've tweaked.

Although so far I've only mentioned instruments being above the noise floor, there are actually three distinct zones created by the noise: totally masked by the noise (inaudible), above the noise (clearly audible), and "melded," where an instrument isn't loud enough to stand out or soft enough to be masked, so it blends in with the noise. I find that mixing rhythm parts so that they sound melded can work if the noise is adjusted to a level suitable for the rhythm parts.

Overall, I estimate spending only about 3% of my mixing time using the injected noise. But often, it's the factor responsible for making the mix sound good over multiple systems. Mixing with noise may sound crazy, but give it a try. With a little practice, there are ways to make noise work for you.

Chapter 23

Using Hardware Control Surfaces

One of the problems with software-based, virtual recording is that it lacks the hands-on, real time control of traditional recording—drawing an envelope is not the same as moving a fader. However, there are now many Cubase-compatible control surfaces, including Steinberg's own Houston controller. Other popular models are the Radikal Technologies SAC-2.2 (with an excellent Houston emulation and very broad feature set), TAS-CAM US-428, and the Mackie Control. Not only can they help you create a more "hands-on" mix, but they can even speed up your work flow and allow for more efficient operation.

Many musicians don't recognize the value of hardware controllers and are content to use a mouse to draw envelopes or move on-screen faders, because this is precise and doesn't require any other hardware. To me, though, that's like step-entering notes in a MIDI sequencer instead of playing on a comfortable, 88-note, weighted keyboard—you can do it with step entry, but playing keyboard makes the process go much more smoothly.

However, before getting into how to install and use control surfaces, we need to understand the history behind them.

23.1   Old School Mixing

Until digital audio came along, all mixing surfaces had one control per function. Large-format consoles were expensive and huge, but this made it easy to tweak anything you wanted in real time. Often, more than one person would be involved with the mixing process—in some cases because it was physically difficult for one person to reach all parts of the board.

But there was one other important aspect to physical mixing: real-time control invited *playing* the mixer, making it more of an instrument than just a way to balance levels. Many engineers would ride gain in time with the music, making subtle—or not so subtle—spontaneous adjustments to add character to the song. When I did a lot of session work at Columbia Records, there was an engineer (who had a lot of hits, by the way) who would get the faders close to the right place, close his eyes, and move them very subtly and rhythmically. I was impressed how much this made the mix more lively, and it was a lesson that has stayed with me.

Part of the reason for fader manipulation was tape's limited dynamic range. Players needed a precise "touch" to play within a range that was low enough to avoid distortion, but high enough to stay out of the noise. So, some of the dynamics would be restored during the mixing process by engineers "playing" the faders.

But moving faders and sends wasn't all. EQs had accessible knobs as well, which likewise invited real-time tweaking. The mixer was not a set-and-forget device, but in the hands of a talented engineer became a dynamic, living part of the recording process. This type of thinking still exists in DJ and "groove" types of music, but overall, it seems mixing has become a more static process as the world of recording has become increasingly digital. It's time to get some of that control and human element back.

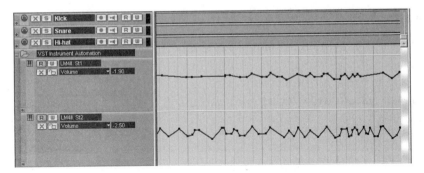

The two automation tracks are for the kick (top) and snare (bottom) parts of a drum track. The snare has a lot of moves to add expressiveness to the level; the upward slopes were often there to increase the level of successive hits.

For example, the screen shot shows the automation moves (done with a hardware controller) for the drum part in a recent mix. Adding dynamic nuances made the tune far more lively, interesting, and human.

Once you're familiarized with the control surface of your choice, using it also helps keep you in that desirable "rigth brain mode" we talked about earlier, because you can just reach out, grab something, and get the desired result without having to think about it. At least to me, a hardware controller is not a luxury, but a necessity if you want a mix to have some of the elements of a "performance," which I feel makes the music more compelling.

23.2 Cubase: Many Ways of Mixing

Cubase allows different approaches to mixing when using a control surface:

23.2.1 Standard Mixing

Hook up a controller and move the faders in real time as you record the output into a CD recorder, DAT, Minidisc, analog tape deck, etc. This is pure "control surface mixing."

23.2.2 Standard Mixing with Automation

This is the same as above, but Cubase "remembers" and plays back your mixing moves. The big advantage here is that if you make a mistake in just a couple of places, you can go back and make any necessary fixes by punching in new automation mixing moves, or by using ...

23.2.3 Graphic Mixing

You can "unfold" a track to see the envelope created by your mixing moves. You can then edit this with the pencil or other tools for very precise edits.

In practice, if you use a control surface, it's likely that you'll record the automation for your real-time moves, then using graphic editing to fix small details.

23.3 Using a Remote Control Device

Cubase supports many commercially-available control surfaces. Go DEVICES > DEVICE SETUP; if you see your controller listed under Devices, you're pretty much ready to go. Make sure it's hooked up correctly (some connect via USB, some need a single MIDI cable, and some need bi-directional MIDI where both MIDI In and MIDI Out go to the device).

If Devices shows a controller you don't have, you can safely remove it. Click on its name in the Devices list, click on the Add/Remove tab, then click on "Remove."

Click on the Device name, and a Setup box appears. Choose the MIDI Input and MIDI Output to which the device connects.

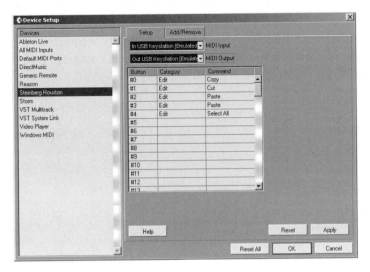

The Setup menu for Steinberg's Houston controller not only includes a place to assign MIDI In and Out, but also lets you assign the buttons to various functions.

At this point, consult your controller's manual to see which knobs are assigned to which Cubase functions. Typically, you'll be able to switch faders in banks (e.g. 1—8, 9—16, etc.) so a limited number of faders can control as many channels as you like. You may also be able to use other controls for various purposes—e.g. switch a set of rotary controls from controlling panning to controlling EQ frequency.

Verify that all is well by moving some controls on your control surface; corresponding controls in the VST Mixer should move as well.

23.3.1   Installing a Supported Device

If you don't see your controller under Devices, go DEVICES > DEVICE SETUP then click on "Add/Remove." You'll see a list of all currently supported devices.

If your controller is on the list, great. Select it and click "Add." This will now show up under Devices, so proceed as described above.

> Even if your controller isn't on the list, don't panic—it may emulate one of the supported devices. For example, many controllers have a mode that emulates the JLCooper CS-10, one of the first controllers. If so, choose that emulation mode and select JLCooper CS-10 within Cubase. As another example, the SAC-2.2 does an excellent Houston emulation, so you can just select Houston if you're using the SAC-2.2 Of course, also make sure you have the correct emulation mode selected at your controller.

23.3.2   Installing an Unsupported Device

If you have an unsupported controller, such as the knobs on something like the M-Audio Oxygen8, or a general-purpose fader box like the Peavey PC-1600, you can still use it as a Generic Remote. To do this:

1   Go DEVICES > DEVICE SETUP then click on the "Add/Remove" tab.

2   In the list click on "Generic Remote."

3   Click "Add."

4   Generic Remote shows up in the Devices list. Click there on "Generic Remote."

5   Click on the "Setup" tab.

6   There are two fields. The top one matches controls on the generic remote to virtual faders. These may or may not correspond to actual Cubase faders, as determined in the next field.

7   The upper field maps controls to virtual faders. If you know the type of MIDI signal being generated, set the MIDI Status, MIDI Channel, Address, Maximum Value, and Flags parameters to correspond to the data sent by the controller (note that clicking on the "Help" button provides lots of useful information on these parameters). For example, if you're using a synthesizer with a volume pedal that transmits controller 7 data over channel 1 and you want to map it to fader 1, the Fader 1 line would read "Controller—1—7—127—R." If you want to map the synth's aftertouch (also on channel 1) to Fader 2, its line would read "Aftertouch—1—(address is irrelevant)—127—R."

With the upper field, you can remove an unused entry by clicking anywhere on a line to highlight it, then clicking the Delete button. Conversely, if you have a controller with a zillion knobs, you can add entries by clicking on Add.

8   If you don't know the signal your controller is generating, no problem. Click on the Control Name that you want to assign, move your controller, and while moving it, click on the "Learn" button. The fader will now respond to the signal generated by the control you were moving.

9   The lower fields maps parameters within Cubase to the virtual faders. Typically, if you wanted to change track levels in a mix, the Device would be VST Mixer, Channel/Category would show the channel you want to control, and Value/Action would show Volume. However, you have a huge choice of what can be controlled—click on a fader's Device or Value/Action field, and you'll see what I mean!

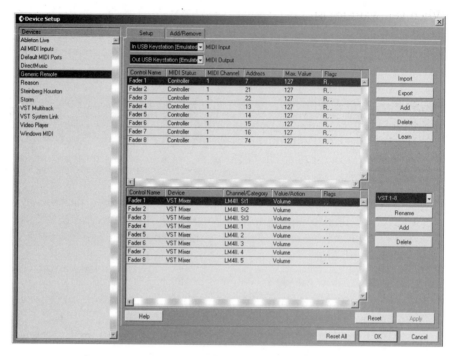

The Generic Remote setup has been used to assign the eight control knobs on the M-Audio Oxygen8 to the first eight faders of the VST Mixer, which control the outputs of the LM4 drum machine. This is only one bank; a second bank (not shown) assigns the same knobs to the faders 9—15 of the VST mixer.

23.3.3 Going to the Bank

Note that the lower field has a drop-down Bank menu where you can create banks of controls. For example, suppose your controller has eight knobs. You could click on the Bank field, click on "Rename," call it "VST 1-8," then map the first eight faders to Cubase parameters (e.g. volume for mixer channels 1 to 8). Next, you could add another bank, rename it to "VST 9-16," and map the first eight faders to additional Cubase parameters (e.g. volume for mixer channels 9 to 16). You could create another bank for Transport control, another for EQ settings, etc.

When you want to use the Generic Remote, go DEVICES > GENERIC REMOTE, and a small window appears where you can select the desired bank. Pretty cool!

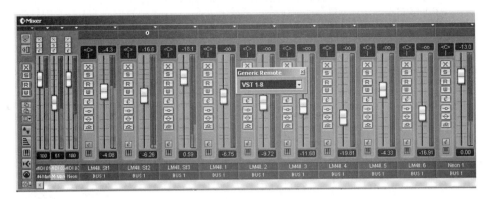

The Bank window for any of the supported controllers, including Generic Remote, is very compact and makes it easy to select different banks of controls.

23.4 How to Choose a Control Surface

I'm sure the folks at Steinberg have a very simple answer to that question: buy a Houston controller. And actually, that's a pretty good answer if your main recording program is Cubase (or Nuendo, for that matter).

But remember that there are two main control surface families: *general-purpose* controllers designed to work with a wide range of gear, and *dedicated* controllers that work with a specific product or line. Houston would be a good example of the latter, and in general, dedicated controllers give the best user experience because of each control's specificity. The catch is that if you use multiple programs, a dedicated controller may or may not be able to accommodate them.

General purpose interfaces start with budget models that have, for example, eight assignable MIDI knobs or faders. Programming these may be a tedious affair involving button presses or more painless if there's a "learn" function (where you send it the controller you want it to transmit). Or, there may be accessory software for programming the device. Not all general-purpose devices are simple; on a novice/intermediate level, Peavey's PC-1600x offers 16 faders and buttons, whereas at the high end, Mixed Logic Studio Electronics offers the M242, a $4,000 control surface with 24 faders, 53 rotary encoders, and more.

Here are a few tips to remember as you seek the right interface:

- Check any general purpose control surfaces for availability of presets or templates that apply to your gear, so you don't have to program your own from scratch.

- Support is a two-way street: not only do control surfaces support software, software sometimes needs to support control surfaces.

- Check whether the controller can also generate general-purpose MIDI controller signals. This is the only way to control some programs and outboard gear.

- You may not really need a controller if your existing equipment can do the job. Several digital mixers include a MIDI fader layer that can be programmed to send out controller information and sometimes, even SysEx. Keyboards are getting into the act, too: Yamaha's MOTIF series has templates for control of several popular sequencing programs. For relatively simple control surface applications, these options may suffice.

- Moving faders increase control surface costs, but simplify the mixing process. An alternative, nulling faders, don't move but include indicators that show whether the fader is above or below an existing programmed value. You set the fader's position to match the existing value, then punch in.

- Check for expandability. That 8-channel moving fader setup may work for now, but then you'll want 16 channels, then 24 ... you know the story. You should at least be able to bank-switch faders to switch to different channels groups (e.g. 1—8, 9—16, etc.).

- Budget systems are proliferating. There are several new USB-based interfaces, such as the US-428 from TASCAM, EZBus from Event Electronics, etc. These include audio interfacing options (such as mic pres, D/A converters, etc.) along with controls like faders and switches—excellent for those on a budget.

- There's more to control than mixing. Find a control surface that will let you tweak EQ settings, aux bus sends, etc.

In any event, try before you buy. A control surface should be simple to use, feel good, and be well-matched to your software you plan to use. If you hook up with the right partner, you will likely find operating your studio to have a vastly improved "feel."

23.5 Recommended Parameters for Real-time Tweaking

Most control surfaces include a main set of faders and auxiliary controls that can work with other parameters. Working with faders is pretty obvious; when people talk about hardware control surfaces, it usually concerns adjusting levels while mixing. While that's an important application, there are other ways a control surface can help make better mixes.

23.5.1 Take a Cue from the Conductor

Before we describe specific parameters to tweak, let's talk briefly about attitude. An orchestra's conductor doesn't just act like a metronome, moving the baton up and down on the beat. A good conductor cajoles, leads, lags, and adds motion to the performance that inspires the players. That's what using a control surface is about: to add the same kind of expressiveness to a mix that a conductor adds to the interpretation of a performance.

Of course, the tracks will hopefully already include some degree of animation. But music seems to lose some of its impact in the recording process, and just as it's common to add a little EQ or harmonic enhancement, real-time changes to various aspects of a mix can create a more satisfying listening experience.

Here are some of recommended parameters to tweak in real time while mixing.

23.5.2 "Pushing" Master Faders

The setup shown below lets you "pump up the volume" in selected places without causing distortion. In this case, the maximizer *must* insert after the Master Gain stage. With Cubase's VST Master Effects window, this means inserting it below the line that says Master Gain.

Here the Waves L1-Ultramaximizer+ is inserted in the master section. Note that the input signal is above the threshold, so the attenuation meter shows some amount of attenuation.

Most maximizers are set for "brickwall" limiting, where nothing can exceed a user-set limit. If you use a limiter, it may have this option as well. Set the maximizer threshold somewhat below 0 (e.g., −2 to −6) and keep a close eye on the attenuation display (if there's a "ceiling" control to set a maximum level, I usually set it slightly below 0, like −0.1).

> If a signal reaches 0 consistently, the assumption is that it's distorted, even if it is not. Some CD duplicators won't accept CDs that hit 0 for a certain number of consecutive samples. Setting a ceiling of −0.1 prevents this problem from happening.

As long as there's no attenution, then the maximizer is out of the picture and you're hearing the natural dynamics. As you move the master fader up 0, when its setting exceeds the maximizer's threshold, gain reduction will kick in and the attenuation meter will show some degree of attenuation. Do this during sections of the song where it should sound like it's working hard; the result is a somewhat higher average level, but without adding distortion. Be sparing—just 1dB or 2 makes a big difference.

23.5.3   Sends and Delays

After hearing one of my mixes that used a lot of delay on voice, a listener commented that the delay never seemed to "step on" the vocals or muddy things up. This is because I "worked" the send control in real time to pick up just the end of phrases. Therefore, when the phrase stopped, the echoes would continue—but just before the vocals came back in, the send went back down again. You'll probably want the send control assigned pre-fader.

23.5.4   Sends and Reverb Splashes

I generally don't like to use huge reverberant spaces on mixes, but I often set up a reverb on one aux bus that *does* have a real long decay. Then, if there's an isolated snare hit or held vocal note that needs lots of emphasis (or a dramatic pause that wants a reverb spillover), I just open the send control long enough to send a signal "spike" into the reverb for a tasty reverb "splash."

23.5.5 Sends and Distortion

One of my favorite mixing tricks is sending an aux bus to distortion, usually the Steinberg QuadraFuzz. You can really make a drum set "pop" by turning up the send and giving the sound some "crunch." Because the distortion acts like a hard limiter, the sound's peak level increases by little (if any). But as with pushing a limiter, the softer parts are brought up and because there's distortion, the crunch adds even more sonic interest. In addition to drums, I find this useful on bass and sometimes keyboard pads or "B3" imitations.

23.5.6 Emphasizing with EQ

Be careful when manipulating EQ in real time, because even slight EQ boosts can lead to distortion or excessive tonal changes. But consider a situation where you want some big piano chords to become more prominent, so they "push" the song more (for example in the final chorus). You could increase the level, but that may cause the piano to dominate or lead to distortion. Another option is to automate a parametric stage's boost/cut control (use a fairly wide bandwidth in the 2—4kHz range). When you want the piano to stand out, just add some boost. As the ear is most sensitive in this frequency range, even small differences give the piano more clarity. This technique works with just about every instrument except bass; for that, try boosting in the 1—2kHz region.

23.5.7 Pan Controls

Back in the 60s, when stereo was relatively new, there was a lot more use of panning ("Oh wow man, the guitars are flying across my head! Pass the bong!"). While going back to those gimmick-laden days is probably not a good idea, there's a lot to be said for subtle panning changes. For example, suppose you're mixing a tune with a big, fat stereo pad. If you want the pad to lurk a bit in the background, turn the pan controls so they point to the same place in the stereo field (e.g. center). Then for the Big Chorus, move the pan controls out to widen the stereo field. Also try expanding the sound in steps, so that as the chorus continues, the pad gets wider and wider.

23.5.8 Complementary Motion

This works best with bass and drums, or bass and guitar; the object is to vary them in opposing ways, but in time with the beat. For example, mix the drums slightly louder for one measure with bass slightly back, and on the next measure, kick the bass up a bit and drop the drums a tiny bit. With mono, this is the closest you can get to simulating the placement of stereo; you can place a sound either more up-front or further back in the track. The rhythmic variations build interest and can even give a somewhat hypnotic effect.

23.5.9 Mutes and Solos

Music has learned a lot from DJs, and one popular technique is to solo a track for a break or perhaps mute several tracks. Skilled remixers often create entirely new types of music by simply running multiple loops simultaneously and bringing them in and out—sometimes with level changes, sometimes with mute or solo—to build compositions. A tune might start with a looped pad, then have the kick fade in, then the hi-hat, then the bass, and then have everything drop out except for the bass before bringing in some other melodic or rhythmic element. As with the other examples mentioned so far, you can of course do this "offline." But remember, mixing can be a performance—and sometimes you might get inspired so that you do fader moves and button presses in extremely clever, non-repeatable ways.

23.5.10 Mute or Level Change?

Also note that a mute or solo is a sudden, rapid change that surprises the listener. Doing the same type of thing with faders will always sound somewhat different, because the fader change will not be instantaneous. Thus, moving a fader from full off to full on—even if it's fairly fast—may cause a feeling of anticipation in the listener rather than surprise.

23.5.11 Controlling the A1 Synthesizer

You can of course automate A1 parameters in the usual way, by drawing envelopes or recording real-time control movements. But the engineers at Waldorf are smart and realized that part of what makes playing a synthesizer fun is being able to tweak its controls in real time. As a result, the A1 is very easy to work from a control surface.

As you pass your mouse over a control, look at the info strip located just above the filter envelope graphic. The right-most parameter in the strip indicates the MIDI controller number assigned to that parameter. Assuming you can assign specific controller numbers to your control surface, it's an easy matter to map the desired physical controls to the desired parameters on the A1.

The cursor is over the Filter Cutoff Mod control; note how its corresponding MIDI controller number shows up as the right-most parameter (circled for clarity) in the information strip above the filter envelope.

Chapter 24

Interfacing with the Physical World

Steinberg really started something with Virtual Studio Technology, which folded more functions that ever before into a computer, while relying solely on a host processor—not additional cards to provide extra processing power. When VST was introduced, computers were underpowered for the task at hand; track counts were limited, plug-ins were pretty basic, and virtual instruments weren't a part of the sequencing environment ... yet the potential was there.

Over time, though, it's clear that Steinberg bet on the right horse. As processors have become more powerful, memory less expensive, and hard disks faster and cheaper, it has become not only feasible—but in many cases, desirable—to do as much as possible within a computer environment.

But at some point, signals have to get into the computer, and out of it as well. In other words, Cubase has to deal with the physical world. This could be via something as simple as a consumer-level sound card with stereo inputs and outputs, to a sophisticated, multi-output audio interface that interfaces with a physical studio setup involving traditional elements like mixers.

> As the point of this book is mixing and mastering with Cubase, not installation and hardware, we'll describe just enough hardware basics so that the rest of the chapter makes sense.

24.1 Using an External Hardware Mixer

Despite the fact that you can pretty much do everything in Cubase, there are still times when using an external mixer makes sense. For example, I have a digital mixer (Panasonic DA7) with superb-sounding digital EQ as well as reasonably good dynamics and a noise gate on every channel. It also has a fader bank that can send MIDI control messages, so it provides a useful control surface when mixing audio or MIDI.

By using Cubase with a multi-channel audio interface and sending those outs into the mixer input channels, I can use the DA7's EQ and some of my more esoteric analog outboard effects, while relieving the host processor of having to do these functions. Thus, there's more power available for processor-hungry plug-ins like software synthesizers.

Being able to trim faders instantly and move several of them at once, is another reason why using a mixer works for me (normally a control surface would be enough, but as I said, I like the EQ). Another advantage of an outboard mixer is you can use its aux busses to feed a high-end hardware reverb, which is likely to sound better than the average reverb plug-in.

Overall, using an external digital mixer can be a good way to derive maximum benefits from a computer-based system as well as gain the advantages of a more standard, hardware-based studio. Before getting into mixing with this sort of setup, though, we need to cover how signals get from Cubase to the audio interface.

24.2 Audio Interfaces

The simplest audio interfaces usually have stereo in and stereo out. Thus, you can record two channels at a time into Cubase through the inputs and play back two channels (i.e., stereo) from Cubase. If you decide to use the mixer in Cubase for mixing and you plan to release your music on CD, then two channels is really all you need so you can monitor what it's going to sound like.

However, you may need more than two channels while mixing if you are

- mixing in 5.1 surround (Cubase SX only) or
- sending the outputs to an external mixer.

Multichannel sound cards very often have an ADAT optical interface, as part of the card or an add-on option, suitable for interfacing with a wide variety of digital mixing consoles. Steinberg has designed a special, cross-platform driver for multichannel sound cards called ASIO, and I *highly* recommended you use a sound card's native ASIO drivers. (By "native," we mean that the ASIO drivers were written specifically for that card, rather than as some sort of emulation.) This gives the lowest latencies for control motion when mixing, which is pretty important if you want a good mixing "feel."

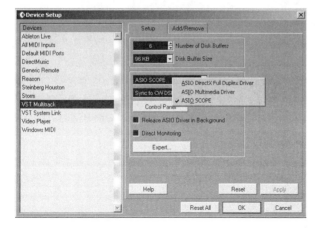

After installing CreamWare's PowerPulsar DSP board and audio interface (based on their SCOPE system), Cubase could select from one of three drivers. However, only the ASIO SCOPE one was written specifically for the CreamWare system, thus guaranteeing optimum performance. ASIO DirectX and ASIO Multimedia drivers also work, but their latency is unacceptable compared to the more efficient ASIO SCOPE driver.

When you install a multichannel audio interface, Cubase runs a test to check out the configuration. Once that's done, the program knows how many inputs and outputs you have. You can check the number of outputs by going DEVICES > VST OUTPUTS. Drag a corner of the window to its full size to reveal the available number of outputs, presented as output busses. Each Bus has an enable/disable button in the upper left corner except for Bus 1, which is always enabled.

The particular CreamWare audio interface being used by Cubase has two ADAT ports for input and output (as well as analog I/O and SPDIF digital I/O). Each ADAT port has eight channels, which are usually configured as four stereo pairs. So, with two ports, there are eight stereo pairs. Cubase sees these as eight stereo busses, labeled BUS1 to BUS8 (but can be renamed). Sending a signal to one of these busses causes the signal to appear on the matching stereo pair in the ADAT port.

24.3 Connecting to Outboard Gear

Continuing on from the previous example, my DA7 has 32 inputs and two ADAT ports. Channels 1 to 16 are analog inputs, while channels 17 to 32 are fed by the ADAT ports. The DA7 channels are mono (but can be ganged for stereo operation). Therefore, Bus 1L goes to channel 17, Bus 1R to channel 18, Bus 2L to channel 19, Bus 2R to channel 20, and so on until all 16 ADAT channels are assigned to the channels provided by the interface's eight stereo busses.

Inputs work similarly. Within the PowerPulsar setup, even though there are also two ADAT input ports, I elected to use only one because I seldom need to record more than eight channels simultaneously; the fewer input and output drivers you use, the less hard the computer has to work.

24.4 Making Bus Assignments within Cubase

Okay, let's recap: We installed a multichannel audio interface in the computer running Cubase; Cubase has recognized the channels and allocated them internally. We've also chosen the proper multichannel ASIO driver, opened up a window that shows the eight busses, and hooked up the audio interface outs to a digital mixer by using two ADAT ports. So far, so good. Now it's time to assign channels within Cubase to the busses.

Beneath each fader is the track name and bus assignment. Clicking and holding on the bus assignment button causes a list to appear of all the available output busses (i.e. those that are enabled in the VST Outputs window).

The Electro Drums track is being assigned to Bus 5. Note how the two Thin Drums tracks, which are both mono, are assigned to Bus 6. However, Thin Drums is panned full left, while Thin Drums 2 is panned full right. Therefore, when Bus 6 arrives at the hardware mixer's ADAT port, the bus's left channel goes to one mixer channel and the right channel goes to another mixer channel. They therefore appear at the hardware mixer as two individual mono channels.

When using an external mixer that doesn't have stereo channels, you need to use two channels for stereo signals (panned oppositely) and one channel for mono signals. However, each bus feeding the mixer is stereo, so how do you send mono signals to individual mixer tracks and be able to adjust their levels in the VST Outputs window?

Each bus in the VST Outputs window has an "unlink" button (the rectangular button located above and between the two faders). When unlinked, the stereo bus becomes two mono busses, with independent level control for each bus. Thus, mono tracks can be assigned to an unlinked bus, but panned full left or full right to appear exclusively on one or the other bus channel.

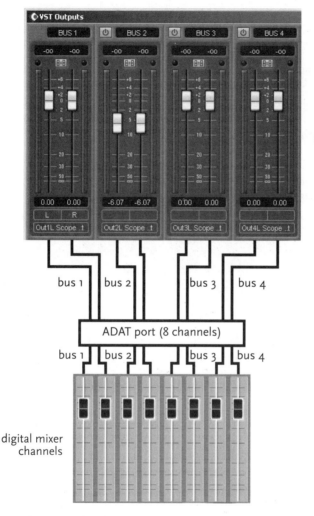

This summarizes how signals get from Cubase busses to digital mixers via an ADAT interface. The bus outs go to the audio interface's ADAT port. It sends the four busses over an optical cable to the digital mixer. The bus left outs and right outs go to individual channels within the digital mixer, because the mixer channels are all mono. For stereo signals, mono mixer channels can usually be linked in stereo.

For some of my mixes, 16 channels isn't enough. In that case, I send related instruments to one bus. For example, with drums I often have separate mono tracks for kick, snare, toms, and hi-hats, and stereo tracks for overhead mic and room mic signals. If each of these went to its own output, I'd use up four stereo busses just for drums. So within Cubase, I pan each track as desired, set levels, EQ, sends, etc., then assign all these tracks to a single stereo bus. Essentially, I'm premixing the tracks within Cubase's mixer, then assigning them to the bus.

At the DA7, the sounds are already set to the right levels and are in the correct stereo positions. Thus, the DA7 fader becomes more like a subgroup fader where I can bring the entire set of drums up or down. If I need to change the levels of individual tracks, that's easily done using Cubase's automation. I get the best of both worlds: Cubase's plug-ins, soft synths, automation, and editing, along with a mixer for great-sounding EQ on every channel, a control surface with real faders, and the option to throw analog effects into the mix.

Granted, for most people, mixing within Cubase will be fine; and mixing within Cubase using a control surface is even better. But for those who regard mixing as an extension of performing, where knobs and faders are meant to be moved spontaneously in real time based on your mood while mixing, being able to team Cubase up with a mixer can be a wonderful combination.

24.5 ReWire and Mixing

We'll close out this section by returning to the virtual world from the physical, because the ReWire protocol allows doing the sort of tricks that required interfacing with outboard, physical devices, but within a virtual environment.

Before the virtual studio, during mixdown MIDI instruments were often added in real time to the mix. The MIDI tracks in a sequencer would be distributed to a synth rack with various instruments, and their outputs were mixed into the console, just like other audio tracks. (In some cases, the MIDI instrument outs were "bounced" to the multitrack so they could be handled as audio tracks.)

Cubase SX/SL does much the same thing with virtual instruments, but instead of living in a rack, they live within the sequencer and feed directly into the mixer. Generally these are loaded in the VST Instruments device, but there's another way to add an entire "synth rack" of instruments: the ReWire software technology developed by Propellerhead Software, which tightly integrates two (or sometimes more) complete *programs*—not just instruments—to work together. If one of the programs is an "all-in-one studio" program like Propellerheads' Reason, Arturia Storm, Image-Line's Fruity Loops, or Cakewalk Project5, these essentially become a giant synth rack for Cubase. MIDI tracks can be sent to these instruments, whose outputs can then become part of the final mix (or, as in the old days, bounced to audio tracks if you'd prefer to handle them in that format or if your CPU can't handle the extra instruments).

With ReWire, Cubase is the "host" or "mixer" program, while the other is a "client" or "synthesizer" program. Note that some programs, like Storm and Ableton's Live, can be either a host or client. When you ReWire a client into a host, the client's outputs go into the host's mixer and show up as individual digital audio tracks.

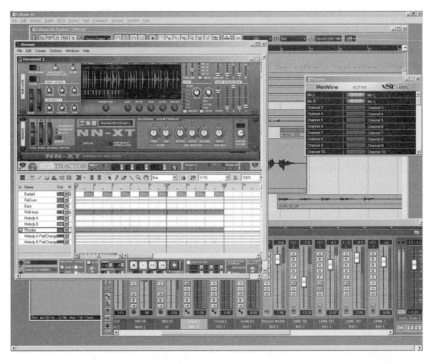

Reason has been rewired into Cubase. In the Reason device toward the upper right, two tracks for the final mixed output have been enabled. It would also be possible to have the individual outs of every Reason instrument go into the VST Mixer, thus allowing them to be processed, have individual level automation, etc.

For example, if you have MIDI tracks recorded in Reason's sequencer and want to add vocals, guitar, piano, etc. (remember, Reason doesn't do digital audio recording), ReWire it into Cubase and record the audio in Cubase. With ReWire2-compatible applications like Cubase, MIDI data recorded in the host can also flow to the client, allowing for client parameter automation via MIDI controllers.

ReWired programs also share transport and sync functions, with single-sample accuracy. Furthermore, any of the client's syncable instruments or processors will respond to the host's tempo.

24.5.1   Can Your CPU Handle ReWire?

There's a misconception that ReWire uses considerable computer resources, but it's just an interconnection protocol. However, by definition, you'll be using another digital audio program with Cubase, and these programs tend to be processor-hungry. Most modern Windows and Mac machines can handle this if you have sufficient RAM and a relatively fast processor. To save CPU power, you can export ReWired instrument tracks to digital audio tracks in the host so that the ReWired device is no longer necessary during mixdown. Unfortunately this gives up some flexibility if you decide to make a last-minute change to the instrument sound.

24.5.2   Loading ReWire Devices in Cubase

To ReWire a program into Cubase:

1   Open Cubase, the ReWire host.

2   Go DEVICES > "NAME OF REWIRE APPLICATION."

3   Enable the ReWire outputs you want to use in the ReWire Device that appears.

4   Open the ReWire client.

5   The enabled outputs appear automatically in Cubase's VST Mixer.

24.5.3   Your New Synth Rack

Cubase does not ship with an integrated sampler or REX file player (although Cubase can recognize and play back REX files), but rewiring Reason 2.0 provides two excellent samplers, the Dr. Rex file player, the Malström graintable synthesizer, SubTractor analog synth, and ReDrum drum machine. You can open up multiple instances of these within Reason to expand the palette even further.

24.5.4 Recording Controller Tweaks in Real Time

Varying parameters in real time helps considerably in terms of giving a good "feel" to synthesized music. Fortunately, Cubase can receive MIDI data and pass it along to ReWire2-compatible clients.

For example, suppose in Reason you want to tweak SubTractor's Amp Env Decay parameter via MIDI (or for that matter, any parameter listed in Reason's MIDI implementation chart). According to the chart, this parameter responds to MIDI Controller #9. So ...

1   Create a MIDI track in Cubase and put it in record mode.

2   Assign the output to the desired instrument in Reason.

3   Set up your controller so that it transmits data over Controller #9.

4   Assuming your MIDI channels, ports, assignments, etc. are set up correctly, test the connection by putting the focus on Reason and varying the controller.

5   The "Amp Env Decay" slider should follow your motions.

6   Record the controller motions in the host, and after stopping, verify that they're recorded.

7   When you go back to the beginning and press Play, the controller changes should affect Reason.

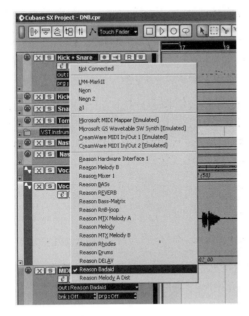

Selecting the output parameter for the MIDI track brings up a list of available MIDI destinations, including the various Reason instruments loaded into the Reason "rack." Select the one you want to control, then record the controllers so that they can affect Reason while you're mixing down.

Part 6

Mastering with
Cubase SX/SL

Chapter 25

Mastering Basics

Traditionally, mastering is the stage between mixing and the pressing plant, where you add any final edits or enhancements (fade in or out, compression, dithering, etc.) to your stereo mixed file, then assemble your tunes in the proper order. As the final link in the CD production chain, mastering can make or break a project—which is why people often pay big bucks to a veteran mastering engineer for an objective viewpoint. Unless you have much experience, hiring someone who really knows how to master could be the best move for your music.

> If you plan to take your mix to a professional mastering engineer, do not "pre-master" the song—export the raw, unprocessed mix to a WAV or AIFF file. Don't even add fades; add them while mastering.

However, in many cases mastering can be handled a bit more casually. Samples need to be mastered, as do commercials. And if you do go to a professional mastering engineer, you can at least try your hand at it first so you can communicate your needs better. Besides, if you do enough mastering, hopefully at some point you'll get good at it.

Do remember that mastering is not intended to salvage a recording, but enhance an already superb mix. If there's a problem with the mix, remix the tune—don't count on mastering to solve the problem.

25.1 Mastering—Then and Now

Prior to the digital revolution, mastering had a very defined set of functions. You would bring your finished mixes on tape to a mastering engineer, who would often "bounce" them to another tape through various signal processors designed to sweeten the sound. The tunes would then be assembled in the desired order, and vinyl test pressings would be made so the final product could be evaluated prior to mass-producing albums.

Mastering was rightly regarded as an arcane, mystifying art. Few musicians had access to the high-end, expensive tools needed to do mastering, nor did they have the experience of someone who had listened to thousands of recordings and knew how to make them ready for mass production.

Today, the situation is quite different. Mastering tools are within the financial reach of just about everyone, and the highly specialized expertise requires to master for vinyl are, except for some small vinyl-oriented markets, no longer an issue. However, experience is still not something you can buy as a plug-in. Given the importance of the mastering process, even those with mastering tools and decent mastering techniques will almost always go to a professional to insure the highest level of quality, as well as an objective viewpoint.

25.2 Mastering Tasks

The mastering process addresses several issues:

- Equalization. This balances out a track's overall frequency response. EQ can even affect the apparent mix by emphasizing the frequency range of particular instruments. For example, if the bass wasn't mixed loudly enough, EQ can raise the level of the bass to where it will sound like it was mixed louder.
- Fade ins and fade outs. You can add these by automating your moves with Cubase's Master Channel fader.
- Compression/limiting/level maximizing. These are all variations on the same basic process, which is to even out the dynamic range, resulting in more apparent loudness.
- Occasional effects. Adding a bit of reverb may help give an additional feeling of "space" and stereo imaging.

- Cleanup. This is your last chance to remove any remaining noise, hum, pops, clicks, crackles, etc.

- Dither. This process helps create the best possible sound quality when going from high-resolution audio (e. g. 24 or 32 bits) to lower-resolution audio (16 bits). There's more on dithering later in this section.

Cubase contains the plug-in tools needed to perform most of these functions (surprisingly, there's no available EQ for mastering; the only EQ shows up in the VST Channels), however, some people prefer to use their personal favorite plug-ins anyway, particularly for critical mastering applications.

Steinberg itself makes a "Mastering edition" set of plug-ins suitable for use with Cubase, as do other companies such as Waves (whose products are particularly well-regarded for mastering). A popular DirectX program by iZotope, Ozone, contains a mastering suite of tools consisting of equalization, multiband compression, harmonic exciter, stereo enhancer, maximizer, etc.; IK Multimedia's T-Racks also does dynamics and equalization processing, but specializes in a creating a more vintage, "tube-like" sound. Bottom line: you have a lot of options in a very subjective field.

Chapter 26

Mastering within Cubase

Most mastering is done with a two-track digital audio editing program, such as Steinberg Wavelab, Sonic Foundry Sound Forge, Syntrillium Cool Edit Pro, BIAS Peak, TC Works Spark, and so on. These offer superb navigation facilities, the ability to zoom in on waveforms, pencil tools to draw out clicks, and include plug-ins for mastering tasks along with the ability to host other plug-ins.

Cubase's Master Channel allows for mastering-type functions within Cubase. The principal difference is that with digital audio editors, you are working off-line with a previously-generated file. With Cubase, you are adding and tweaking mastering effects in real time. Of course, though, these effects can be applied and the results exported as an audio file.

As a result, even after mastering within Cubase, you may still want to import the file into a digital audio editing program for final touch-up and then into a CD-burning program (if the editing program doesn't have those capabilities) so you can assemble tunes in the desired order and burn a reference CD.

However, there are certain other advantages to using mastering effects within Cubase. It's not uncommon to do a mix, take it to a mastering engineer who adds some compression, and then find out that compression changes the mix subtly, requiring you to go back and do a quick remix. By patching a compressor into the master channel, you can get a better idea of what the music will sound like when mastered, and mix accordingly.

If you decide to use a pro mastering engineer, it's also worth creating a version of the tune that uses mastering effects to give the engineer an idea of the type of sound you seek. The engineer can then translate your ideas into something perhaps even better, yet retain the "feel" you want.

26.1 The Master Channel

The Master Channel is where mastering functions take place. This affects any channels assigned to Bus 1; if channels are assigned to other VST output busses, they will not be processed by any effects in the Master Channel. (Typically, multiple output busses would be used to send Cubase channels to an external mixer for mixing, which itself may have physical insert jacks for master effects.) The situation is different for surround mixing (available only in Cubase SX).

To view the Master Channel from the mixer, click on the Show Master button. The Master fader then appears toward the right of the mixer. You can also call up the VST Master Effects device through the Devices menu, or by clicking on the Master Channel's edit ("e") button. Next to the edit button is a button that bypasses the master effects—a very handy feature when doing "reality checks" to determine how the master effects change the sound.

In Cubase SX, the VST Master Effects device also shows how the effects are patched into multi-output configurations, such as Quad or 5.1 Surround, as well as a File button to load or save banks of presets or individual presets. Also in Cubase SX, the expanded Mixer view shows the eight effects slots above the master fader.

opened
patch editor

patch editor
window

expanded view shows
master effects slots

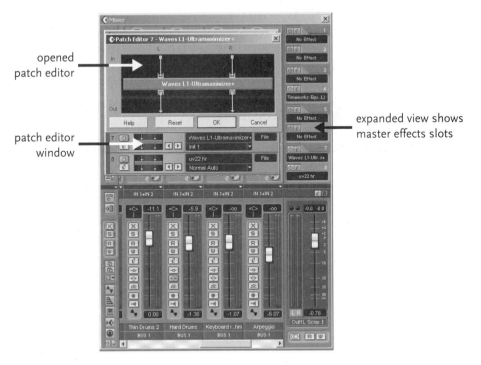

The Patch Editor shows two channels for stereo, four for Quad, six for 5.1 surround, etc. You can determine which channels an effect will process. For example, with surround, a stereo reverb could process only the rear channels.

Choosing effects is the same as with Insert or Send effects: click on the Effect field and choose the desired effect from the pop-up menu.

26.2 Pre and Post Master Gain Effects

Note that the top six effects slots are located before the master gain control, whereas the bottom two are located after it. Generally, you will put your effects before the master gain control, so that pulling down the gain also attenuates any noise that the effect may create (compressors are particularly prone to add noise).

However, suppose you are mixing a tune and you want an abrupt end rather than a fade out, that goes through a delay set for lots of feedback so the sound echoes off into nothingness. If you play the delay before the Master Gain, then when you pull down the gain for the abrupt end, the echo will stop too. If the delay follows the Master Gain, then the echoes will still be heard, even after you bring down the levels.

Another potential application for a post Master Gain effect is loudness maximization. Although this would normally go before the Master Gain, consider a scenario where you want to "push" the sound harder while mastering so sections that are supposed to be more intense become more "squashed," thus giving a higher level (this is described more in the section on Control Surfaces). If you set the loudness maximizer threshold down a few dB, increasing the level will force the maximizer to work harder and attenuate more of the signal, thus squashing the dynamic range more.

In the picture, the Waves L1-Ultramaximizer+ has been inserted post Master Gain. The threshold is set around −4dB and the output ceiling at −0.1dB. Any signal louder than −4dB will force the maximizer to start attenuating the signal. Here the input signal is well above the threshold and is being attenuated by 3dB, yet the signal doesn't exceed the −0.1dB ceiling. Note how Cubase's output meters are at the absolute maximum, yet the clipping/overload indicators remain unlit.

Finally, note that dithering (see later for a discussion of dithering) is always the last processor in the chain. If placed pre-master fader, then changing the master fader will process the signal in 32-bit floating point resolution, thus negating the effects of dithering.

26.3 Proper Setting of Master Levels

Individual channels are processed with 32-bit floating point math, which allows a huge amount of headroom. You generally don't have to worry if the individual channels go into the red zone, but the Master Channel represents the sum of these channels, and overloading can occur. You must be careful about this to avoid distortion in your final mastered mix. Fortunately, the Master Channel provides useful feedback to help prevent this.

Your first line of defense against distortion are the clipping indicators above the meters. If they light, then you need to pull back the master level control.

> Some digital devices build in a "margin of error" and indicate that clipping occurs just before the actual clipping point, as a warning. Cubase "tells it like it is" and does not work this way—if the clip indicator lights, clipping has occurred.

The two numbers above the master fader represent the "margin"—the difference, in dB—between the highest level attained and the maximum available headroom. For example, an indication of "−1.2" indicates that the highest level attained was 1.2dB *below* the maximum available headroom. You can reset this by clicking on the clipping indicators or by moving the master fader. An indication of "2.3" means that the o level was exceeded by 2.3dB.

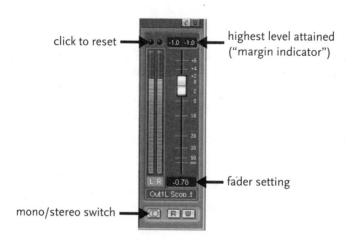

The Master Channel provides a variety of information to help you obtain the highest possible level short of distortion.

The number below the fader indicates its nominal level setting; a negative number indicates the amount of attenuation (level reduction) provided by the master fader. If the reading here is "o" and you send in a signal that reaches –2.0dB, then the margin indicators should also show "-2.0dB." If the master fader indication is "–1.5" and you feed in the same –2.0dB signal, then the margin indicators would show "–3.5dB"—the original margin, minus the amount of attenuation provided by the master fader.

You want to set the master fader for the highest possible level short of distortion. I recommend a maximum level of –0.1dB below maximum (this means that with peaks, the margin indicator would show no more than "–0.1"). The reason for this is that if a tune has peaks that hit o for more than a few milliseconds, it may be rejected by a CD pressing plant on the assumption that those peaks represent distortion.

To reach the optimum level, first reset the margin by clicking on the clip indictors, then play the tune through from start to finish. When it's over, check the margin indicator and note the reading. Let's say it's "−2.3." As you want the margin to read "−0.1," that means the overall level needs to be raised by +2.2dB.

Now note the fader reading. We'll assume it shows "+1.2." We want to add another 2.2dB of level, so if we set the fader reading to "+3.4" (1.2 + 2.2), then the next time the song gets played from start to finish, the margin should indicate −0.1dB.

26.4 Checking for Mono Compatibility

Periodically switch the output into mono to check for mono compatibility. Some effects alter the phase of one channel compared to other, and when combined in mono, there may be filtering or partial cancellation effects. If the mono output sounds weak, thin, or filtered, bypass effects until you find out what is causing the problem. And don't forget to switch back to stereo when exporting the file!

Chapter 27

Mixing for Better Mastering

In theory, doing a great mix would eliminate the need for mastering. But this is rarely the case; the analogy I'd use is putting dressing on a salad. You could put a certain amount of dressing on each piece of lettuce, tomato, etc., then when combined, you should have the same results as putting dressing on the entire salad. This would be like optimizing every track, and assuming that when put together, something would sound "mastered." But in my experience, I've never heard a mix—no matter how good—that couldn't benefit in some way by quality mastering.

Nonetheless, before we get specifically into mastering, let's look at some techniques you can use while mixing to make the mastering process go more smoothly, whether you do your own mastering or hand the project over to someone else.

27.1   Matching Timbres

If you use loops in your music, be aware of loops whose characteristics are wildly different from other loops. For example, let's suppose most of the loops were taken from a drum machine you use, but you also inserted a few commercially-available drum loops. It's likely that the latter were already "pre-mastered," perhaps with some compression or treble-boosting. As a result, they might sound brighter than the loops you created.

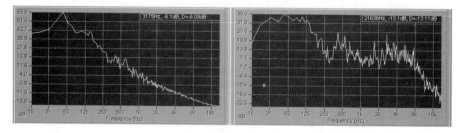

These graphs use Cubase SX's spectrum analyzer function (not available in Cubase SL) to plot amplitude vs. frequency for two different drum loops. Although the level calibrations aren't perfectly matched, the sound on the left—recorded from a drum machine—is quite different from the one the right, which came from a commercially-available sampling CD. The right curve is clearly more compressed with respect to dynamic range and has a much brighter high end.

If you decide to boost the track's overall brightness while mastering, the commercial loops will now seem "over the top" in terms of treble. I had this happen once when re-mastering a stereo track where everything needed a little extra brightness except for a hi-hat loop. It took seemingly forever to use notch filtering to find just the hi-hat frequencies and reduce those, while boosting everything else.

This kind of inconsistency can also happen if you use a lot of analog synths, which tend to have a darker sound, mixed with a few digital synths, which tend to be brighter. This will also give problems when mastering, because if you bring down the highs to tame the digital synths, the analog synths will sound much duller; if you bring up the highs, the digital synths may screech.

The solution is simple: to ensure that changes made during mastering will affect all sounds pretty much equally, before mixing, bring "minority" tracks into timbral alignment with the majority of the track's timbres. However, don't go overboard with this; some differences between tracks need to be respected (e.g. you might want a track to sound brighter or duller than others, regardless of any equalization done while mastering).

27.2 Bringing Peaks into Place

Another issue involves peak vs. average levels. A lot of engineers use mastering to increase a tune's average level, thereby making it seem louder (regrettably, some engineers and artists take this to an extreme, essentially wiping out all of a song's dynamics). To understand the difference between peak and average levels, consider a drum hit. There's an initial huge burst of energy (the peak) followed by a quick decay and reduction in amplitude. You will need to set the recording level fairly low to make sure the peak doesn't cause an overload, resulting in a relatively low average energy.

On the other hand, a sustained organ chord has a high average energy. There's not much of a peak, so you can set the record level such that the sustain uses up the maximum available headroom.

Entire tunes also have moments of high peaks and moments of high average energy. Suppose you're using a hard disk recorder and playing back a bunch of tracks. Of course, the stereo output meters will fluctuate, but you may notice that at some points, the meters briefly register much higher than for the rest of the tune. This can happen if, for example, several instruments with loud peaks hit at the same time, or if you're using lots of filter resonance on a synth and a note falls within that resonant peak. If you set levels to accommodate these peaks, then the rest of the song may sound too soft.

You can compensate for this while mastering by using limiting or compression, which brings the peaks down and raises the softer parts. However, if you instead reduce these peaks during the mixing process, you'll end up with a more natural sound because you won't need to use as much dynamics processing while mastering.

The easiest way to do this is as you mix, play through the song until you find a place where the meters peak at a significantly higher level than the rest of the tune. Loop the area around that peak, then one by one, mute individual tracks until you find the one that contributes the most amount of signal. For example, suppose a section peaks at 0dB. You mute one track, and the peak goes to −2. You mute another track, and the section peaks at −1. You now mute a track and the peak hits −7. Found it! That's the track that's putting out the most amount of energy.

Zoom in on the track and use automation or audio processing (AUDIO > PROCESS > GAIN) to insert a small dip that brings the peak down by a few dB. Now play that section again, make sure it still sounds okay, and check the meters. In our example above, that 0dB peak may now hit at, say, −3dB. Proceed with this technique through the rest of the tune to bring down the biggest peaks. If peaks that were previously pushing the tune to 0 are brought down to −3dB, you can now raise the tune's overall level by 3dB and still not go over 0. This creates a tune with an average level that's 3dB hotter, without having to use any kind of compression or limiting.

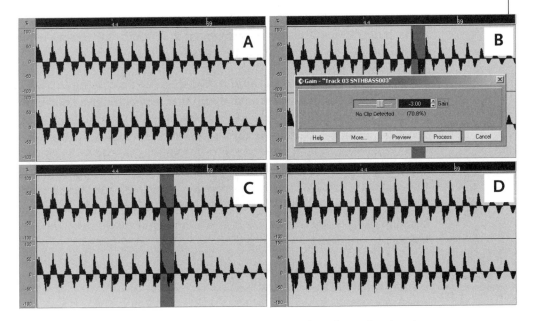

(A) shows the original signal. In (B), the highest peak has been located and is about to be attenuated by –3.00dB. (C) shows what happens after attenuation—it's now only a little higher than the other peaks. In (D), the signal has been normalized up to 0.00dB. Note how the signal has a higher average level than in (A), but there was no need to use traditional dynamics processing.

27.3   Getting Rid of Subsonics

Digital audio technology can—and sometimes does—record and reproduce energy well below 20Hz. This subsonic energy has two main sources: downward transposition/pitch-shifting and extensive DSP operations that allow control signals, such as fades, to superimpose their spectra onto the audio spectrum.

I ran into this problem recently when doing a remix of a soundtrack tune. I was adding some limiting to the finished mix, and in some sections, the level went way down, as if some hugely powerful signal was overloading the limiter's control signal. Yet I couldn't hear anything out of the ordinary.

Looking at the two-track mix showed a massive DC offset. After a bit of research, I noticed that these dips corresponded to places in the song where there was a long, rising tone. I had transposed the tone down by several octaves so it sounded like it was coming up from nowhere, but that transposition had moved it down so far into the subsonic region it created a varying DC offset. That's the signal to which the limiter was responding. Adding a filter to remove as much as possible below 20Hz solved the problem.

You can also use a sharp low-cut filter with already mastered material to cut out subsonic frequencies, but it's much better to do this type of processing *before* the files are mixed together, as this can lead to a cleaner mix.

Chapter 28

Mastering-Oriented Plug-ins

Plug-ins for mastering are not that different, at least conceptually, from ones designed to be insert or send effects. However, mastering effects will often require more CPU power, as more power is "spent" on the highest possible sound quality. An EQ that's just taking some top off a bass track doesn't have to be a marvel of sophistication; but if it's adding very refined EQ to a mixed stereo track, that's another story.

Of course, just because a plug-in says it's a "mastering plug-in" doesn't mean that it is. Your ears should be the judge.

Following are some of the most common plug-ins used for mastering.

28.1 Multiband Compression

With a traditional compressor, a strong signal that exceeds the threshold brings down the gain, but this affects all frequencies. So, if a strong kick drum hits, it will bring down the level of the cymbals and other high-frequency sounds as well. Multiband compressors, which are used a lot in mastering, split an incoming signal into several bands (typically 3 to 5)—like a graphic equalizer. A compressor follows each band, so that each compressor affects only a specific band of frequencies. This gives more transparent and effective dynamics control than single-band compressors. (The compressors can also usually serve as limiters or expanders.)

If you just want a hotter, louder sound, that's the simplest application: just split the signal into bands that divide up the spectrum, and set the compressor parameters similarly. In this case, the multiband compressor acts like a standard compressor, but gives a more transparent sound because of the multiple bands.

Using a multiband compressor to fix response problems is more complex. For example, suppose you're mastering a tune, and the bass end sounds kind of muddy because the kick and low toms ring too long, the high end is shrill, and the vocals in the midrange sound buried in the mix. You don't want to compress the low end and make the mud louder, nor do you want to emphasize the high end. But you do want to compress the midrange to bring the vocals more to the front.

Once you've assessed what you need to do, determine the optimum frequency ranges. Most software multiband compressors let you edit the frequency range, from narrow to broad, covered by each compressor. Generally, you can also solo individual bands to hear what they contribute to the overall sound. Set the compressors for a 1:1 ratio and high threshold so they don't affect the signal, then solo a band and listen. In our example above with the muddy low end, you might omit compression entirely and add some expansion to reduce ringing. Tweak the band's range so that it covers the muddy bass area but nothing else.

As most multiband compressors have level controls for each band, I initially treat the device like a graphic EQ. If turning up a band improves the sound, that may indicate the need for a little compression. If turning a band down helps, then I generally don't compress it or use subtle expansion to emphasize peaks more while de-emphasizing lower-level signals.

Next, adjust the compression ratio settings. This is tricky, because anything you do in one band affects how you perceive the other bands. For example, if you compress the midrange, the treble and bass will appear weaker.

Avoid going over 1.5:1 or 2:1 compression ratio at first and keep the threshold relatively high, such as −3 to −9dB. This will tame the highest peaks, without affecting too much else of the signal. Listen after each change and give your ears a chance to get acclimated to the sound before making additional changes. If your multiband compressor lets you save presets, save them periodically as "temp 1," "temp 2," "temp 3," etc. That way you can go back to a previous, less radical setting if you start to lose your way.

In general, it seems best to work on any "problem bands" first. Get them sounding right, then tweak the other bands to work well with them. For example, suppose you compress the upper midrange to better articulate voices or bring out melodic keyboard lines. Once that's set, adjust the bass to support (but not overwhelm) the midrange, then tweak the treble to suit.

> CD track 27 plays part of tune that's mixed but not processed, followed by the same piece after undergoing subtle multiband compression. Note how the second version sounds fuller, brighter, and more present.

Finally, after the dynamics are under control, my final tweak is usually adjusting each band's output level for the best overall balance. In fact, one of the nice things about a multiband compressor is that some bands can compress while others expand, and still others just do nothing—if set for zero compression, they act like bands in a parametric EQ.

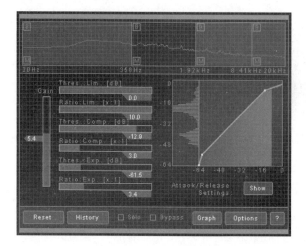

The multiband dynamics processor from iZotope's Ozone mastering suite. Note the four bands; each has separate parameters for limiting, compression, and expansion. The display shows the value for the lower-midrange band. Here, there's a bit of compression for the peaks and some low-level expansion to get rid of noise and hum.

28.2 Mastering EQs

Mastering EQs fall into two broad categories:

- Multi-stage parametric EQs designed for precision signal shaping. Unlike the 4-band EQs in Cubase's VST channels, mastering EQs may have 6, 7, 8, or even more stages. At least some of these will typically have adjustable responses, such as bandpass, notch, high shelf, low shelf, etc. These also tend to eat a lot of CPU power because they are designed for the most transparent processing possible, which is very important when you're processing complex program material as opposed to an instrument in a single track. (It's not that individual tracks aren't important; they are. But practically speaking, compromises must be made in native-based systems—CPUs don't have unlimited power—and less refined EQ will be far less noticeable on individual tracks.)

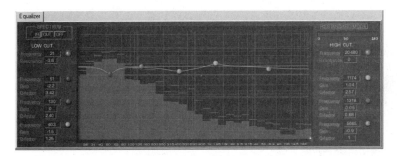

The Timeworks equalizer provides six parametric stages and separate high cut/low cut sections. It also includes a spectrum analyzer that can switch between monitoring the incoming signal's spectrum so you can see where peaks and valleys lie, or monitoring the output so you can see the results any equalization has on the spectral response. This is a very neutral-sounding EQ; with subtle amounts of equalization, you don't even know it's there.

- "Vintage" EQ circuits designed to add some particular attribute or flavor rather than solve specific, detailed response problems. For example, the Pultec equalizer, a studio mainstay during its heyday in the 60s and 70s, was essentially a passive EQ with very gentle curves. The alteration it produces is very gentle and also has a certain warmth (probably due to the use of inductors in the circuitry). Software emulations of these hardware classics range in terms of quality, but some are exceptionally good. If you want to give a gentle high end lift, add some power to the low end, or get rid of a little mud in the 300—400Hz range, emulations of vintage classics can often do the job in a very pleasing, natural manner.

28.3 Level Maximizers

With the trend toward ever-louder CDs, new and more potent strains of dynamics control have appeared called level maximizers, loudness maximizers, level optimizers, etc. These restrict dynamic range by essentially re-drawing peaks to go no higher than a user-settable threshold. It's then possible to increase the overall file's level by whatever amount the peaks were reduced—sort of an automated version of the peak reduction method mentioned above in the section "Mixing for Mastering." Although not as flexible as traditional limiting or compression, for a given perceived increase in level, maximizers can produce fewer obvious audible side effects.

We've already shown a maximizer from Waves in action; let's look at the controls on Steinberg's Loudness Maximizer, part of their Mastering Edition set of plug-ins.

Like most maximizers, Steinberg's Loudness Maximizer is designed to do only one thing and has a very simple set of controls.

The "Possible Gain" meter shows how much headroom is still available. You increase the "Desired Gain" control until the possible gain goes no lower than 0. I generally make sure that the possible gain doesn't go much lower than +1 or +2, otherwise the effects can become very audible.

The "Boost" button adds a level boost regardless of what's going on with the other controls; it also seems to boost the high end a bit. The "Soft/ Hard" switch is like a compressor's knee control—it sets how hard the maximizer clamps down on a signal that needs to be attenuated.

"More Density" makes the sound a little thicker, while "Desired Gain Done" shows if the maximum available headroom is being used.

Note also the input and output level meters. In particular, the output meter's maximum range is only 10dB—and most of the scale covers the range of −2.0 to 0.0dB. This helps show how often your signal is hitting the maximum amount of "hotness."

Because it's possible to really push these and not hear too many audible artifacts, it's tempting to just keep pumping up the volume. But if you're working with a reasonably well-mixed tune, boosting it by 3dB or so will be plenty. Unrelenting loudness and lack of dynamics ultimately leads to listener fatigue.

> CD track 28 plays an excerpt from the cut "Abdullah Smokez Rock," from the Rei$$dorf Force CD "Smart Dust." The first part has been maximized to be as loud as possible; the second part had been mastered previously, but without the same amount of maximization and upper midrange boost. The processing for the first part was done through Steinberg's Loudness Maximizer.

28.4 "Warmers" and Other Distortion Devices

It may seem heretical to add distortion to a final mix, yet the concept isn't as strange as it sounds: in mixing to tape, engineers would frequently hit the levels really hard so the tape would distort a bit. Many companies have tried to emulate this sort of effect in the analog world, with varying degrees of success.

One popular option is PSP's Vintage Warmer, which combines "old-school" compression, overdrive, and high/low frequency equalization. It's not supposed to be sonically neutral; instead, it gives you the option to "hype" the sound and give it a bit more "crunch."

PSP's Vintage Warmer doesn't just strive to give vintage sounds, it also emulates the look of vintage gear.

Cubase itself includes three distortion-based devices. DaTube and Overdrive are intended more for use as insert or send effects, but the QuadraFuzz is ideal for mastering applications as well as individual tracks. It is a multiband device, so you can add (for example) a bit of low-end distortion while leaving the high end alone.

> You may want to add an equalizer before distortion to trim the highs a little bit, as distorted high frequencies can sound extremely brittle and unpleasant.

You have to be *very* careful; you don't want your mix to turn into a muddy, distorted mess (well, maybe you do—that's cool too!). But some engineers use light, subtle distortion as their "secret weapon" for mastering.

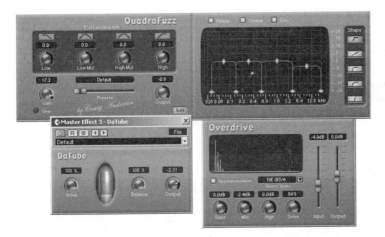

The QuadraFuzz is shown "folded out" so you can see its editing window. This is where you set the width of the band being distorted, as well as the distortion shape. In this case, the default preset is being edited to add a light amount of distortion. Below are the DaTube and Overdrive modules.

CD track 29 demonstrates that a little bit of distortion from the QuadraFuzz doesn't have to wreck a track, but it can sure add some punch and a volume increase.

28.5 Bass Enhancers

In addition to EQ, there are other ways to enhance bass. The Waves Maxx-Bass adds harmonics to the bass, so it can stand out better in systems that lack good bass response (such as music intended to play over computer speakers). Psycho-acoustically, when you hear the upper harmonics, your ear tends to "fill in" the bass's fundamental.

The MaxxBass isolates the signal's original bass and generates harmonics from it. You can then adjust the blend of the original bass with the bass contributed by the MaxxBass.

Other plug-ins take an opposite approach, adding sub-harmonics to give the bass more depth. Yet another approach is to add a stage of compression, optimized for low frequencies, to bring out the bass.

28.6 Stereo Image Enhancers

These create "super-stereo" effects that widen the stereo image, particularly in the high frequency range where the ear is most sensitive to directionality. Some of these devices use phase changes or delay to enhance the stereo image, and therefore may give unpredictable results if played back in mono. Always check the response in mono when using any plug-in or device that alters stereo separation.

28.7 Harmonic Enhancers

This type of plug-in adds a high-frequency "sheen" without the use of EQ. As with bass enhancement, there are many ways to do this. One approach is to add a very slight amount of distortion, use a steep highpass filter to remove everything but the highest harmonics of the distortion, then mix this signal back in with the main signal. If used sparingly, the minute amounts of high-frequency distortion can give increased clarity and stereo separation, without the "tinniness" you might encounter with standard EQ.

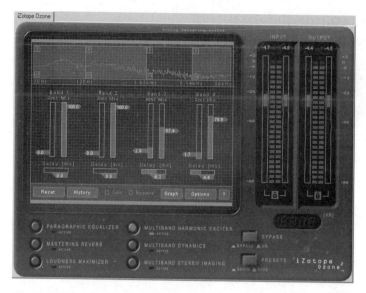

iZotope's Ozone includes a multiband harmonic exciter that increases the sharpness and "definition" of audio within the selected frequency ranges. As with most mastering effects, be subtle—a little goes a long way.

28.8 Reverb

Reverb is not used a lot in mastering, but there are circumstances where it can help. If material was mostly recorded direct (i.e. instruments plugged directly into the console rather than being recorded via microphone), reverberation can add a little space. Although usually this is done during the mixing process by adding reverb as a send effect, you may encounter a final mix that lacks "space" or depth. In this case, a subtle amount of reverb can fill out the stereo image.

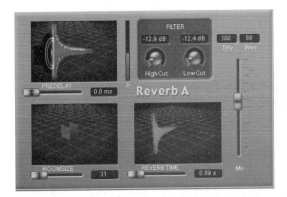

Cubase includes two reverbs, A and B. When used for mastering, I generally set a relatively small room size and decay time with only a little bit of "wet" (reverberated) signal. However, most of the time it is not necessary to use reverb as I add it during the mixing process.

Chapter 29

Dithering

Some hail dithering as the "miracle drug" of digital audio that restores sweetness to digital's supposedly "harsh" sound. Others say that dithering is overrated and doesn't matter to most music anyway. But as with so many aspects of digital audio, the truth lies somewhere between the extremes.

Processing digital audio data involves math processes such as addition, subtraction, multiplication, and division. Most digital audio editors process 16-bit files using higher resolution, like 24, 32, or even 64 bits, because processing two 16-bit signals can produce results that exceed 16 bits of resolution. (An analogy: multiply 4 times 4; although each number is only one digit, you need two digits to express the result.)

However, even though Cubase processes signals internally with 32-bit floating point resolution and most modern audio interfaces can record and play back with 24 bit resolution, the result ends up on a 16-bit CD. (Maybe next year it will end up on a 24-bit DVD-Audio release, but for now, let's deal with the real world.). So, all that wonderful dynamic range goes away when the 16 least significant digits (i.e. the ones with the lowest numeric values) are discarded on their journey to CD compatibility. It just doesn't seem fair to those 16 bits (particularly after having been called the "least significant" bits all their lives).

Cutting off bits is called "truncation," and one common misunderstanding about dithering is that it sidesteps the truncation process. Yet dithered or not, when a 32-bit signal ends up on a 16-bit CD, 16 bits are truncated and never heard from again. The advantage of dithering is that it manipulates those 16 least significant bits so that they influence the sound of the most significant bits. It's almost like even though they're gone, their spirit lives on in the sound of the recording.

29.1 The Problem with Truncation

Truncation removes the low end of the dynamic range; during long fades, reverb tails, and the like, at some point the signal just ends abruptly rather than fades out. At the end of the decay, you'll also hear a slight buzzing as the least significant bit, which tries to follow the audio signal, switches back and forth between 1 and 0. Of course, there are varying levels between that "on" and "off" condition, but the resolution simply isn't there to reproduce those changes. This buzzing is called "quantization noise," because the noise occurs during the process of quantizing the audio into discrete steps.

Remember, though, that we're talking about very low-level signals. A 16-bit signal has a theoretical dynamic range of 96 dB, and even though real-world specs aren't quite that good, we're still talking about low-level signals that are barely audible in most listening environments. For a punk rock mix where all the meters are in the red, you probably don't even need 16 bits of resolution; 8 or even 4 bits would likely do the job. But if you're trying to record the ambient reverb tail of an acoustic space, you need good low-level resolution.

29.2 Dithering and the Art of Adding Noise

The dithering process adds random noise to the lowest 8 bits. This noise is different for the two channels in order not to degrade stereo separation. (Technically, we're "re-dithering" the output because some dithering may have already occurred internally in the system, but this is a fine point and we'll continue to refer to the output process as "dithering.")

It may seem crazy that adding noise can improve the sound, but one analogy is the bias signal used in analog tape. Analog tape is linear (distortionless) over only a very narrow range. While most people know that distortion occurs if you hit tape with too hard a level, signals *below* a certain level can also sound horribly distorted. So, the bias signal adds a constant supersonic signal (so we don't hear it) whose level sits at the lower threshold of the linear region. Any low-level signals are *added* to the bias signal and make it into the linear region, where they can be heard without distortion.

Adding noise to the lower 8 bits increases their amplitude and pushes that information into the 16th bit. Therefore, the 16th bit no longer correlates directly to the original signal, but to a combination of the noise source and information present in the lower 8 bits. This reduces quantization noise, providing in its place a smoother type of hiss, modulated by the lower-level information. The most obvious audible benefit is that fades become smoother and more realistic, but there's also more sonic detail.

But isn't adding hiss bad? Well, yes. But this is where psycho-acoustics comes into play. Because any hiss is constant, our ear has an easy time picking out the content (signal) from the noise. We've lived with noise long enough that a little bit hanging around at −96dB or so is tolerable, particularly if it allows us to hear a subjectively extended dynamic range.

However, there are different types of dither, with varying degrees of audibility. For example, the Waves IDR (Increased Digital Resolution) system has two types of dither. One is wideband and trades off the lowest distortion for slightly higher perceived noise. Another uses a much narrower band of noise and sounds quieter, but some extremely low-level distortion remains.

29.3 Refined Dithering through Noise-shaping

Audio engineers are stubborn in their pursuit of the ultimate sound and have come up with some ingenious ways to minimize the audible effects of dithering. "Noise-shaping" distributes noise across the spectrum so that the bulk of it lies where the ear is least sensitive (i. e. higher frequencies). Some noise shaping curves are extremely complex—they're not just a straight line, but also dip down in regions of maximum sensitivity (typically the midrange and upper midrange).

Again, this recalls the analogy of analog tape's bias signal, which is typically around 100kHz to keep it out of the audible range. We can't get away with those kinds of frequencies in a system that samples at 44.1 or even 96kHz, but several noise-shaping algorithms push the signal as high as possible, short of hitting the Nyquist frequency (i.e. maximum theoretical frequency for a given sampling rate).

Different manufacturers use different noise-shaping algorithms, which are jealously guarded as trade secrets. Digital audio editors sometimes offer variations on their dithering and noise-shaping algorithms so you can choose the combination that works best for specific types of program material. Suffice it to say, not all these algorithms are created equal, nor do they sound equal; deciding on whose brand of dither you like best is not unlike wine-tasting. Dithering algorithms can involve tremendously complex calculations using very high internal resolution (64 bits or more), and some systems need to do this offline—real-time auditioning isn't really practical.

29.4 The UV22 and UV22 HR Dithering Plug-ins

The UV22 (included with Cubase SL) and UV22 HR (included with Cubase SX) are high quality dithering devices using algorithms by Apogee, a company well-known for their digital audio expertise. With the UV22 HR, you'll generally select "Normal" dithering, then select the target resolution (16 bits for CDs). "Autoblack" mutes the dither noise during silent passages, which may or may not sound unnatural when transitions occur from program material to the silent space between cuts.

The UV22 and UV22HR are very similar, except that the HR version can dither to 8, 16, 20, or 24 bits.

Note that because Cubase runs at 32-bit internal resolution, you may even want to add dithering when creating a 24-bit master file. However, it is doubtful you'll hear any real difference—whereas you'll likely hear an improvement when dithering to 8 or 16 bits.

The UV22 operates similarly, but its dithering is fixed at 16 bits.

29.5 The Rules of Dithering

The one inviolable rule of dithering is: Do not dither more than once. Dithering should happen only when converting your high bit-rate source format to its final, 16-bit, mixed-for-CD format.

> Always keep an undithered copy of your unmastered audio. If you need to make changes later, work on the original and re-dither rather than work with dithered audio.

Never take material that has already been dithered and re-dither it. For example, if you are given an already dithered 16-bit file to edit on a high-resolution waveform editor, that 16-bit file already contains the dithered data, and the higher-resolution editor should (hopefully) preserve it.

When it's time to mix the edited version back down to 16 bits, simply transfer over the existing file, without dithering. The results will likely sound better than if you redither.

Another possible problem could arise if you give a mastering or duplication facility two dithered 16-bit files that are meant to be cross-faded. Cross-fading the dithered sections could lead to artifacts; you're better off crossfading the two, then dithering the combination.

The best way to experience the benefits of dithering is to crank up some really low-level audio and compare different dithering and noise-shaping algorithms. Proper dithering can indeed give a sweeter, smoother sound free of digital quantization distortion; if your music has any natural dynamics in it at all, you *will* hear a difference.

29.6 Why You Should Master in 24-bit Resolution

Even if you recorded your tracks with 16-bit resolution, the processing that goes on in the master section will likely calculate internally to a higher level of precision. It's worth mixing to a 24-bit file and saving that as a backup; then dither down that file for your final 16-bit master for CD duplication.

Chapter 30

The Final Stages of Mastering

30.1 Comparisons with Commercial CDs

When mastering, compare the results of what's coming out of Cubase SX/SL with a well-mastered CD. Listen closely to the timbral balance; check for excessive differences in terms of high-end brightness, low end power, and midrange definition. Also listen for differences in dynamics—is the commercial CD more "squashed" sounding or has a much louder sound? If so, you need to decide if you want to add more compression or loudness maximization, or whether you want to retain a more natural dynamic balance.

Note that there are programs, such as Steinberg's FreeFilter, that can analyze one tune's spectral response and apply it to another tune. A "morph" slider determines how closely your tune adopts the reference's curve, from a very slight influence to an exact match. However, this is an "offline" process that cannot be done in real time using Cubase; you need to use a program like Wavelab.

While useful, this type of program has limitations. If the reference tune has a strong kick drum and weak bass, the curve will show a strong bass bump because of the kick. If you apply that to a tune with a moderate kick and strong bass, the bass will likely be boosted too high. Nonetheless, programs like FreeFilter can, if nothing else, educate you regarding the spectral response of various pieces of music.

30.2 Mastering for Data Compressed Formats

Mastering for a data compressed format such as MP3, Ogg Vorbis, Real Audio, WMA, etc. requires a somewhat different skill set compared to mastering for standard, uncompressed formats such as WAV or AIFF. This is because many tradeoffs are involved, such as deciding whether small file size or fidelity is your highest priority.

Data compression is important because high-quality audio generates over 10 Megabytes per minute for stereo, 44.1kHz, 16-bit sound files. Yet non-broadband phone lines choke on that kind of data stream. A typical, dial-up, 28.8kbps connection can transfer about 2.5 kilobytes of data per second if there's no net congestion. So, sending or receiving a 4-minute, CD-quality pop tune takes hours. Because it takes so long to download a piece of music (let alone have it "stream" in real time, like a radio broadcast), you must make compromises to present music on the web.

30.2.1 Data Compression vs. Data Omission

True data compression, as found in programs like StuffIt or WinZip, restore the exact same original file when uncompressed. On the other hand, audio compression schemes are more accurately labeled data *omission*—a process like MP3 throws away "unneeded" data. For example, if there's a lot of high-level sound going on, the algorithm might assume you can't hear lower-level material and decide for those sections you only need 24dB of dynamic range. This requires only 4 bits of resolution—25% the amount of data required by 16-bit resolution.

Unfortunately, it's difficult to retain quality when music is data-compressed. When you save a file in a compressed format (FILE > EXPORT > AUDIO MIXDOWN), you need to make various choices about its characteristics; exporting a file in Cubase using a data-compressed format presents you with plenty of options.

In any case, data compression is not about subtlety. You'll get the best results when encoding if you feed in a signal with a really high average level, which spends most of its time in the very top (loud) end of the dynamic range. Compression is not always the tool of choice, as overcompression can actually lead to inferior results when encoded. I prefer using loudness maximizing tools, which increase the perceived loudness in a more intelligent way than normal limiting or compression. I generally increase the amount of maximization until the sound is as loud as possible without sounding "squashed."

30.2.2 Which Compression Format is Best?

Here are some comments on each format.

MP3

This is the most universal file format. It allows several levels of encoding, so you can generate just about any size audio file, with a corresponding loss of fidelity as the files get smaller. There are numerous free or shareware MP3 players for computers, as well as portable MP3 players into which you can transfer files from your computer (Apple's iPod is probably the best-known). Many "boomboxes" and DVD players can also play back CDs with files in MP3 format.

Real Audio

This is currently the most popular format for streaming video on the web and produces acceptable quality even on dial-up connections. The audio isn't bad either, and a few musicians prefer to release music in the Real format for streaming (for downloading, most musicians remain committed to MP3).

Ogg Vorbis

Although not as common as MP3, this is an open standard that (unlike MP3) requires no licensing fee. Most listeners consider the sound quality as superior to MP3 for a given file size, and as a bonus, file sizes tend to be very small. It's a good choice if you're sharing files with a collaborator like a songwriting partner, assuming you both have the means to generate and play back files. Unfortunately, few portable devices can handle the Ogg Vorbis format.

Windows Media Audio

This rising star has the power of Microsoft behind it. At really low bit rates, like 24 or 32kbps, WMA doesn't have MP3's annoying "underwater" sound, but the tradeoff is a very artificial-sounding high end. At 64kbps, WMA sounds better than MP3; at 96kbps, the difference is less dramatic, but I'd give WMA the edge. At 128kbps and above, differences in sound quality tend to be more quantitative than qualitative. Microsoft has big plans for WMA: Version 9 delivers surround-compatible files over the web, and they've signed licensing agreements with many companies so that products from car stereos to portable players can play back WMA format files. Although not as common as MP3 files, that situation could change in the years ahead.

30.2.3   Exporting as a Compressed File

After getting your project to sound exactly the way you want, go FILE > EXPORT > AUDIO MIXDOWN and you'll be greeted with a screen where you can specify the file type. After selecting it, other options will be presented. Here are the options for different file types.

MP3

I usually adjust the lower parameters first. You want to check "Automation" and "Effects" (these parameters are available for all compressed file format exports) so that your MP3 file sounds just like the way your hear your sequence when you press Play.

The choice of channels is crucial. Mono or stereo files are the same size, but the mono one will be higher-quality because the stereo is basically like two mono files. In other words, if you encode at 128kbps in stereo, each channel is running at 64kbps. In mono, the file runs at 128kbps. For lower data rates (under 64kbps), I strongly suggest mono. For data rates of 128kbps and above, stereo is acceptable. 96kbps is a sort of "gray area"; use your ears.

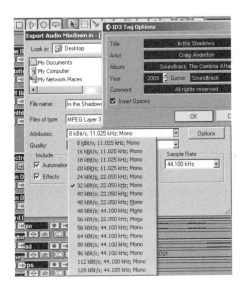

Cubase's MP3 export parameters are very flexible. Don't forget that mono will give better fidelity for a given file size than stereo. The options window lets you enter data that may appear with some MP3 players.

"Sample Rate" sets the maximum possible sample rate. You can reduce file size by choosing 32kHz (not bad) or 22.050 kHz (somewhat dull-sounding, but not too terrible). I think sometimes, a file sounds better at a lower sample rate despite not having as good a high end, because the overall fidelity required to produce a nice high end isn't worth it.

"Quality" is a no-brainer: choose Highest. This affects the time required to "render" the MP3 and has nothing to do with file size.

For "Attributes," chose the bit rate that works best for your application. For dial-up streaming, choose 20kbps to stream with a 28.8k connection, or 32kbps if you expect to serve a 56kbps hook-up. You can bump these up a notch to 24kbps and 40kbps, but if the net's congested, the audio could break up or pause for varying amounts of time—not a seamless listening experience. For broadband or corporate networks, 80 to 100kbps should work just fine. For personal MP3 players, 128kbps is a good compromise between fidelity and memory usage. If you plan to make a CD with MP3 files, go for 256 or 320kbps—you won't be able to fit quite as many files on the CD as you would with lower bit rates, but the improvement in sound quality makes it closer to a CD-type listening experience.

The "Options" button calls up a window where you can tag info about the title, artist, genre, and other information.

> CD data folder "MP3 Encoding" shows examples of the same file encoded through two different programs at different rates, in both mono and stereo. You may be surprised at just how different they all are.

Ogg Vorbis

The choices here are basically the same as those for MP3, except there's no attributes parameter. However, the Quality parameter serves a different purpose as the Ogg Vorbis format uses variable rate encoding, which means that the amount of compression varies from moment to moment, depending on the content (this also slows the encoding process a bit). "Fast" creates the smallest file sizes, "Highest" creates the largest.

Real Audio

Real Audio tries to simplify things as much as possible. Basically, just choose the desired bit rate under "Coding" (which also describes the typical communications medium, such as 56k modem, Single ISDN, etc.), then choose the type of content. Under content, choosing "Music" is the only stereo options; all others are mono. Oddly, for mono files sometimes "Vocals with Background Music" produces better results than "Music + Vocals." Experiment to see which works best.

Options works differently compared to MP3. You can specify Title, Author, and Copyright information, which will show up on most Real players. However, you can also select whether the user will be able to download the file (Selective Recording), do a partial download prior to streaming for low data-rate connections (Perfect Play), and the ability to download the file with a web browser (Mobile Download).

Windows Media Audio

This is the easiest to adjust of them all: choose from one of the options (e.g., 56 Dial-up High Quality Stereo is intended for 56kbps modem connections), enter any desired Title/Author/Copyright data in the Options box, click on Save, and you're done.

General Rules

Regardless of which format you choose, save a file using a variety of bit rates and sampling frequencies, in mono and stereo, then determine which combines best sound with smallest file size. Different source material works differently with different encoders; there is no "one size fits all" perfect option.

Finally, if you end up posting your song on the web, download it and/or stream it to make sure the process actually works, and no glitches crept into the process.

What's on the CD

The accompanying CD is a mixed-mode CD with both audio and data tracks. Audio examples are generally presented in three formats: WAV (Windows standard), AIF (Macintosh standard), and Red Book Audio (audio you can play on a standard CD player). The only exceptions are three data-only folders: one includes examples of a file encoded to MP3 format at various bit rates, the second contains different mixes of the song "Fate of a Heart" to illustrate the huge impact different mixes can make to the same song, the third contains Cubase example Projects that are used in the book.

> Please note that all material on this CD is copyrighted by their respective owners and is licensed non-exclusively to the readers of this book for their private, non-commercial use.

CD tracks 01 to 09 show a variety of equalization effects applied to audio. Track 1 is the original waveform, track 2 does a 6dB bandpass boost at 1kHz with a 1-octave bandwidth, track 3 is the same but has a 6dB cut, track 4 is a highpass filter starting at 1kHz, track 5 is a high shelf filter that's boosting 6dB starting at 1kHz, track 6 is a high shelf filter that cuts by 6dB starting at 1kHz, track 7 is a lowpass filter starting at 1kHz, track 8 is a low shelf filter that's boosting 6dB starting at 1kHz, and track 9 is a low shelf filter that cuts by 6dB starting at 1kHz.

CD track 10 first plays a bass figure without envelope attack, then with envelope attack added by increasing the AutoGate's attack time.

CD track 11 shows how changing the threshold control in real time changes the sound of a loop being processed by the AutoGate.

CD track 12 plays the original drum loop without reverb, followed by the same loop with reverb added from the extracted snare.

CD Track 13 shows how a short release setting affects drums. This produces an effect often used for "psychedelic" 1960s drum sounds, where hitting the cymbal modulates the entire kit with a pumping kind of sound (drum loop courtesy Discrete Drums, www.discretedrums.com).

CD Track 14 plays three sections: five hits through Reverb A then one second of silence, five hits through Reverb B then one second of silence, and finally, five hits through both reverbs as described in this section. Note how the reverb sound is far better in the last example.

CD Track 15 first plays a sampled piano by itself, which is definitely lacking bass. Next you'll hear the same part in a duplicated track, set to compress only the bass range. Finally, the two tracks play together. Note how the final piano example sounds much fuller than the original one.

CD track 16 plays a figure in mono; after the short pause, the same material repeats but using the channel EQ/splitting technique described in this section. The difference isn't huge, but the second figure definitely has a more ambient, bigger sound. This difference is particularly obvious when listening with headphones.

CD Track 17 first plays a drum part with no delays. After a one-second pause, the next section uses fixed short delays, followed by a one-second pause, then mod delay with 5+8ms of delay, another pause, and finally, mod delay with 10+12ms of delay.

CD Track 18 shows off what the Native Instruments Spektral Delay plug-in can do. The first part is a straight piano sound, followed by the same part played three more times through different effects.

CD Track 19 plays a straight guitar part (from a "Technoid Guitars" sample CD guitar preset, played via HALion), then through a shifting parametric frequency without cancellation effects, then through the "canceled" wah-wah effect described here.

CD Track 20 first plays a power chord from the Technoid Guitars CD, then processes it with the sample-and-hold technique.

CD Track 21 plays some power chords (again, from a Technoid Guitars sample CD preset) without processing, then with the rhythmic tremolo effect.

CD Track 22 plays the same rhythm guitar power chord six times as it traces the evolution of its sound through signal processing. The first chord is as the guitar was recorded. The second chord goes through Sonic Foundry's Smooth/Enhance plug-in, which takes off some of the highs. The third chord goes through the VST parametric EQ to give a bit of an upper midrange life. The fourth chord is processed by the compressor in Steinberg's Mastering Edition to give some more sustain, while the fifth chord goes through Steinberg's WunderVerb. Finally, the sixth chord goes through Steinberg's Stereo Expander plug-in; the seventh chord merely repeats the original first chord for comparison. The difference isn't huge, but the processed version has a wider stereo image, sounds more defined, and sits in a track better.

CD Track 23 illustrates how panning and delay can change the sound. In the first part of the file, the 16th note ostinato figure is generated by a string of 16th notes feeding Steinberg's Neon, and the LM4-Mark II tom part has no echo. After the pause, in the second part, the Neon is being fed with quarter notes (everything else about the part is the same), and the 16th notes are being generated by delay and panned off to the side via the DoubleDelay effect. The tom part has delay that pans across the stereo field (also courtesy of DoubleDelay). The second part sounds much more animated than the first part. Other notes about the mix: the kick drum is going through the Quadrafuzz, the snare drum is being bitcrushed down to 6 bits, and the Waves L1-Ultramaximizer+ is inserted as a master effect to provide about 3dB of loudness maximization.

CD Track 24 demonstrates the drums and bass, playing together. The first two measures have the exciter enabled, the second two measures do not. Note how the drums in the first two measures are much more prominent compared to the bass.

CD Track 25 plays a patch from the Technoid Guitars sample CD through Steinberg's HALion sampler. The first part does not have the pitch envelope added; the second part has an added downward pitch bend, which makes the attack more prominent in a subtle way.

CD Track 26 consists of 60 seconds of pink noise that you can use to try mixing with noise. The file is crossfade-looped if you want to load it into a sampler, otherwise you can just drag in enough instances to last the duration of the song you're mixing.

CD Track 27 plays part of tune that's mixed but not processed, followed by the same piece after undergoing subtle multiband compression. Note how the second version sounds fuller, brighter, and more present.

CD Track 28 plays an excerpt from the cut "Abdullah Smokez Rock," on the Rei$$dorf Force CD "Smart Dust." The first part has been maximized to be as loud as possible; the second part had been mastered previously, but without the same amount of maximization and upper midrange boost. The processing for the first part was done through Steinberg's Loudness Maximizer.

CD Track 29 demonstrates that a little bit of distortion from the QuadraFuzz doesn't have to wreck a track, but it can sure add some punch and a volume increase.

CD data folder "Cubase Projects" contains Cubase example Projects that are used in this book.

CD data folder "MP3 Encoding" shows examples of the same file encoded through two different programs at different rates, in both mono and stereo. You may be surprised at just how different they all are.

CD data folder "SSS Mixing Project" includes 25 different mixes of the song "Fate of a Heart," written by George Toledo III. For more information, see Appendix B.

About the Sound, Studio, and Stage Mixing Event

Author Craig Anderton currently hosts a bulletin board at www.music-player.com called "Sound, Studio, and Stage." This is one of the longest-running boards in the industry; it started on AOL in 1995, moved over to a temporary home on engineer Lynn Fuston's web site (www.3daudio.com) in late 1998, and finally settled into the MusicPlayer site in January 2000.

This was not the first time an online mixing project had been attempted, but was a first for SSS. Although originally done just for the fun of it, when the project was complete it seemed like the perfect complement to a book about mixing and mastering. It shows, in very obvious detail, how much mixing can change a song, and how different people can give radically different interpretations of a song.

But it also gives a glimpse into the future of mixing, where thanks to the internet, collaborations can span time zones, nationalities, and transcend language differences. There were participants from Europe and North America, including Spain, the Netherlands, Sweden, Canada, and the United States. The talent ranged from Grammy award winners and engineers with Platinum records, to hobbyists who had recently gotten into recording.

Let's have the organizer of the event, Bunny Knutson, describe how it all came about ...

"George Toledo III, a musician/engineer from Tampa, Florida, volunteered to supply the tracks from one of his original songs for us to mix. That was fortunate, because George is a talented guy. He supplied a really good song with 15 substantial tracks, featuring a variety of instruments, mostly played by George himself. When it was agreed that a more comprehensive set of live drum tracks would enhance the mixing event, Lee Flier, a musician/engineer from Atlanta, offered to record live acoustic drum tracks for the song. Lee brought her friend Eskil, a talented session drummer, into her studio and recorded six tracks of live drums."

"We used two methods for distributing the tracks to the event participants, depending on the individual's internet connection speed. Those with dial-up connections were sent CDs by mail. For those with broadband connections, I posted the track files on my web site for them to download. I compressed the files with a lossless compression program called Shorten. Recipients then decompressed the files and dumped them into their digital audio workstation (or analog rig) of choice."

"We agreed early on that this event would not be a contest, and that we would have few rules. Mixers could choose to do a 'purist' mix, sticking to the tracks provided. It was also acceptable to drastically edit, sample, loop, and add parts. Even extreme 'remixes' were considered fair play, as long as they contained some recognizable part of the original song. This lack of ground rules made the mixing event very conducive to creativity and expression. Participants had six weeks to work on their mixes. Final versions were sent as MP3 files (the same ones you'll hear on the CD), and posted for everyone to hear."

"Furthermore, there was no input from George himself, either in terms of his vision of the song or a representative mix from him, so the participants could treat the song in any way they felt was appropriate. In retrospect, this was one of the most important aspects of the mixing project, as it led to the diversity you'll experience as you listen to the various interpretations."

Thanks, Bunny. After getting everyone's permission to use their mixes on the CD, and from George to use his song, Craig Anderton asked everyone to send a brief bio and some notes on their mix ... so here they are. Some of the techniques they described are sure to inspire you as well. It was not essential that they use Cubase SX (although several did use Cubase), because these mixes are provided to give insight into the mixing process itself rather than applications for any one particular program. In fact, mixdown occurred on everything from Cubase SX (of course!) to other software, all-in-one studios, and traditional multitrack recorders with consoles.

Here are bios and mix comments from the participants, arranged in no particular order.

Bob Phillips (20to20soundesign)

Bio: After tinkering with telephones and tape recorders as a tot, Bob Phillips began recording actual musicians in 1980. In 1995, he formed Stillsound Studios, one of the first digital/hard disk recording facilities in northeast Indiana. Since 1999, he's owned 20to20soundesign, a multitrack recording, mastering, and graphics design studio complex.

Mix notes: "I started by passing each of the tracks through a FATSO/ Avalon747 chain, just to get a little Tape/Tube/Tranny effect happening. To me, the intro had an ambient vibe happening, so I expanded on it by doing the old Eno trick of dropping the tape speed by one half, thereby doubling the length and also lowering the pitch by an octave (just in the intro section). Of course I'm not actually using tape, so I performed that trick by flying the Intro Submix out to my Alesis Masterlink, then flying it back into the TASCAM MX-2424 hard disk recorder at an 88.2k sampling rate, then dropping the rate back to 44.1k ... voilà!"

"In the 1st 'rap vox' section I treated the voice with multiple pitch transpositions, moderate compression, and then gating to clean up the gaps; against the main vocal, I slightly delayed the 'analog-ed' track for a kind of slap-back/rock voice. I used both the ArpeggiOrgan and the original hi-hat throughout, albeit nearly subaudibly, by 'auto'-panning them L-R, R-L; synched with the tempo. Finally in the outro, I let all of those cool Ted Nugent guitars wind down by extending the original drum tracks and synth bass by several measures. After a classic 'fake fade-out,' the drums come back in with only the synth bass and a reprise of the Enossified Intro Section."

Anon-a-Monster (this participant wishes to remain anonymous)

Bio: Anon-a-Monster started at Criteria Recording Studios in Miami in 1973 and assisted some of the greatest engineers and producers around at the time, from Tom Dowd to Phil Ramone, to Ron and Howard Albert to Karl Richardson.

He graduated to first engineer and recorded many popular albums at Criteria, from artists like The Allman Brothers, Stephen Stills, Rod Stewart, Andy Gibb, Wishbone Ash, and Kenny Loggins. He also had a varied and full recording tutelage from the owner Mack Emerman, who engineered big band dates three or four times a year, as well as his jazz combo sessions, and was very grateful for the experience.

In 1980 he moved to Los Angeles and engineered/co-produced a best-selling Crosby, Stills and Nash album and recorded/mixed many songs for film and full length concert specials. He also worked at CBS Songs with hit songwriters to gain further experience in the process of the birth of a song (for which he offers the following insight: "they write as many bad songs as anyone else!").

Anon-a-Monster has been in a shadow mode for the past few years as he says he is "not partial to hip-hop, what is passing for R&B, or boy/girl group domination, and am not a fan of the overly edited, auto-tuned production style of the moment ... but it will soon change."

Mixing Notes: "The remixes were composed in Acid, with some survival mastering done in Wavelab."

Bunny Knutson

Bio: Bunny is the founder and president of San Francisco's 4:20 Records Group, which combines four independent California labels. He has produced three albums released by 4:20 Records, Puzzlefish's "4:20" and "Bouncenplod," and Budderball's "The Great Pepper Shaker in the Sky." He is currently working on his debut solo album.

As lead guitarist and key songwriter for Puzzlefish, Bunny has played live alongside such bands as Mr. Bungle, The Deftones, and the Deli Creeps featuring Buckethead, now of Guns N' Roses fame. Puzzlefish's first demo featured Brain (Brian Mantia of GNR, Primus and Praxis) on drums. Puzzlefish's Bouncenplod was recorded in part with John Avila of Oingo Boingo; Avila had hooked up with Puzzlefish after spontaneously jamming with them onstage.

In his early reckless years, Bunny toured though Europe and the USA as lead guitar for punk rock pranksters No Use for a Name. In the late 90s, Bunny played in an experimental Oakland-based groove band with Prince Lasha of old-school jazz notoriety. He lives in the San Francisco East Bay Area with his wife and two sons.

Sites: www.420RecordsGroup.com, www.mp3.com/bunnyknutson, and www.bunnyknutson.com.

Mix Notes: "I edited, recorded (bass), mixed, and mastered in Cakewalk Pro Audio 9, and didn't place anything on a tempo grid, because I liked the organic feel of the recording.

"First, as several tracks were shared by multiple instruments throughout different sections of the song, I isolated each individual instrument or part to its own track. I also added the acoustic drum tracks provided by Lee Flier and Eskil. I then recorded a new bass track, to get the bass syncopated better with the newly recorded drums. I ended up with around 32 tracks, using all but four of the original tracks provided."

"I liked the rhythm guitar track a lot, so I didn't EQ it much, but I compressed it pretty heavily. I panned the dry original track pretty hard left, then copied it, offset the copy by a few milliseconds, and panned the copy hard right at low volume with a touch of reverb. I used the synthesizer guitar track, at low volume and panned at about 2:00 o'clock, to fill out the guitars. Organs and other keys were layered behind the guitars."

"Compressing the lead vocal seemed to suck the life out of the track, so I ditched the compressor to maintain the dynamics. Instead, I rode touchy parts with a volume envelope. I didn't EQ the vocal much; slight high-end boost, slight low-end roll-off. I added reverb (panned center) and quarter note delay (panned 11:00 o'clock). In the intro, I added backwards reverb and a boosted track of midrange-EQ vocals."

"I ran the intro pads and the bass through a tape simulator plug-in. There was a Farfisa organ hook that I looped and placed in all the post-chorus sections. The last time this figure repeats, it's distorted by an amp simulator. I kind of exaggerated the ending by placing a copy of the intro pads over it, creating a climactic surge of energy before a tasteful fade ... at least, that was my intention."

Christopher Kemp

Bio: Christopher is a guitarist and audio engineer currently living in Stone Mountain, GA. He was trained in studio recording (analog 2"!!) before beginning a live audio, television audio, and performing career of over 10 years. He currently works for Klotz Digital America, programming logic for digital audio equipment, and playing for love (for the time being). **Site:** http://franknputer.complexero.com

Mix notes: "Early on I played with some of the drums, but the track really came alive for me when Lee Flier provided Eskil's drums. At that point, I decided to go in a more live band direction: a drum-bass-guitar-organ thing that used bits of the synth stuff to complement it."

"The slower arpeggiated hook stuck in my head, so I cut that one short phrase out, pasted it where I wanted it to go, then added the delay doubling to give it some bounce."

"I decided that I wanted to play some different guitar parts than what was there, so I used my gold PRS bolt on through a Johnson J-Station, selecting different tones that I felt fit what I wanted to do in various sections, and just going for it. They are mostly unedited tracks, except for the chord swell at the beginning of the lyric. That is a C chord run through the J-Station harmonizer, which I reversed in Audacity (a free cross-platform wave editor)."

"I mixed the track with Digital Performer 2.7 on a G3 power Mac with a G4 upgrade. Audacity was used for track edits. Monitoring was done with AKG 240 headphones, as well as through Yamaha NS10s with a Hitachi HTS5 subwoofer."

C. W. (Bill) Miltenberger

Bio: Bill is in the start up phase of DakLander Music, a small, independent publishing, recording, booking, management and web site development company located in Temecula, California. He is fairly new to mixing, and generally is a live performer who plays with a band called Dakota Night as well as being a solo artist. He writes and collaborates on original songs which he records and mixes on his computer system. Bill is affiliated with ASCAP, a member of 'Just Plain Folks' organization, and networks with other JPF members and members of the Music Player forums.

Site: www.daklander.com

Mix notes: "My recording/mixing system is very basic: Marshall Electronics condenser mics into a Phonic mixer to a SoundBlaster Live soundcard, recorded via n-Track Studio. All WAV files are edited using Acoustica. CDs are burned using EZ CD Creator. Conversion to mp3 is via MusicMatch."

"All recording and mixing is accomplished on an Athlon Thunderbird PC with 512 MB of RAM. The GT3 project was imported into n-Track Studio where I manipulated the levels and added processing as I felt were warranted. My goal was to keep as much of the original feel of the song, without changing too much—though the final version included Eskil's acoustic drum tracks."

"The acoustic drum tracks were equalized and compressed with FaSoft plugs, purchased with n-Track Studio. Anything with organ/synth had echo or tremolo added, as well as some light EQing and compression. The vocal/guitar tracks were also equalized and compressed. All were processed as individual tracks and I also applied some very light compression on the main out. I also used some Fish Fillets plugs, primarily Blockfish, and Ruby Tube to add some sparkle here and there."

Lance Hayes (a.k.a DJ Drunken Master)

Bio: Lance has scored three tracks to be included in the Warner Bros film 'Animatrix (The Picture),' done sound design for Reason 2.0 software, Photoshow 2 software, and event music contribution for the National Organization of Radio Broadcasters at EMP in September 2002. There were over 80,000 downloads of his material on MP3.com in the first year on the site; the cut 'This is DJ Drunken Master!' reached the #24 spot (all genres) and #4 spot (electronic) in August 2002."

Recent project responsibilities include being the liaison to Sirius Satellite in NYC for The Jones Radio Network, and representing Jones Radio in the area of talent coordination, audio file management, and talent content editing. He is currently in the process of transitioning into a position as VP of Promotions for Lightning CD (www.lightningcd.com).

Site: www.mp3.com/DJ_Drunken_Master

Mix notes: "I went for a 60s live arena rock sort of thing. I did not try to remix it and was instead trying to work on my straight mixing skills rather than my "mix-mastering."

"I used exclusively Cubase VST 5.1r1 for almost the entire project. There was a lot of tomfoolery in the area of EQ on most of the tracks and many, many VST effects, some vocal doubling, etc. I think the thing I enjoyed most is the sound I managed out of the organ which I ran that through my own modified patch on the Cubase Rotary Emulator plug-in. That and the Guitars are processed heavily with a global overdrive on them all at their mix bus. Other interesting things include lots of tape style Karlette delays on the tracks (also Cubase) for a more old school sound on the instruments. Loads of fun!"

"While my version sounds pretty reverb thick in comparison to some of the others I was thinking of the Hendrix "Live at Winterland" album with its static panning of the instruments and the strange sense of depth that the concert had. Not really having a rock mixing background I took it as a challenge to try that direction. I had a bit of fun with it!"

David Tkaczuk

Bio: David is currently arranging/recording/mastering projects for singer/songwriters, radio and televison commercials, and call on hold recordings. Clients include Thinkway Toys, Naylor Event Management, FIFA World Cup, The Cottage Life Show, Academy of Learning, Kumon Math & Reading, Canadian Electronics Show & Sale, Sporting Life, Healthy Choice, CTV, Saatchi & Saatchi, Grey Canada, DMB&B, and Context Marketing & Communications. He has worked as a keyboardist, writer, or arranger on "Surveillance" by Triumph (MCA Records), "Absolutely" by Rik Emmett (Duke Street/MCA/Charisma Records), Patti Jannetta's "Breathless" and "Mark On My Heart" (Trilogy Records), Danny Brooks "After the Storm" (Duke Street Records), and many other independent CDs.

Site: www.d-dmusic.com

Mix Notes: "My computer is an Apple G3/233 desktop with an XLR8 CPU upgrade. Running Cubase VST32 5.0r2 on a Yamaha DSP Factory. External processors are a Lexicon MXP1 and two MPX100s; plug-ins used in the mix include the Waves Gold Bundle, PSP MixPack/Stereo Pack/PSP84/PSP42/Vintage Warmer, and BBE Sonic Maximizer. The project was mixed down to a TASCAM DA30 DAT and monitored over Mackie HR824 speakers."

George Toledo III

Bio: George is a 23-year-old songwriter, multi-instrumentalist, and recent graduate of USF. He co-founded Musicalife (www.musicalife.org), a non-profit organization devoted to developing the talents of the underprivileged, with Mike Pinera (Blues Image, Iron Butterfly, and Alice Cooper) and his father, George Toledo Jr.

"Fate of A Heart" was his first use of a digital recording system or a synthesizer. The bass was played by Patrick Osman, a good friend of George's. As George says, "One of my goals was to bring together divergent musical influences, yet still make a song that sounds totally natural—and most importantly, moves you. It's great that so many people have put their own spin on the song; I can feel a lot of 'heart and soul' in the mixes."

George is currently recording his first album and developing a stage show, and is searching for talent of all kinds.

Contact: musicalife1@aol.com.

Mix notes: "The mics I used were AKG C1000, MXL 2001, Shure KSM 32 (vocals), SM 57, and Beta 52. Preamps were the HHB Radius 40 and Focusrite Tone Factory; recorders were two Roland 1880s and a TASCAM 488. Instruments included a Gibson 'Lonnie Mack' Flying V, Gibson ES-347, Fender '68 Telecaster, Musicman Stingray Fretless, Roland R-8 mkII, Roland XP-80, and a vintage Gretsch/Ludwig drum kit."

Jim Holland

Bio: Jim was college educated in music (guitar/composition). He played guitar professionally and did sound on occasion for 10 years on the road with cover bands; he currently plays guitar with a seven piece Latin dance band and does live sound from time to time. Three years ago he got into recording, and is presently finishing up his home studio and getting his record company, Seaweed Music, off the ground.

Mix notes: "I mixed this tune in Sonar with a mouse and a lot of envelope drawing. I took the voice out to my Distressor, and also ran it through a Waves multiband compressor (C4) and Cakewalk delay. I also erased all the noise on a few tracks and replayed the bass line on my 'Tune' bass with a pick through the Distressor, direct into a MOTU 2408 audio interface."

"The drums are loops that I set up in Sonar; two are layered at some points. After mixing the tune I ran it through the Waves L1 Ultra-Maximizer and got another 5dB or so average level increase."

"Most of my time with this tune was spent cleaning up existing tracks and deciding which parts to use—there was a lot to choose from. I ended up creating some new parts out of what was there by cutting loops or short sections and repeating them."

"I brought a couple sounds out that I didn't hear others use, like the jet plane type sound (under 'get on top of you') and 'the jangley thing that blows in the wind on your grandma's porch' sound (end of breakdown in middle of tune). I also found a real buzz on the end of one of the keyboard tracks and spattered that around a bit. It probably sounds like a mistake but I thought it was hilarious."

"I felt the tune's structure lacked an interesting momentum, so I changed that too. I like the idea of a nice clean ending that is reminiscent of the start. I also felt it needed some resolution in the middle."

"I'm a guitar player and a big fan of solid riffs rather than a bunch of notes. I felt this song should focus on the lyric and message within the lyric, so I tried to bring that to the forefront. Thus, I didn't use any of the soloing at the end of the tune, and I tamed down the part in the middle substantially. Near the end I took that #9-type chord riff and turned the rhythm around; I liked it better that way and thought it sounded strong with the ascending power chords so I repeated that a bit."

Mark Hensley

Bio: Mark is an engineer in both audio-post and music who was born in the US, grew up in England and The Netherlands, and now lives in Vancouver, Canada, after 5 years in San Francisco where he started as an Intern at The Plant. He has just started a band after 15 years, and is recording a CD; he's also a grandfather.

His first engineering gig for a major label occurred when he arranged for some cheap studio time at The Plant one weekend for the 4 Non Blondes, so they could come in and re-record "What's Up." The record went Platinum (sold more than 3 million copies world wide). His remixes for the album "Introspection" by Mythos resulted in the 1997 PMIA award for best dance album of the year, and a 1998 Juno nomination for best instrumental album. He also mixed the second Mythos album, which hit the Top Ten in Billboard's new age charts, and assisted with engineering on various major label albums including John Lee Hooker, Santana, Sheila E., Tracey Chapman, Celine Dion and Mariah Carey. He now owns his own studio and works only on music that interests him.

His postproduction experience includes mixing, sound effects editing, dialog editing, ADR and pre-lay recording for various cartoons, including Film-Romans Animated Classics. He's also mixed various documentaries and movies, and done digital editing for the Kids in the Hall movie "Brain Candy."

Mix notes: "My plan of attack was to first time correct everything that needed it (drums, some loops). I fixed some of the bass (tuning problems) and keyboards. Then I tried to figure out how to structure the song so it would make sense from a more 'pop' point of view."

"I cut and pasted whole sections around to create a structure that had a couple of verses and choruses, as well as a bridge. I only used elements that were provided; there was no additional recording or samples added.

"I mixed from the Fairlight MFX3.48 using the Mackie D8B mixer. All compression was done from the Mackie, and EQ was from the Fairlight. For effects I used the TC System 6000 as well as the single Mackie MFX card. I then recorded directly into Wavelab and had my friend Yanni Fyssas master it for me (he does all his mastering in Wavelab). I find him the best mastering guy here in town."

Marc Siegel

Bio: After a couple of audio production courses at SUNY Purchase and a brief stint at Berklee College of music, Marc started his professional recording career at Normandy Sound in Warren, RI. As an assistant engineer he worked with a variety of bands, including John Cafferty and the Beaver Brown Band, Melanie, and Leeway, as well as producers Jimmy Miller and Maurice Starr.

After leaving Normandy, Marc became an independant engineer and producer, working with bands Asche Tuesday, Beyond Reason and Alan Joe Rondo. Marc's latest project is with guitarist Robert Sequoia.

Contact: birdnhand@aol.com

Site: www.robertsequoia.com

Mix notes: "I created my mix in Sonar using Waves plug-ins and a Layla audio interface, running on an Athlon 1.2GHz machine. Monitoring was through Mackie HR824s."

James Baker

Bio: James is a musician with over 15 years experience. He began is career in recording over 5 years ago. Hailing from Ottawa, Canada, James owns and operates his own recording studio.

Site: www.dirtydogstudio.com

Mix notes: "The mix was done using the Mackie D8B digital mixer, HDR 24/96 hard disk recorder, and HR824 studio monitors. All effects used were internal patches on the D8B MFX cards. No outboard equipment was used."

"I wanted to stay true to the artist's vision by using as much of the provided material as possible. The only tracks that were replaced were the original drums, for which I used Eskil's drums. Every track was used to varying degrees; the song was then compressed and normalized in Sound Forge."

Josep Tvrdy

Bio: Josep is a 32 year old audio engineer from Barcelona, Spain. His entry to the music business was as a guitar player in a university band for about five years; he was also in charge of doing live sound and recording the band's demos on a 4-track recorder and cheap microphones. When the band broke up, he continued recording demos for other bands and installed his own small studio.

Over time he found himself buying more gear and recording lots more peoples' demos, and after eight years his studio is based around a Pentium III 800 MHz running Windows 98SE, Logic Audio 5.1, Sound Forge, and Waves plug-ins; his main console is a TASCAM M700; while recorders are ADAT HD24, ADAT (black face), ADAT XT, and Fostex D5.

Mix notes: "I kept the original structure intact, but used Eskil's drum tracks with some modifications—like using the drums from the end of the track and pasting them after the first verse, as I felt it was fresher and gave more attitude towards the next verse due to its use of more dynamic hi-hats."

"All the tracks were dumped into Logic Audio and EQed, then all the individual tracks were sent through the MOTU 2408 to the Alesis HD24. The tracks then went through the mixer where I mixed, added reverb, and compressed a bit. The bass went through a Joemeek VC1; all the guitars, voices and keyboards went through the dbx266A. The final mix was sent to the ART ProVla using a very slight amount of compression (2 to 3dB at a 2:1 ratio) and finally, a little more general EQ was done with an SPL Qure. The final mix went to a Fostex D5 DAT machine."

Ken Lee

Bio: Ken Lee was born in Frankfurt, Germany, and moved to the US at an early age. He started classical piano lessons at age six. When he was 10, his parents gave him a portable tape recorder. It broke, so they bought another, but somehow Ken had fixed the first one, so now he had two. He started experimenting with the two of them to see what results he could get, as well as run the batteries down for special effects and record things outside to see what they sounded like later.

Ken has played keyboards and other instruments (he can play some guitar, bass, Javanese gamelan, and percussion) in Hollywood-area bands such as Holy Sisters of the Gaga Dada, Twist of Fate, Pendu Femelle, and I Am Love (which included the engineer/producer for Henry Rollins and Filter as well as the singer from Danse Society). He records his music as Eleven Shadows at Mensh Tracht, Gott Lacht (Man Plans, God Laughs) Recording Studios in Los Angeles, California.

In addition to his many musical influences, Ken has been heavily influenced by his travels throughout Northern India and the Himalayas, as well as Hong Kong, China, The Philippines, Japan, and Singapore.

Site: www.elevenshadows.com

Mix notes: "This was the first time that I've ever mixed on Pro Tools LE 5.1 (Mac OS 9.1). It took about four hours, and it was fun. The monitoring system was a Kenwood A/V stereo receiver powering Yorkville YSM-1 nearfield monitors. I did not add any new elements to the mix or edit anything, but rather, went for a relatively straight-ahead mix."

Ken Favata

Bio: Ken is an audio production hobbyist and aspiring songwriter. Trained as a physicist, his day job is working for a large company where he has been involved in technology and product development, product planning and business strategy—but music remains his passion.

Like many musicians, a deep appreciation for music seemed to be genetic and was apparent at a very early age. He grew up near New York City in the late sixties/early seventies, and attended many of the gigs and venues that made up the exploding rock music scene at the time.

His garage band career was left behind for a few years after college. However, his musical ambitions were stoked up again during the mid-nineties. "I was lucky to have had the chance to live and work in Tokyo for five years—it's a great music town. This led me to build a project studio and develop some production skills. Interestingly, my training as a physicist turned out to be quite relevant to the audio production world."

Ken's goals are to continue to improve as a songwriter and producer and to write at least one truly great song that the world gets to hear.

Today Ken lives and works in Rochester NY with his wife and two kids and almost-Weimaraner-Shadow.

Mix notes: "This was fun to do. It was the first time I mixed material that I did not record—and there were no track notes provided. So, all decisions were made purely by ear. This felt a little strange."

"Tracks were loaded into a Yamaha AW4416 workstation. Sampled toms, a kick, hi-hat and cymbal crashes were added from an E-mu sampler through an AES digital interface (to eliminate a set of conversions). A synth sound in the intro was added from an Ensoniq KS-32."

"The tempo was increased 3.5% to get a more driving rock feel that the song seemed to want. I went for a sound that a live rock band could reproduce—not too many elements at any one time, not too many fancy production tricks."

"I compressed the bass and let the kick own the very lows; I sidechained the channel containing only the very low components of the compressed bass with the kick so they wouldn't fight below 140Hz or so. I EQed a number of tracks, mainly to prevent buildup in the lows; almost all EQ was subtractive."

"I chose not to use several of the tracks provided in an attempt to focus the song sonically. A number of fader moves were automated as necessary to give! the mix some life, and shift the focus around. I added a few outboard effects—nothing fancy. As one of those happy studio accidents, I left in timing beeps in the outro as they happened to fall in a spot that made them sound like they belonged there."

"I did little to the voice. If I had it to do over again I think I might do more with the vocal treatment—maybe compress a little more add a little more ambience/delay."

"The final mix went through a TC Electronic Finalizer to normalize/maximize levels, and performed no more than 2dB of compression to the mid band."

Lee Flier

Bio: Lee Flier grew up in Los Angeles and began playing guitar at age 12. Developing a deep affinity for the music of the 1960s British Invasion despite being a teenager of the 70s, she became something of a teen prodigy in L.A.'s "Paisley Underground" scene of the late 70s and early 80s, playing in bands with older musicians who understood the music she loved. She also played occasionally with members of many popular L.A. based bands of the time including the Plimsouls, Tom Petty's Heartbreakers, the Textones, Phil Seymour, Lone Justice, and others.

At age 18, Lee also decided to tackle the field of engineering. She began interning at any local studio that would let her hang around, eventually becoming a freelance engineer who logged many hours in studios both large and small.

Lee's real dream was to have a home studio and a long term band, in which she could pursue her fondest creative interests both in performance and production, free from dependence on record labels and the fleeting nature of mainstream trends. In 1992 she moved to Atlanta, Georgia and bought a house, complete with a basement where she could build that dream studio. She now plays, writes songs, and records with her band, What The?, who are all committed as she is to keeping the passion for rock'n'roll alive.

Mix notes: "I mixed with a Yamaha AW4416 all-in-one workstation, using only its internal effects and mixer. Also, when several other participants in the mixing event lamented the lack of real drums on the tracks provided, as a passionate lover of drums I offered to recruit a drummer and record drum tracks to share with all participants. That drummer was Eskil Wetterqvist (see his bio below), and the drums were recorded at my studio on the AW4416, using only its internal preamps. Eskil played my Gretsch Broadcaster drum kit, which I recorded to six tracks with the following mics: kick, EV ND-868; snare, CAD E-100; overhead, Beyer M-160 ribbon; room/front of kick, Rode NT2; rack tom, Shure SM58; floor tom, Sennheiser MD-421."

Eskil Wetterqvist

Bio: Eskil began playing drums at the age of 11, and has been playing professionally for over 25 years. His played his first gig at 12, and won the "Distinguished Musicians Award" and the "John Phillip Sousa Award" in High School while continuing to pursue his original music projects, and learning guitar, bass, and keyboards in the process.

Eskil has continued that pursuit to this day, performing and recording with many bands, and composing his own music. Highlights include winning 2nd place nationally in "The Marlboro Music Talent Round-up" with The Chris Kenny Band, making the semi-finals in the "Yamaha Music Showcase" with the band Rain House, and being nominated for

"Best Local Band" in the "Georgia Coca-Cola Music Awards" with Big Sky, a band whose members included former Steve Morse Band bassist Jerry Peek, and which was produced by Kansas drummer Phil Ehart.

Eskil also performed live with former Kansas violinist David Ragsdale to support his CD "David and Goliath." Recently he toured the UK with singer/songwriter Sue Wilkinson, for whom he also directed/edited a music video for her song "Box." The video won 1st place in a contest on online TV station now.com for their mp3tv channel. More recently, he toured Europe with the eclectic original blues band, Mudcat. He presently resides in Atlanta, Georgia.

Maarten Ligtenberg

Bio: Maarten is a guitar player living in Holland. He graduated from GIT in LA in 1993, and has been playing in several bands in Holland since, along with holding a normal day job in software engineering. He started recording his own demos on a TASCAM 4-track in the late 80s, and moved on to recording on PC when he got his first version of Cubase.

Mix notes: "The setup used for the mix consists of a Pentium 4, 2.53GHz PC with Windows XP Pro, 1GB of RAM, RME Digi 96/8 pst + RME ADI8-AE, TC Powercore, and Cubase SX version 1.051. I mostly used TC Powercore effects on the mix (Classic Verb and 24/7 C limiting amplifier), with some Waves L2 for mastering."

Håkan "Master Zap" Andersson

Bio: Master Zap has been releasing music online at www.Master-Zap.com since 1995 and selling it since 1997, when his debut indie CD "The Curvature of Space" appeared, now a sold-out collectors item. He also produces music videos and music for "Nina—Goddess of Dance."

Site: www.NinaGoddess.com

Mix notes: "I mixed it 100% within SONAR using mostly Waves plug-ins. First I tried to find the groove ... for the beat, the "grooviest" thing (to my ears) was the drum loop, which after EQ and a massive compression, combined with judiciously edited version of the bass guitar track, created a nice grooving bottom to work from."

"I then dropped in the pieces that still 'fit' this groove-oriented base, and removed those that did not, which actually was quite a lot of the tracks, percentage-wise."

"By spicing up the lead vocal with EQ, compression and a bit of chorus I got a more distinct and airy sound. The vocal was intervoven with pieces of the original instrumentation where I felt it was needed. The cool 'bass drop' from earlier in the song was copied, pitched down and re-used in front of the rap-break, which was stripped down to only drums and rap, again with the 'use the elements that groove' logic."

The 2-bus was compressed with a Waves C1 compressor during the entire mixing process. Mixing into a compressor can yield interesting results, just be careful not to pump so much in you drive it all the time ... which is what I did."

Salvatore Orlando

Bio: Having studied jazz improvisation as well as computer science, Sal got involved with the web at its very beginning. By 1996, with Spotted Antelope Multimedia, Sal created the first large-scale web site to use Dynamic HTML, bringing Netscape's 1996 online Annual Report to life with rich animations and interactivity. Sal was also instrumental in a complete redesign of the Netscape Web site at this time, which demonstrated the potential of the then newly-released Navigator 4.0 browser.

In 1997, Sal's pioneering work on "The Groovolator," the first online musical synthesizer, as well as "Snoovler," a children's Web site which combined Flash, Shockwave, and Beatnik technologies to present an online interactive storybook, led AV Video & Multimedia Producer Magazine to name him one of the Top 100 Multimedia Producers of 1997. Sal was also a finalist in the 1997 NewMedia INVISION awards.

Sal went on to create high profile content for sites including Yahoo.com, MTV.com, Intel.com, DavidBowie.com and many others. One of his most successful creations, in collaboration with Thomas Dolby, is the Mixman eMix (a.k.a. Beatnik GrooveGrams) which enables users to remix popular songs and share them with friends via email in a bandwidth-friendly digital format, an experience enjoyed by over seven million Web surfers to date. Featured artists include Britney Spears, David Bowie, Moby, N'Sync, Puff Daddy, Nine Inch Nails and dozens more.

Sal's latest project is an online Flash-based remixer which enables users to remix songs in their Web browser, which can then be purchased and sent to any cellular phone which supports polyphonic ringtones.

Contact: sss@salorlando.com

Site: www.salorlando.com

Mix notes: "In mixing 'Fate of a Heart', I decided to approach the project as if I was working for a client, and therefore tried to stay true to the intent of the song as closely as could be inferred without direct input from the artist. I used a Power Mac G4, and mixed and edited entirely in MOTU Digital Performer 3.11."

Rim Rivera

Bio: Rim has been passionate about music since childhood, and learned to play piano and guitar mostly from instructional books borrowed from the local public library. He even composed two ragtime pieces that were recognized by the Long Island Composer's Alliance while in high school. Playing acoustic guitar semi-professionally in college, he never joined a band until seven years after graduating. Currently, he is still in local bands but has a growing interest in audio recording, having set up an audio recording studio in his bedroom called Rim Speed Studio (www.rimspeed.com) to use for personal projects as well as other local artists' endeavors, on a limited basis. His studio work has consisted of demo recordings as well as albums planned for limited commercial release. He currently lives in the Washington, DC metro area and plans on staying there.

Mix notes: "I mixed George's song on an AMD XP 2200+ PC running Pro Tools LE on Windows XP. My monitoring setup includes a pair of M-Audio SP-8B powered speakers and an M-Audio SP-8S powered subwoofer. The plug-ins I used were from Waves' Gold Native Bundle and Digidesign's DigiRack (included with Pro Tools). The mastering was done using iZotope's Ozone and IK Multimedia's T-Racks 24."

Sruly Nachfolger

Bio: Soundscape Studios in Passaic, NJ is owned by Sruly Nachfolger who also happens to be an ordained Rabbi (a Rockin' Rabbi, that is). At age 23 he has worked in all facets of the recording industry. Starting out at age 8 playing keyboards and going professional at age 12, Sruly is well known on the NYC Jewish wedding/bar mitzvah circuit. This led to many gigs playing with the top "A" list Broadway musicians, who also frequent the Jewish circuit. Keyboards eventually led to an interest in recording, which resulted in a successful studio. To date, Sruly has produced radio spots which have aired on WCBS, WABC, Bloomberg News, and many others. The Jewish recording scene has also seen prominent releases from Soundscape Studios. A recent project including the Israeli Philharmonic has garnered rave reviews in the press.

Mix notes: "The song was mixed on a Roland VS-1680 with a little 'cool verb' on the vocals, which were panned hard L-R to achieve space. The original tracks included a close vocal in addition to a 'far' vocal. The vocals were additionally processed through a D. W. Fearn VT-2 tube preamp to impart some warmth, with a bit of compression from a Neve System 9098 Compressor."

"The mix is obviously sparser than other's mixes—this is a minimalistic approach that, in my opinion, works well for this situation. I added a pad, and a bell phrase to begin the song. All the added sounds are Korg Triton factory presets. I then added an acoustic guitar patch to serve as the chordal foundation of the song. I took some liberty in changing the song to a minor theme in the middle. Fretless bass rounded things out; all that was left was the synth lead solo at the end. This is actually a homage to Jordan Rudess—one of my influences."

urk10

Bio: Urk10 has played music since he was 12 years old, and has toured around the world playing in various bands and shows in France, South Korea, Japan, Canada, Australia, USA, Singapore, Malaysia, Cayman Islands, and Hong Kong. He is currently working on a project CD in his home studio.

Mix notes: "For this mix I used only Cubase SX and the factory plug-ins. I used a lot the dynamics plug-ins for the bass, drums and vocal. I doubled the vocal for a stereo effect with some distortion on one of them. I rolled off every track up to 45Hz. I wanted to do more a rock mix, so that's why I didn't use the keys tracks a lot. The delay effect at the beginning is only one of the vocal tracks shifted earlier. I really enjoyed doing this project!"

Craig Anderton

Bio: By his 22nd birthday, Craig had recorded three albums with the group Mandrake, toured most of the USA east of the Mississippi, and played Carnegie Hall.

He has played sessions on both guitar and synthesizer for Epic, Metromedia, Columbia, RCA, United Artists, and other labels, and was mixdown/production consultant on "Valley in the Clouds" by David Arkenstone (which remained on Billboard's Top 20 new age chart for over a year). In 1989, Narada Records released "Forward Motion," a CD written, recorded, and mixed by Craig in his home studio with noted keyboardist

Spencer Brewer. Rolling Stone called it "one of those rare instrumental electronic albums that is not mere New Age tapioca." He has also done sound design work for Alesis, Digitech, Discrete Drums, E-mu, Native Instruments, Peavey, Prosonus, Steinberg, TC Electronic, Wizoo, and Yamaha. His most recent sample CDs are "Technoid Guitars," distributed through Steinberg, and "Turbulent Filth Monsters," a CD of hardcore drum loops distributed by Discrete Drums.

Craig has given seminars on technology and the arts in 37 states and 10 countries, while authoring over 20 books and thousands of articles on musical electronics.

In 1998 he started playing on a semi-regular basis with Rei$$dorf Force, a German experimental electronic music band headquartered in Cologne, as well as performing solo under his own name. Several of his tunes have been remixed for the European market and released on compilation CDs.

Site: www.craiganderton.com

Mix notes: "I picked up on a sort of Dylanesque vibe in the vocals, and built the mix around that. I was trying for a 60s sort of sound, with trashy drums and upfront instruments, and wasn't concerned about any tuning or timing issues—I wanted a raw feel. I added no new tracks nor did I change the arrangement, although I did cut pieces of tracks and insert them elsewhere, like the snare hits that follow some of the breaks. I also added some rhythmic slapback on the bass so it felt a little more in the pocket."

"I particularly liked cutting out parts to give dramatic pauses, and to provide a more psychedelic feel, went for synched echo on the vocals. The only vocal processing was a significant amount of Waves L1—no EQ or compression. Mastering was done in Wavelab."

"My goal with this was to have fun mixing it, and to try to give the song a different kind of slant. I've been calling it the 'New York City 1966 Mix;' hopefully it applies the fresh, raw, experimental vibe of that time to George's song, which I personally find quite optimistic and moving."

Index